Contents

The Pyramid Approach to Education in Autism

Andy Bondy, Ph. D.
and
Beth Sulzer-Azaroff, Ph. D.

Pyramid Educational Products, Inc.

ISBN: 1-928598-03-X

Foreword

The Pyramid Approach to Education is aptly named. Metaphorically, it has much in common with the Great Pyramid of Giza in Egypt, as a marvel of construction. The Great Pyramid is supported by a solid foundation of 2.5-ton blocks. *The Pyramid Approach to Education* is solidly founded on scientific principles. As described in Chapter 1, these principles were derived from uniform observations of facts about how certain events (antecedents and consequences) influence what we do and how we learn. These facts and relationships are the building stones of behavior analysis, and their organization into principles of behavior provides a firm foundation for The Pyramid Approach to Education.

The height of a pyramid is a function of the size of its base—the larger the base, the greater the height. As the highest stone structure in the world, the Great Pyramid has an enormous base. So, too, the base of the Pyramid Approach to Education is not only solid but ample. When systematically analyzed across many different populations, situations, and types of behaviors, virtually thousands of times, the principles of behavior have been broadly demonstrated to hold. In fact, the examples distributed throughout this text allow us to see not only how the lives of students are influenced by those principles but also how our own lives are impacted by them. The key is that once we understand and are better able to predict the effects of environmental events described by these principles, we are empowered. Now, new possibilities present themselves for rearranging conditions for the betterment of our students' and our own lives. This book offers specific, practical strategies and empirically validated behavioral principles and procedures for doing just that; in so doing, it guides our students toward reaching their highest goals.

Estimated to have taken 30 years to complete, the Great Pyramid consists of 2,300,000 blocks. These are arranged in a series of steps forming the buttress walls, along with packing blocks to fill the steps, and then overlaid with casting blocks for smoothness. Analogously, rising from its base of principles of behavior, the Pyramid Approach to Education has developed numerous strategies and procedures for promoting learning and adaptive repertoires. These strategies have been positioned, one by one, also over the period of approximately 30 years, when applied behavior analysis first was introduced. They have been applied systematically to effect improvements in various aspects of performance and across diverse domains. As additional needs and challenges have been identified, behaviorally based procedures have been developed and evaluated to address them. As these strategies have been tried and tested, they have been further refined. The Pyramid Approach to Education incorporates them here into a coherent and useful model. This book provides teachers with the steps on which to build and buttress their students' skills; from planning of functional curricula to choosing and implementing strategies to achieve the goals—from acquisition, to fluency, to generalization—and adapting those strategies to meet the students' needs in relevant contexts and settings.

The triangular shape of a pyramid gives it stability. Thus, the Pyramid Approach to Education appropriately emphasizes the importance of (1) functional objectives that directly address skills the student needs to perform in his or her daily environment, (2) powerful reinforcement systems to promote learning and performance of those skills, and (3) management of contextually inappropriate behaviors that could otherwise interfere with the student's learning and successful performance. Clearly, all three of these issues must be given consideration. Neglecting any one of them will undermine the benefits of the other two.

The Great Pyramid was designed to last indefinitely; and it has survived for over 40 centuries. The Pyramid Approach to Education, derived from the field of behavior analysis, also has been designed to endure. Because it focuses on objective measurement of observable behavior, only those procedures that produce actual change toward the desired performances survive. This built-in accountability has allowed behavior analysis to withstand the encroachment of "fads" (such as "facilitated communication") that do not live up to their promise, and it ensures that ineffective practices will be replaced by effective ones.

Finally, the apex of a pyramid points upward, an entirely fitting symbol for the progress that can be achieved with the Pyramid Approach to Education. The sky is the limit.

Nancy A. Neef, Ph.D.

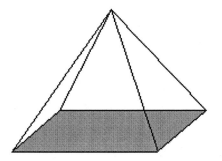

The Pyramid Approach to Education

A little girl with a head full of soft blond curls lisps, "It's your turn." Her tongue pokes into the space where her new front tooth is just breaking through the gum line. A boy, a bit taller, pulls his gaze away from his flicking fingers, looks at the girl, and spins the spinner. "Where do you have to go?" the girl asks. The boy points to a box on the board depicting a cookie. "Yes, you can go to the cookie square," and he moves his marker to the correct spot.

In another classroom, a teacher is seated with three children. They read their primers in unison, "Billy and Tommy are sailing their boats." "Put your finger on Billy's boat. Good Carlo. Good Heather. Uh oh, Victor. You've found Tommy's boat." The boy quickly switches his finger over to the other object. They practice pointing to different objects, switching ultimately back to Billy's boat. This time Victor gets it right. "Okay. Now each of you gets an ice cream cone token." The children each take a foam rubber symbol and place it into their token boards. "Just one more for each of you and we can go for our ice cream."

The next scene is set in a middle school science laboratory. The students are drawing pictures of the algae they have scraped from the side of the fish tank and viewed under the microscope. They are preparing reports to present orally or turn in for grading. One boy renders an almost photographic fac-simile of the specimen, but when an aide asks him the name of his drawing, he does not say the term aloud. Instead he writes it down.

The last setting is a residence for eight young adults. Posted on the wall is the schedule for the day, a set of pictures, and words fastened to a Velcro strip. A tall young man has just moved a picture of a toothbrush into the upper portion of the schedule board to indicate that it is time to progress to the next activity. Now he, another youth, and a more mature woman, the group home manager, stand before a washing machine. "How much soap powder do we need?" "A half cup," the two boys answer. "Okay. Go ahead." One of the boys reaches for the measuring cup, using it to extract just the right amount, and pours the powder into the tub, then turns on the machine. "Good for you," says the woman. "You figured it out all by yourself."

What is so remarkable about these events? After all, kindergartners play board games, youngsters in primary grades learn to read, middle schoolers participate in science lab, and most young adults operate washing machines, don't they? Suppose we were to tell you that all but the little girl playing the board game and the group home manager have been diagnosed with autism or another developmental disability? Yet this scenario is exactly the sort of thing you will see in educational programs operating according to the precepts of the Pyramid Approach to Education.

Notice that each of the students is actively engaged in a meaningful learning experience and that none are misbehaving or totally tuning out. Those major accomplishments have resulted from a long history of effective teamwork among staff performing at the highest-quality level and willing parents.

Unfortunately, while success stories like these are becoming more familiar, they are not as widespread as they might be. Many people still regard good teaching as an inborn trait, incapable of being improved. As a case in point, a few years ago, a principal of a local school rebuffed an offer of staff development services from one of the authors. "Son, its really simple, good teachers just are born that way." Apparently, once they stepped foot into the classroom, according to that principal, it was already too late.

Others fail to recognize the universality of laws of learning: An elementary teacher asked for help in managing a particularly active student. When the conversation veered in the direction of effective instructional strategies, the teacher asserted flat out, "Look, you teach him how to sit in that chair, and I'll teach him how to read!" "But," the consultant wondered to himself, "if she truly knew how to teach him to read well, wouldn't she also know how to teach him to sit?"

Maybe. Assuming that she used good practices to teach reading, she could have used similar methods to encourage his remaining seated; but that probably was not apparent to her and may not be to many others. This is one of the main reasons we have written this book. We hope to share with you what we have learned about how to successfully apply established learning principles to teach may different kinds of things: academic concepts and skills; effectively communicating and otherwise effectively interacting socially, remaining safe and healthy, and becoming physically adept and emotionally controlled. As a result, even though the main focus here is on students with autism and related disabilities, you should be able more effectively to design effective educational environments anywhere regardless of whether the setting is a regular or a special education one or whether your students are infants, children, youth, or adults with specialized or typical needs.

This is not to suggest that becoming an excellent teacher is a simple matter. If it were, deficiencies in academic performance and conduct would not be as widespread as they are today. It takes little exposure to the classroom for most teachers to realize that like so many other deceptively simple approaches, effective teaching demands well-honed skills. Good results depend on teachers who are able to choose, organize, and sequence optimal instructional experiences, reinforcing student progress along the way. Skills like those apply regardless of the nature of the student body.

The two of us share considerable experience as teachers and performance managers. We have taught just about every category of student: business executives and managers, school administrators, professional and research psychologists, health and human services providers, teachers, economically and culturally advantaged and disadvantaged children, and those with special talents and with educational and developmental delays. We have found that, indeed, the fundamental principles of effective education and training apply universally. It is only in the specifics of the execution that the differences arise—in selecting what to teach, where, when, and how in particular.

To illustrate, while serving as head administrator of a statewide public school program for children and adolescents with autism, one of us joined his colleagues in devising a powerful staff development and training system. In general, staff, parents, and other family members working with children, adolescents, and adults with various types of developmental disabilities learned to apply those methods in different types of settings—classrooms, the gymnasium, the lunchroom, job sites, workshops, group and private homes, and elsewhere. Soon students were making major improvements academically, socially, and otherwise to the extent that the state education department felt that it no longer needed to send students out of state to residential treatment facilities.

Objective assessment of student and teacher progress has demonstrated that applying solidly established principles of learning in manageable ways has produced impressive results across the gamut of student conditions.[1] In *The Pyramid Approach to Education,* we describe the practices that we and

---

[1]See two volumes of collected papers published by the Journal of Applied Behavior Analysis, one on behavior analysis and developmental disabilities, the other on behavior analysis and education in general.

our colleagues have found most effective and user-friendly for educating students with special needs like autism. Our intention in the pages that follow is to elaborate on the approach to enable teachers and other educators[2] to do the best job they can and derive pleasure from the process.

Features of the Pyramid Approach to Education

Relatives and professionals ("teachers") responsible for teaching students with autism or related disorders[3] and those training and/or supervising those teachers seek effective, user-friendly methods. An organized, manageable educational design based on solidly established principles of learning and behavior is just the thing, especially when paired with the tools allowing them to determine whether their methods are having their intended effects.

You might wonder why we use a complicated symbol like a pyramid instead of a simpler design to describe our system. Because effective teaching demands that we attend to a number of factors at the same time: *why, what,* and how we are doing things the way we do and *how well* those efforts are paying off (see Figure 1.1). A visual image of a system like this also should help you recall its critical parts.

The Base of the Pyramid: The Why of Behavior—The Science of Learning

Remember, as Professor Nancy Neef reminds us in the Foreword, the pyramid is one of the most stable geometric forms known to humanity. While the forces of nature may cause palaces, office buildings, factories, and homes to crumble, the pyramids of the Pharaohs remain intact after thousands of years. As they did, we must begin with a solid base before constructing the main body of the three-dimensional pyramidal structure. We will use this same analogy to present a sequence of critical educational issues to address, beginning with its firm foundation.

This base is composed of the science of learning and behavior. This science has produced enough evidence to spawn many general laws of learning. These laws explain much about why people do what they do.[4] The fruit

---

[2]Throughout this book, we use the term *teacher* to refer not only to certified classroom teachers but also to anyone (including parents, siblings, speech therapists, psychologists, paraprofessionals, classroom teachers, consultants, and so on) engaged in the activity of promoting learning.

[3]Henceforth, for the sake of brevity, we use the term autism to include that condition as well other related disorders.

[4]Biomedical researchers are beginning to discover factors related to malfunctioning of the central nervous system among people with autism and related disabilities. As is becoming

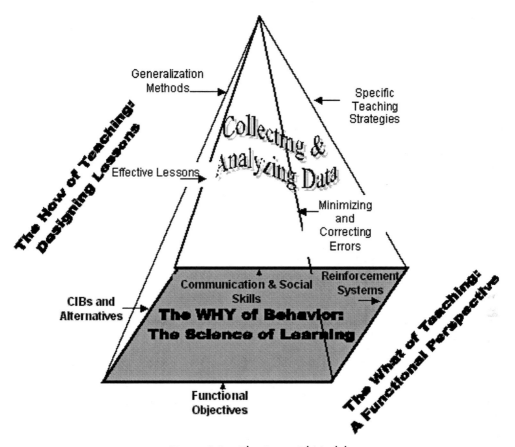

Figure 1.1   The Pyramid Model

of these efforts is a set of principles or rules of behavior change that we can use to teach successfully. As implied earlier, this knowledge base is our reason for choosing the science of behavior as its foundation on which to erect the pyramid. Chapter 2 elaborates on this fundamental concept of "the *why* of behavior."

Firming the Foundation: The What of Teaching

Once we begin to understand why people do what they do, we then need to consider *what* to teach. We reason that when we want to teach a child something, we want to change the things they say or do—their behavior. Two areas

standard practice in the treatment of true attention-deficit/hyperactivity disorders, ultimately we may find ways optimally to combine medical and behavioral interventions to minimize the damaging effects of these conditions. Because this book is directed toward the teaching role, we restrict our discussion to the areas in which it is appropriate for teachers and parents to intervene.

of behavior generally demand the attention of those working and living with children with autism:

1. The **presence** of challenging behaviors. The list is large and includes hitting, screaming, tantruming, biting, spitting, throwing objects large and small, running around at amazing speeds all day, self-stimulating at high rates (rocking, finger flicking, spinning objects, and so on), echolalia (or perseverative speech), and countless other upsetting actions.
2. The **absence** of important key behaviors, such as functional communication (whether via speech or other modalities), eye contact and other orienting reactions (like looking in the direction of a teacher's pointing finger), appropriate toy play, social skills involving adults or peers, staying in an assigned area, attending to a group task, and many related deficits.

We plan our lessons to enable students to do something differently afterward than they could do before the lessons. That is, our lessons are aimed at reducing the acts in the first category and increasing those in the second; but which should we address first?

Problem behaviors like those in the first category seem to demand instant relief. Think about your last conversation about your job with someone close to you. Were you more likely to have reported, "You know, 73 percent of the time, he independently followed 17 steps in the right order to tie his shoes," or "He scratched me again. Look!" It is those bothersome behaviors that tend to command our attention and gain us sympathy. That is why many choose to begin by eliminating the problem behaviors: stop the child from self-stimulating, running, hitting, and so on as a way to get the student "ready to learn." As we soon will see, this tactic is a mistake.

First of all, the commonly used phrase "ready to learn" concerns us greatly because it seems to imply that the child is not yet capable of learning. Everything we know on the subject, however, suggests that children can and do learn, even under all sorts of conditions and at various times and places. It is not necessary for them to be sitting quietly in a chair with their hands in their laps for 10 seconds before responding to a teacher's single instruction. They can learn while sitting on the floor, running around the room, or playing with dirt on the playground. To us, the more critical question should be, Is the teacher ready to teach?

Another broad concern about beginning by attempting to eliminate behaviors is that unless certain things are in place, our efforts will not pay off. Numerous research studies have shown that some children hurt themselves, by scratching or biting, as a way to gain attention. Let us assume that certain methods allow us to stop a child from doing that. However, when the child sits motionless, what is she now lacking? Right, attention! Maybe we have taken away her only means of getting it. That outcome would be unusually harsh for someone so dependent on others for her wants and needs. Furthermore, we should hardly be surprised when she reverts to scratching herself or devises on her own a different, possibly more damaging technique, like hitting her head or hurting others. If a child is not likely to generate an effective new solution, it is up to us to teach one. Now we begin to see that a better place to start is by building new, effective, and presumably healthier attention-seeking skills. Unless we pair a *constructive functional objective* with our efforts to eradicate inappropriate behaviors, the intervention will not succeed.

Building skills, then, is the primary emphasis of Chapter 3, "Functional Objectives," our first chapter in the *what* category. That does not mean that we intend to ignore dealing with disruptive, damaging, and dangerous behaviors, only that we postpone the topic until we have provided teachers with the means to devise constructive alternative objectives. Choosing optimal functional objectives is not always easy, though. Chapter 3 will help you by offering a set of guidelines for generating instructional objectives that are developmentally appropriate and useful to the student in various ways.

People learn for a reason, usually because it does or promises to provide something people want or need to know or get or to rid them of something they do not. The material in Chapter 4, "Powerful Reinforcement Systems," describes ways to encourage students to keep trying. There, you will find out how to enrich the environment by providing many opportunities for your students to experience reinforcement as a result of their efforts. When you use these tactics to optimal advantage, any necessity to resort to coercion will be minimized.

Learning addresses not only interactions with the physical environment—tying shoes, drinking from a cup, catching a ball, and so on—but also those within the social environment. People also must learn to communicate and relate effectively to others in other ways. Chapter 5, "Functional Communication and Social Skills," addresses appropriate goals and procedures for teaching toward those goals. The last element of the base of the pyramid concerns itself with those remaining student behaviors that interfere with their own or others' learning and well-being. Chapter 6, "Preventing and Reducing Contextually Inappropriate Behavior," describes ways to reduce those troublesome behaviors that remain.

Teaching teams often are composed of staff with different levels of expertise. Despite any such differences, though, all members should find that the chapters in this part of the book provide them with some valuable problem-solving tools. It is hoped that the material will counter the team's general tendency to want to assign a new student's disruptive actions top priority. Instead, if any effective long-term solution is to be found we urge teachers to take the Pyramid Approach by first putting in place the other elements of the base: functional objectives, powerful reinforcement systems, and functional communication skills.

Getting There: The How of Teaching

Once we have addressed why people behave the way they do and what to teach, we are ready to consider the question of *how* to teach. By telling us how to achieve our teaching aims, this section is the one that transforms the pyramid into its full three-dimensional structure. The strategy will be to ask very broad questions before narrowing in on more specific topics. Therefore, before we begin to teach a lesson, we should be clear about where it eventually will lead. That is, we need to remind ourselves what should take place, where, and when by the end of the lesson. It is not enough to teach a student to do something with a particular object only for a teacher in a classroom or for a parent at home. The intention usually is broader than that—extending the skill beyond, to other times and places, and with different people. Consequently, from the very start, we will need to build into our methods strategies to promote *generalization,* the subject of Chapter 7.

Once we understand the full nature of the lesson we want to teach, it is time to attend to some broad guidelines that are outlined in Chapter 8; "Designing Effective Lessons." Chapter 9, "Specific Teaching Strategies," describes the type of temporary help teachers can provide students and how best to withdraw that assistance. Furthermore, while our general approach will always be to try to minimize student errors, we must have specific lesson plans for responding to them when they do occur. These issues are detailed in Chapter 10, "Minimizing and Correcting Errors."

Assessing and Evaluating: Collecting and Analyzing Data

Finally, everything that we do in our attempt to understand our students and ourselves, to set worthy objectives, and to design and implement effective lessons requires careful assessment and evaluation. We need to know what conditions are supporting behaviors of concern and which ones have been interfering with learning. We have to develop useful methods for finding out whether our efforts are working; whether we need to consider making some changes. Therefore, the Pyramid Approach to Education requires that we collect, summarize, and analyze data to be certain that our methods are having the intended positive effect. In essence, data are tied to every element of the pyramid: the principles of learning on which it is founded, what and how we choose what to teach, and the way we go about educating students with autism. Strategies for collecting and analyzing data are reviewed in Chapter 11, "Collecting and Analyzing Data."

Putting It All Together

At this point you may be feeling overwhelmed, wondering how all the pieces of the pyramid puzzle join together and operate. Diane Black, a consultant for Pyramid Educational Consultants, Inc., understands your concern. She, like the rest of us, has had to work hard to learn to apply the Pyramid Approach effectively in her own classroom. So, in Chapter 12, "A Typical School Day;" she invites you into her preschool classroom for a day to see for yourself one instance of the Pyramid Approach operating successfully. Invisibly cloaked so as not to disturb the routine, you will be able to watch and listen to what happens from the moment her students arrive until they depart. You can read the chapter first to gain a sense of the pyramid reality and then later review it to identify each of the elements of the pyramid. That will help you begin to fashion your own school or home-based instructional design and to conduct and assess progress. While there is no guarantee your students will be able to progress through school unassisted, we can promise that if you learn and abide by the principles and practices suggested in this book, you will see considerable improvement in your students' progress.

Summary

Today, thanks to the field of applied behavior analysis, students with autism and related developmental disabilities have been able to make greater strides than anyone might have imagined just a few decades ago. They can enter and succeed in school, care for themselves at home, become gainfully employed, and function effectively in social and community situations. This encouraging state of affairs has resulted from the recognition that the laws of learning can be applied to change the behavior of anyone, as long as the specific procedures stemming from those laws are optimally arranged within a supportive environment to suit the student's current set of skills.

The *Pyramid Approach to Education* describes the most fundamental of those laws and procedures and describes how to apply them effectively. In a systematic fashion, this book will teach you to plan *what* to teach by setting functional educational objectives and ways to organize a reinforcing environment, promote effective communication skills, and minimize behaviors inappropriate in particular contexts. Then it will guide you through the process of selecting and applying methods for achieving those aims. You begin by organizing for generalization from the onset, designing and carrying out specific lesson plans accordingly. Assessing and evaluating your choice of procedures and their effectiveness will allow your instruction to be self-correcting. If progress is in the direction and at the rate anticipated, you continue on course. Otherwise, you try another approach, saving precious time and other resources in the process.

This book contains many concepts and guidelines. Chapter 12 permits you to see one case of how everything fits together. That should give you some ideas for adjusting the Pyramid Approach to your own particular situation. Learn your lessons thoroughly, apply them with care, and watch your students progress.

Suggested Readings and Viewings

To	Read
Share one family's experience in coping successfully with their children's autism	Maurice, C. (1993). *Let me hear your voice: A family's triumph over autism.* New York: Ballantine Books.
Gain a layperson \-parent's perspective about the value of an applied behavior analytic approach to intervening with students with autism	Maurice, C. Why this manual. In Maurice, C., Green, G. & Luce, S. (Eds.) *Behavioral intervention for young children with autism.* Austin, TX: Pro-Ed, 3–12.
Become informed consumers of treatment for your child	Harris, S. L., & Weiss, M. J. (1998). *Right from the start: Behavioral interventions for young children with autism: A guide for parents and professionals.* Bethesda, MD: Woodbine House.
Find out the answers to questions parents commonly ask about children with autism	Luce, S. & Dyer, K. Answers to commonly asked questions. In Maurice, C., Green, G. & Luce, S. (Eds.) *Behavioral intervention for young children with* early intervention with*autism.* Austin, TX: Pro-Ed, 345–358.

To	View
Watch children with autism and their families experience intensive early intervention education	Groden, J., Spratt, R. J., Fiske, P. & Weisberg, P. (1998). *Breaking the barriers III. Intensive early intervention and beyond: A school-based inclusion program.* Champaign, IL: Research Press.

2

The Why of Behaving:
The Science of Behavior

"This time it's going to be different," we vow to ourselves on New Year's Day. "I'm going to exercise and eat healthy food and get enough sleep." We stick to this regimen for a week or two, then begin to slack off. Eventually we are right back where we were, gobbling down fatty fast foods; convincing ourselves that we are too busy to exercise, absolutely having to check out what our favorite late-night talk-show host has to say, or surfing to just one more Web site. Periodically, we scold ourselves, "Why, why don't I have more willpower?"

We pose these same sorts of questions about other people, too: Why does a person commit a given act of evil or heroism? Where do qualities like dependability, persistence, disloyalty, or impulsiveness come from? Why is it that some people seem to take everything at face value, while others catch subtler meanings? All these illustrate things people *do* that many of us find confusing.

Those of us living and working with children with special needs continuously find ourselves trying to understand their odd behavior. Why does Louis, a four-year-old diagnosed with autism, scream when a detour sign forces his mom to take a different route to school or when she brings his sandwich wrapped with any but yellow paper? Why does he rock in his chair endlessly or arch away from anyone who tries to hug him? Are those acts determined by forces from without or within, or do they just happen?

Possibly an even more important question for many who come in daily contact with youngsters with severe special needs is, Given the situation, is there anything that can be done to change it? If so, how?

Science and Human Behavior

Humans have been pondering questions like those for a long time. Now, at the dawn of a new millennium, science is bringing us ever closer to finding the answers. Among others, neuroscientists are learning more about how the brain is structured and operates. Behavioral scientists are describing patterns of behavior and how they relate to social, genetic, and other factors. *Behavior analysts* are among this group. These specialists continue to make important discoveries about the relation between people's environments (what occurs inside and outside our bodies) and their actions.

It is this last focus, the science of behavior analysis, that forms the basis for our Pyramid Approach to Education. Why? Because, as we soon will discover in this chapter, behavior analysis helps explain the two things we want most to understand about ourselves and others:

1. How people learn: why they do what they do and when they do it
2. How to teach: how to alter when, where, and how people act

Notice that our main focus here is on what people *do:* where, when, and how a person shouts, rocks, laughs, cries, reads, or reasons aloud in some particular way and what *conditions* are influencing the way it happens. When we discover events that consistently affect the behavior, often we can do something about it. After all, changing behavior is what teaching—and preaching, training, managing, counseling, and therapy—is all about. The person shouts or rocks *less,* reads *more* of certain things, reasons in a *more* logical fashion, or laughs or cries *sometimes but not others,* according to socially acceptable norms.

Note also that we do not place our main focus on people's thoughts, impulses, or feelings. There is a good reason for this. It is only by analyzing people's actions or behaviors[1] directly that we can discover what factors are regulating or "controlling" those behaviors and then possibly do something to alter the situation.

How, then, can we find out what those controlling events are? We need to be able to detect them in some unbiased way. Similarly, we need to measure objectively how those events relate to the behaviors of concern. Louis's mother wants the flexibility of picking up his lunch from several (not just one) fast-food restaurants. Yet Louis smiles and eats his sandwich only when it is wrapped in a familiar yellow wrapper. He cries and pushes the food away if it is wrapped in white. We know this because we have observed and counted

---

[1]We use the term behavior to describe anything the person does or says, good, bad, or indifferent.

laughing and crying and eating or pushing the food away according to whether the wrappers were yellow or white. If there were no objective ways to observe and measure any change in those behaviors when we try to educate him differently, it would have to become a guessing game. That is why thoughts, feelings, and impulses are not our main focal point.

Does that mean that we consider "internal events" unimportant? Not at all. Surely people think and have feelings, and we assume that these are affected by the same principles as any behavior. The difference is that because we cannot detect thinking and feeling directly, we can only guess what is happening on the basis of what our own senses tell us, including what people say about themselves. Whether what they say matches exactly what is happening within them is not possible to determine. Although changing what people report can be the main focus, as in many forms of psychotherapy, probably readers of this book are more concerned with actions than words. When, for instance, we are trying to find out what a girl really likes to do, we can monitor the following:

- How long she stays with a particular activity
- Whether she attempts to escape from the situation
- How frequently she selects or rejects it when given a choice
- Whether she smiles, laughs, frowns, or cries while involved in a certain situation

Assume that we already had run that kind of test with Louis and found out that indeed he accepted yellow-wrapped and rejected white-wrapped sandwiches. Now suppose that we want to see whether we can do his mom a favor by eliminating his unpleasant reactions to sandwiches wrapped in white. We locate wrapping paper in varying hues from deep yellow to lighter and lighter yellow to white. Then every five days we wrap the lunch sandwich in a slightly lighter wrapper. To find out whether this tactic works we measure how Louis responds during the process (Figure 2.1). We are convinced that this "fading"[2] method is effective because while we are introducing the white wrapper, Louis nearly always continues to accept and eat his food at school, at home and even at local fast-food restaurants without crying. Unable to see inside his head and locate his likes and dislikes, we are doing the best available thing: watching his behavior.[3] Had we not continued to observe carefully, we might have been tempted to give up the one time, part way through,

---

[2]This method is described in greater detail later in the section on prompting (Chapter 10)
[3]Today, sophisticated instruments can detect things happening in areas within the brain, even groups of neurons firing. No one, though, claims to be able to decipher the "content" of these events.

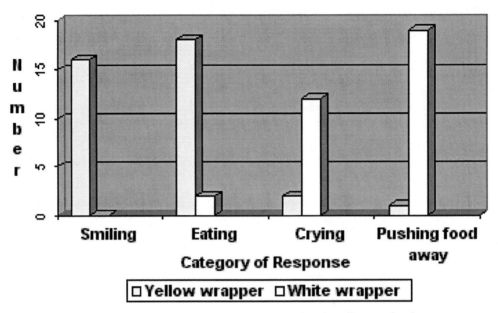

Figure 2.1   Louis's Response to Sandwiches Wrapped with Yellow and White Wrappers before Any Systematic Teaching

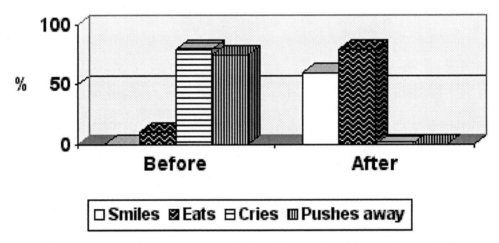

Figure 2.2   Louis's Reactions to Sandwiches Wrapped in White Before and After

when Louis pushed his lunch away or the two times he cried. After the full lesson is complete, we keep count of Louis's reactions for a few more weeks. To everyone's delight, as Figure 2.2 shows, Louis no longer seems to care about whether his sandwich wrappers are yellow or white.

In the previous example, we portrayed both learning and teaching. Where does it all begin? From infancy onward, how we react to events—in a broad sense, our behaviors—are continually changing. When those behavioral changes are relatively long lasting, we say we are learning. Moving from needing to be fed to being capable of preparing one's own meals; having no numerical concepts to the ability to determine the amount of money to pay for something and what to expect in change; feeling frightened when setting foot into a strange classroom to confidently entering the place—all these exemplify learning. The methods of change, a fading procedure in Louis's case, illustrated teaching. The change in the rate of his various behaviors demonstrated learning.

Learning about Teaching and Learning

For many years, behavior analysts have been studying how learning occurs by systematically measuring changes in behavior in relation to events that come before (antecedents) and after (consequences) the action. Whenever they find that certain arrangements of consequences and/or antecedents produce consistent results across species, locations, individuals, and so on, that is cause for excitement. The discovered rules describing the nature of these relationships are called **principles of behavior.**

The heart of this book consists of a description of practices based on well-established behavioral principles. We illustrate how they have been applied, especially to teach students with various kinds of developmental challenges, and suggest how you in your role as an educator can make use of these techniques. The principles hold true for everyone: you, us, children developing typically, those experiencing developmental challenges, rocket scientists, people living in poverty, bankers, professors, construction workers, migrant laborers, the aged and infirm, star ball players, and, yes, cats, dogs, and parrots. The differences may crop up in the individual's rates of learning, the form or medium of the response (most people and some parrots speak, and toddlers and some children and adults communicate primarily by means of gestures), how broadly they apply what they have learned; how long the new learning lasts, and the resources necessary to achieve the best possible results. Knowing basic principles of behavior empowers us because we then can use this knowledge to help us better understand, learn, and teach. Let us, therefore, begin by exploring how learning occurs.

How Does Learning Come About?

The systematic behavior change we call learning can be simple in nature or more and more complicated. One of the most basic forms is called **classical conditioning.** Here is the way classical conditioning takes place: Just about every complex individual (organism), animal or person, is born with a tendency to respond to certain events in predictable ways. When there is a loud sound, baby responds with a startle. A puff of wind or a sudden bright light before her eyes causes her to blink. Pavlov's dog salivates when meat powder is placed into his mouth. We call the events that elicit the responses **stimuli (S)**. When the stimulus **(S)** is seen to produce or elicit the behavior or **response (R)** just about every time, independent of the individual having any particular experiences related to the response, we call that eliciting stimulus, an **unconditioned stimulus (UCS)**, and the reaction an **unconditioned response (UCR)**. Figure 2.3 shows the series of events in this kind of classical conditioning.

So far, no learning has occurred. In fact, the "unconditioned" **(U)** in "UCR" and "UCS" is the same as "unlearned." We say this because infants blink the very first time a light flashes before their eyes. Learning enters the picture when a different stimulus, like the sound of a bell or mom touching the light switch, regularly coincides with the unconditioned stimulus *and* the individual responds almost identically as when the UCS was presented. Because they are paired closely in time, now baby blinks when mom touches the light switch; Pavlov's dog begins to salivate when the bell rings. The new working stimulus is called a **conditioned stimulus (CS)**, and the response it produces, one almost identical to the unconditioned response, is called a **conditioned response (CR)** (see Figure 2.4). The event is called classical

Figure 2.3   Unconditioned Response

Figure 2.4   Classical Conditioning

conditioning. When our mouths begin to water at the smell of fresh bread or we feel nauseated by the sight of a particular food that previously made us sick, classical conditioning is responsible. Most of us would use the word *learning* to describe these kinds of changes in patterns of behaving.

Operant Conditioning

We assume that parents and educators of students with special challenges usually are less interested in the kinds of teaching just described and more concerned about schooling of a different variety. This is where the concept of **operant conditioning** enters. B. F. Skinner, the name of the individual most closely associated with the concept of operant conditioning, selected that term because the classes of behavior of interest here are those that "operate on the environment." An antecedent stimulus is not essential to operant behavior. Randomly, baby smiles, points, or waves his hand—an **operant behavior (B)**. The learning occurs when that operant is useful (or instrumental) in producing a dependable effect or **consequence.** The response increases in rate when that consequence is satisfying or **reinforcing (R+)** (see Figure 2.5).

Baby smiles; mommy picks him up and feeds or hugs him. Daddy heralds baby's first hand wave with an enthusiastic, "Good boy! You're waving to daddy." Guess what? Baby begins to wave more often, especially when he sees his daddy (Figure 2.6). This increase in behavior (B), especially when

Figure 2.5   Operant Conditioning

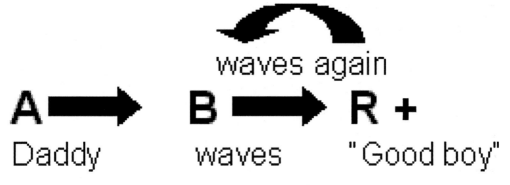

Figure 2.6   Operant Conditioning

certain antecedent cues (As) are present, is primarily what we seek as educators. As you will see later, many of our teaching objectives involve increases in the number of words spoken, read, spelled, or written; in the variety of job tasks performed correctly; and in the number of children with whom a youngster plays or the number of minutes she sticks to a task. In essence, rapidly promoting enduring learning of functional objectives is what quality education is all about.

How do we accomplish this purpose, though, especially with students who learn slowly, for whatever reason? They have so much catching up to do—so many new challenges facing them. Despite this, today we can count ourselves fortunate. Thanks to thousands of operant learning experiments, many dependable principles of behavior are available to us. These principles provide us with the tools for delivering a high-quality education to anyone.

Take the example we offered previously in which Louis was taught to "tolerate" a white wrapping on his sandwich. How did that relate to operant learning research? In many ways. Embedded in the procedure are the essentials:

- The reinforcer—food that Louis enjoyed
- The behavior—consuming the food

However, the connection between the two was blocked by Louis's emotional response to the antecedent stimulus: the unfamiliar color. The teacher's task was to teach Louis to accept a wrapping of a different color, minus the interfering response. The dilemma is shown in Figure 2.7.

The teacher was able to turn to related research showing that errors, which typically provoke unpleasant emotional reactions, could be avoided. That had been accomplished by means of an "errorless learning"[4] method, first found to be successful with pigeons and now known to be as effective with people.

This strategy consisted of the following:

(1) Starting with an effectively working A-B-R+ connection (here, where A = yellow paper and the behavior, B = accepting and the consequence, and R+ = consuming and enjoying the reinforcer)
(2) Very gradually introducing hardly noticeable differences in the A
(3) Obtaining the same results (consuming/enjoying) as before
(4) Gradually continuing the very slight adjustments in A until it was really quite different, in this case, white

---

[4]H. S. Terrace, Discriminative Learning with and without Errors, Journal of the Experimental Analysis of Behavior 6 (1963): 1–27.

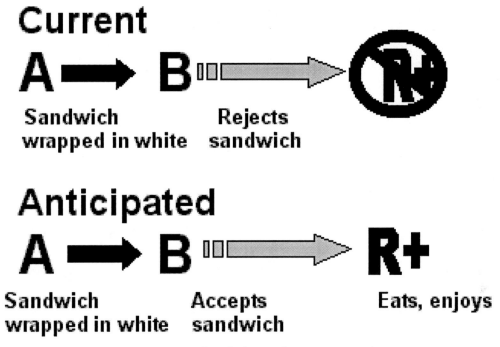

Figure 2.7   Louis's Original and Changed Reactions to White Wrapper

This is not to imply that we know how to teach everyone everything, but it does mean that, regardless of developmental barriers, if we understand how to support behavior change, we can make the most of our efforts. When we see what conditions reliably influence behavior, we can use that information to broaden our knowledge and hone our skills as educators. The outcome is that we teachers, administrators, supervisors, parents, coaches, communication specialists, and other professionals can help our students make the most of their capabilities.

The A-B-Cs of Behavior Change

As you now see, discoveries about the nature of the relationships between a particular behavior and what came before and after it may enable us to design powerful instructional methods. These associations are the reason that it pays for us to get a better handle on what these relationships are all about. For instance, we know that particular events like reinforcers (R+s) or other consequences (Cs) that follow a behavior may influence the way that behavior is repeated later on. If the consequence is a reinforcer, the change will be an increase in the rate of the behavior. We also saw an illustration of how antecedents, the things that happened before the behavior of interest (daddy's presence), affected the outcome. Let us look more closely at how this happens and how one might arrange these antecedents and consequences to promote meaningful change in the behavior of interest. We will begin with context, move on to prompts and cues, and then shift over to the powerful role that consequences play in this drama.

Context

Learning happens somewhere, in a **context** or setting that can encourage or discourage the rate of change. Just as a field of grain needs to be plowed and fertilized to nurture optimal crop growth and yield, educational contexts must be prepared to support productive change in the behavior of concern. Supportive contexts can help students and teachers focus on the task at hand or put out their best effort. Different contexts actually alter the relation between the behavior and its consequences. The very same behavior, say, yelling and screaming, might be reinforced within the context of a soccer game but punished within the context of a wedding ceremony. The context produced by eating a great deal of salted popcorn will increase the reinforcing value of drinking fluids.

It would be wonderful if there were one ideal context for learning, but sadly that is not so. Some students learn better in an environment free of distractions; others when they can observe other students engaged in work or see items or activities they would like to have or do. The different sounds and sights to which students attend can vary also. Some want to touch certain objects; interact with particular people, or watch or participate in given activities. Others might be repelled by those stimuli. Time of day, weather conditions, noise, minutes since one's last meal, and health status (yes, contexts can be internal, too), may also influence what happens.

Antecedents

Antecedents are events that precede the behavior of interest more immediately. Those stimuli are especially important when they are related to specific consequences. Prompts and cues like hints, gestures, rules, oral and written instructions, signs, pictures, symbols, sounds, or the behavior of others serve this purpose in educational settings. They signal to the person the chances a particular behavior has of being reinforced. We saw how daddy's presence eventually became a signal for baby to wave. Daddy's being there made it more likely that he would wave back, smile, talk to baby, and so on. After all, if he or anyone else were not there, waving would produce little. "Time for snack. Let's clean up," signals that the behavior of cleaning up will lead to getting a snack, especially if it has previously.

Have you noticed that, contrary to popular belief, these stimuli do not guarantee the response we would like to see? They only alter the probability that the behavior of concern will follow. Getting the response depends on the student's **learning history,** particularly the frequency and regularity with which the behavior has resulted in reinforcing consequences in that context, when cued by that particular stimulus.

Threats and promises are good examples of this point. If a parent promises a child a preferred treat after he cleans his room but then regularly fails to deliver, eventually the promise will have little effect on how often he cleans his room. However, if the promise is always kept and the treat remains a powerful incentive, the child will begin to "trust" the promise and act accordingly.

We adults are no different. Recall your own driving patterns, say, when the posted speed limit is 55 miles an hour. If you typically drive faster than 55 miles an hour in a particular region and nothing directly or indirectly unpleasant results, there is a good chance that you will continue to speed there despite the posted or cued limit. Instead, if you have seen others detained by the police or you yourself have received speeding tickets when exceeding the limit in that area, you probably slow down there.

Consequences

Later, when we go into the details of successful instruction, we will talk about how to manage prompts and cues effectively. For the moment, let us concentrate on the most essential element of the learning process, the consequences (Cs) of the behavior of interest. One of several things can happen as a consequence of any given behavior:

- It can produce an item or event, one the person chooses or works to get at the time. This consequence is called a **positive reinforcer** (**R**+). Assuming that the rate of the behavior increases or persists at a high level, we call the process **reinforcement.** (Realize, though, that what is a "wanted consequence" for one individual at one time may mean nothing for that person at a different time or nothing or the opposite to a different person. We return to this point in Chapter 4.)

Examples

Harry hits himself in the chest (the behavior). His mom looks at him for a moment (the consequence: getting attention, something Harry "wants"). Harry hits himself again and again (result: increase in behavior following receipt of consequence).

How Do We Know whether a Consequence Is a Reinforcer?

The only way to know whether a consequence is functioning as a *reinforcer*—either positive or negative—is to see whether the rate of the individual's behavior increases when it leads fairly regularly to that consequence, that is, if the behavior tends to be repeated more often after it has resulted in or been instrumental in producing or removing that consequence.

Sally says "milk" (the behavior). Her mom giver her a little milk. Sally says "milk" again (result: increase in behavior following receipt of consequence).

- It can produce an item or event; one the person "prefers" to escape from or avoid at the time. This consequence is called a **punisher** (or an **aversive stimulus**). When the rate of the behavior decreases thereby, the process is called **punishment** (not negative reinforcement).

Examples

Harry hits himself on the chest (the behavior). His mom shouts, "Stop hitting yourself" (the consequence of yelling provides something aversive). Harry stops hitting himself (decrease in behavior following receipt of consequence).

Sally runs toward the street (the behavior). Her mom yells, "Sally, *no*." (the aversive consequence). Sally no longer runs toward the street (decrease in the rate of the behavior following receipt of consequence).

How Do We Know whether a Consequence is a Punisher?

The way to know whether a consequence is functioning as a punisher is to see whether the rate a particular behavior *decreases* when followed regularly by that consequence.

- It can remove an item or event; one the person chooses to or works to get rid of or escape from at the time. The consequence the person is avoiding or escaping from is a punisher (or an aversive stimulus). When the rate of the behavior *increases* thereby, the process is called negative reinforcement (negative because something is subtracted; reinforcement because the preceding behavior increases). (Note that this is not punishment because here the rate of the behavior increases.)

Examples

Harry hits himself on the chest (the behavior). His mom stops urging him to eat his vegetables (takes away something aversive). The next time his mom urges him to eat his vegetables, Harry hits himself over and over (Harry's self-hitting increases). His behavior has been negatively reinforced (increase in behavior following removal of consequence) and so has his mom's terminating her urging.

Sally is seated in the circle with the other children. The others begin to sing a song. Sally asks for a break. The teacher guides her to a quieter spot. The next time the children sing, she asks for a break (increase in behavior following removal of consequence).

- It can remove something the person has worked for and would like to keep or keep doing (a reinforcer or reinforcing activity), resulting in a decrease in the rate of the behavior. Generally, when something reinforcing is taken away, we use the term **response cost** to describe the operation. When the opportunity to continue engaging in a reinforcing activity is removed, the term **time-out** is used as the descriptor.

Examples

Harry has been earning tokens he can exchange for his favorite orange juice when he does his lessons without hitting himself on the chest. When he hits himself on the chest, his teacher takes a token away (response cost). Harry hits himself less frequently while doing his lessons (decrease in behavior following removal of consequence).

Harry hits himself on the chest (the behavior). His mom turns off the television program he was watching for five minutes. He stops hitting himself. His behavior decreases as a function of the cost of the response—the removal of or time-out from the opportunity to watch something he enjoys.

Sally is seated in the circle with the other children who begin to sing a song Sally especially enjoys. Sally starts to scream the words. The teacher has everyone stop singing. Sally stops screaming. They all start to sing again, and this time Sally does not scream (decrease in behavior following removal of consequence).

Sally jumps up and down so forcefully while the group is singing her favorite song that the other children become upset. The teacher removes Sally to a quiet place for a few minutes (time-out). When Sally rejoins the group, she does not jump up and down again (decrease in behavior following removal of consequence).

- It can stop presenting the punishing consequences that previously have been functioning to reduce the behavior. In that case, we can expect the rate or strength of the behavior gradually to return. The term for this process is **recovery.**

Harry has been hitting himself (the behavior) less and less frequently after his mom began to shout at him every time he did that. Now his mom has stopped shouting at him when he hits himself. Within short order, Harry is back to hitting himself as often as he formerly did (the behavior recovers its former rate).

Sally disturbs the group by jumping up and down loudly while they are singing her favorite song. No one removes Sally to a quiet place for a few minutes. Sally's rate of jumping up and down recovers to its original level.

- If the behavior led to positive reinforcement but no longer does, then a process called **extinction** is in effect. After a while, the response eventually decreases.

Examples

Harry hits himself (the behavior). His mom does not pay attention to that any more. After a while, Harry hits himself less frequently (behavior decreases).

When the children start to sing, Sally asks for a break. Her request is repeatedly ignored. Sally stops asking for a break.

Table 2.1 summarizes these behavioral processes, describing the effect on the behavior as a function of the consequences operating on it.

Table 2.1 Terms for Processes Based on the Relation between the Response and Its Consequences

	Operation		
Nature of Behavior	Behavior →	Behavior →	Behavior →
Change	Something added	Something subtracted	Something no longer added or subtracted
Increases	Positive reinforcement	Negative reinforcement	Recovery
Decreases	Punishment	Response Cost/time-out	Extinction

Behavioral Procedures

Maybe you have already noticed that these processes can operate without regard to a person's intentions; that each of these processes is identified by the actual changes in a student's behavior rather than the intended change of the teacher. The true change in a behavior can be determined only after observing many opportunities, not just one episode. For example, we may scold a child for running around the room and notice that the child immediately sits down. From this single interaction, we may conclude that scolding is a punisher—it seems to have resulted in reducing the child's running. However, when we monitor what happens over the course of the entire day, we see that the rate of running around is quite high and sustained. In this case, our interaction with the child—although we tried to scold him—actually provided something reinforcing (most likely our attention) because the behavior of running was maintained or even strengthened over time. We might test this guess that attention is the reinforcer by withholding that consequence—that is, we stop scolding the child when we see him run. If, over time, he runs less and less, then we would feel more comfortable concluding that scolding was a reinforcer because withholding it (i.e., putting the behavior on extinction) led to a reduction in that behavior.

You also may have noticed that there are several procedures that lead to increases or decreases in the strength of a behavior. In other words, there is always more than one way to change a behavior, whether we are trying to increase or decrease its strength. This diversity of options is very important to remember with your students. To decrease a behavior, you do not have to resort to punishment. You may choose instead to reinforce some alternative action. Likewise, you may want to use extinction to reduce the rate of some behavior but realize that you do not control the effective reinforcer—perhaps the reinforcers are provided by peers. In such a case, you may opt to use a response cost strategy involving a point system that you have established. In each case, there are many strategies that you can choose to use.

The Three-Term Contingency

Figure 2.8 is a picture of the **three-term,** or **A-B-C,** contingency, set within its context. Notice how the consequence, C, influences B over and over. As we now know, if the consequence is a reinforcer, the rate of the behavior it follows will increase. We also have just seen that other consequences can have different but similarly powerful influences.

These concepts are straightforward, and one would think they should be easy to apply. However, that is not necessarily so, especially because people have different learning histories and because how badly they want to have or to avoid something changes from circumstance to circumstance. We must understand and adjust for these complexities if we are to teach effectively.

Although some consequences, like food for the hungry, rest for the weary, and money for the poor, are almost universally reinforcing, as we have hinted, many consequences are specific to the person within a given context. While lots of people seek and enjoy companionship and affection, others may not. Viewing a football game may appeal to one audience; an opera to a different one. If you are fortunate, your closest companions enjoy providing

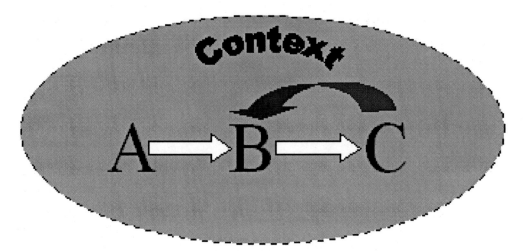

Figure 2.8   The Three-term Contingency Set in its Context

pleasure and support; but have you ever heard of someone who seems to delight in inflicting or receiving discomfort? We all have our likes and dislikes in food, jobs, and recreational activities.

Complex Learning

So far we have talked about the simpler processes of behavior change. As you might have suspected, though, that certainly is not all that there is. Learning is not only about increases and decreases in behavior. Among others, it also involves the following:[5]

- The behavior taking place under one set of circumstances and not under a different set of circumstances, as in dressing for the cold only in winter. The name for this is a **simple discrimination.**
- One behavior occurring under one set of circumstances while another behavior occurs under a different set of circumstances: dressing for the cold when it is snowy or dressing for the heat when it is warm and sunny. Because each behavior is dependent on one of two or more antecedent conditions, it is termed a **conditional discrimination.**
- Practicing the same behavior across differing circumstances: being polite at home, in school, at work, and with authority figures. Behavior analysts call this **generalization.**

---

[5]For a more thorough, technical treatment of this subject refer to Sulzer-Azaroff and Mayer (1986) *Achieving Educational Excellence,* or (1991) *Behavior Analysis for Lasting Change.*

- Continuing the behavior over time, for example, speaking French now as well as you did in school 20 years ago. **Maintenance** is the term behavior analysts use here.

Each of these more complex forms of learning will be included later in this book where they seem especially relevant. In Chapter 7, you will learn more about broadening the circumstances under which a behavior occurs, and in the chapters on teaching strategies, you will learn about narrowing the circumstances for behaving in given ways (**discrimination learning**). Beforehand, though, we begin by helping you decide what to teach and elaborate on how reinforcement can be integrated within systems to produce powerful teaching and learning of productive, contextually appropriate communicative and social skills.

Were you to survey the field of "behavioral education," you would discover a huge and ever-expanding number of examples of effective teaching strategies based on principles of behavior. You might see how the standardized test scores of students in the ghetto have surpassed those of many in the wealthier suburbs; young children have mastered calculus and can perform intricate jobs that many adults find challenging. Learners have included just about every category, from infants to golden-agers, those with developmental delays, business managers and executives, school administrators, scientists, teachers, parents, and regular preschool through postgraduate learners. Curricula have covered training in just about every imaginable academic, social, personal, and vocational skill area. Increases in classroom academic performance, self-help, vocational, interpersonal, leadership and many other skill categories have been the happy outcome.[6]

Limitations on Our Teaching

Before going any further, notice that we do not promise you the ability successfully to teach any or every student all you would like them to learn. First of all, individuals have their own physical limitations. No more than we can spread our wings and fly like a bird or become Olympic gold medalists in the broad jump if our legs are short, neither can we expect to teach people who lack the essential physical attributes to learn and perform exactly as their more fit peers do.

That is the bad news. The good news, though, is that physical abilities (even including brain function) can improve as a result of intensive training

---

[6]Check out the educational pages and links of the Cambridge Center for Behavioral Studies' Web site (www.behavior.org) for sources.

and experience, especially in the early years. Therefore, just as anyone can improve the distance of her broad jump through training, given rich educational experiences, so children with delays of various kinds can increase the length and number of their academic, social, emotional, and physical strides.

More good news is that in the same way humans have discovered they can fly with the help of an airplane, people with physical limitations can make use of technological supports to assist their performance: walkers or wheelchairs to help them go from place to place; glasses and hearing aides to improve the way they see or hear, and picture systems or electronic communication boards to support their ability to interact with others. We need to include optimal use of aides like these within the student's list of high-priority objectives.

The second important constraint is that many aspects of the environment are not under our control. If these events are tied to the behavior of concern and we cannot manage them, we will not be able to change the behavior. Among others, these limitations could include the following:

- Lacking sufficient tangible resources like funds, space, equipment, and supplies
- Lacking intangible resources like sufficient energy, patience, knowledge, and skills
- Internal events, unpleasant ones the person would try to avoid or end, like hunger pangs, aches, and pains, or pleasant ones, like the satisfaction a person derives from moving his body in a particular way
- The actions of others—groups of strangers, friends, family, community members, supervisors, and peers

If we find ourselves unable to continue along a path for the reasons just stated, we have a few choices: Push harder, give up, or find another way. Pressing harder actually is a fairly common response. It worked before—why not now? When we insert money in the soft-drink dispenser and it fails to deliver, we push the lever or button harder and faster. When a student fails to repeat a phrase he was able to say last week, we prompt him again and again and again. Had we successfully taught Kevin, Gloria, and Elvis to operate the washing machine, we probably would repeat the same technique to teach Erica. When she fails to master the skill, we repeat those methods over and over and over, and often all we accomplish is wearing ourselves out. Ultimately, we give up. Then, in our frustration, instead of assigning the responsibility to the teaching technique, where it rightfully belongs, we are tempted to blame the student or some other outside cause. "She is a poor learner." "Her disability is at fault." "What would you expect with parents like hers?"

> We can change only what we can manage.

Giving up, also not unusual under the circumstances, sounds like copping out. Indeed, maybe it is; but often there is another, better way. Good teachers seek to change how they teach by using different tools and new approaches. It may just take stepping back, reviewing the situation, and using a different approach. We might, for instance, break the teaching steps down into much smaller parts or use pictures or diagrams to prompt what is to come next. We could even work backward, instead of forward[7], completing all steps ourselves except for the last—pushing in the dial—which we leave for Erica. Assuming that she is successful there, next we would omit the last two steps—turning the dial to the proper position until she mastered that— and the process would continue in that way until she could complete the entire sequence on her own.

Sometimes, though, a particular alternate way may not be the wisest approach. We need to ask ourselves whether the extra effort, time, material, and other resources would justify the results. Do the costs of achieving this objective warrant the benefits? Using the elaborate method we described to teach Erica to operate the washing machine might take more time than we can spare currently. Perhaps it would make more sense for the present to teach her how to bundle her dirty laundry for us to wash for her. Would it be more advisable to remove the white wrapping from Louis's sandwiches and substitute it with a yellow one? Could the time be used more wisely to teach him how to communicate his wants and needs more effectively? In Chapter 3, we will return to this point. For now, we need to realize that sometimes instead of changing the behavior, it would be wiser to change the instructional objective. Nonetheless, setbacks of this type do not mean that the laws of behavior are at fault; rather, it is a particular set of circumstances beyond our control that limits us.

The good news here, though, is that the behavioral approach to education can also empower students, parents, educators, friends, and companions, who can learn to apply these principles to manage their own behavior as well as that of others. Teach your students or yourself to smile or comment positively about how good it makes you feel when someone compliments you or does you a favor and you will probably find that the number of those agreeable experiences will increase.[8] When a person who craves attention says something you would just as soon not hear too often, such as complaints or

---

[7]The technical term for this procedure is backward chaining.

[8]These examples, though common, are not universal. Later you will learn that not everyone responds identically to the same events. The behavior of many people with autism is not reinforced by compliments or attention, so applying them systematically may not work for you in the beginning. Yet you can teach these students to use those tactics to teach their parents, teachers, and others to do more or less of what they like or dislike.

fault finding, direct your notice elsewhere, and after a while those irritating comments may well begin to diminish.

Summary

The Pyramid Approach treats teaching as a technology for promoting behavior change. Like any effective technology, the principles of behavior we apply are founded on scientific discoveries. At the most fundamental level are laws of classical and operant conditioning. All other assessment and instructional strategies flow from those laws, including the way we analyze and understand what currently is controlling given behaviors and adjust the educational context of the behavior of interest and specifically modify its antecedents and consequences. The broad application of such methods has produced a tremendous number of success stories, empowering educators, parents, and the students themselves. The behavioral approach to education does not promise miracles, especially when we are bound by circumstances over which we have no control. Our best alternative, then, is to rethink what we are attempting to teach. That is the main focus of the next chapter.

Chapter 2 The Why of Behaving: The Science of Behavior

To	**Read**
Discover what the research has to say about early behavioral *intervention with children with autism*	Green, G. Early behavioral intervention for autism: What does the research tell us? In Maurice, C., Green, G. & Luce, S. (Eds.) *Behavioral intervention for young children with autism. Austin, TX: Pro-Ed,* 29–44. Harris, S. L. & Weiss, M. J. (1998). Does early intensive behavioral intervention work? In Harris, S. L. & Weiss, M. J. (1998). *Right from the start: Behavioral interventions for young children with autism: A guide for parents and professionals. Bethesda, MD: Woodbine House.*
Survey, from a behavior analytic perspective, the current research and issues in the field of autism	Frea, W. D. & Vittimberga, G. L. (2000). *Behavioral interventions for children with autism. In J. Austin & J. E. Carr (Eds.) Handbook of applied behavior analysis.* Reno, NV: Context Press, 247–273.

For characteristics, definitions and basic principles of behavior	Michael, J. L. (1993). *Concepts and principles of behavior analysis.* Kalamazoo, MI: SABA.
Learn generally and in depth about applied behavior analysis	Cooper, J. O., Heron, T. E. & Heward, W. L. (1987). *Applied behavior analysis.* Englewood Cliffs, NJ: Prentice Hall. Sulzer-Azaroff, B. & Mayer, G. R. (1991). Behavior analysis for lasting change. Atlanta: Wadsworth Group: Thompson.
Review general inferences based on a survey of basic learning experiments	Catania, A. C. (1992). *Learning,* 3rd Ed. Englewood Cliffs, NJ: Prentice Hall.
Survey learning from a bio-behavioral perspective	Donahoe, J. W., & Palmer, D. C. (1994). *Learning and complex behavior.* Needham Heights, MA: Allyn & Bacon.
Learn the characteristics, definitions and basic principles of behavior and their relation to social and cultural issues	Skinner, B. F. (1974). *About behaviorism.* New York: Knopf.
Become familiar with science in autism treatment	Science in Autism Treatment. Association for Science in Autism Treatment, 175 Great Neck Rd., Suite 406,Great Neck, NY 11021.

To	*View*
See behavior principles in action	Videos by E. P. Reese. Can be obtained via www.behavior.org.

To	*Attend*
Hear about the latest in research, theory and issues in behavior analytic approaches to education and treatment of people with autism	The Association for Behavior Analysis state, regional,national and international conventions The International Conference on Science in Autism Treatment The PECS Forum

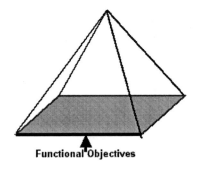

Functional Objectives

3

What to Teach: Functional Objectives

Kelly, a seven-year-old student with autism, has just been assigned to your class. From your earlier observations of Kelly in her previous class and at home, she faces many challenges. You try to learn everything you possibly can about Kelly—by reading records; meeting with the family; talking to the teachers, professionals, and paraprofessionals familiar with her; and participating in a meeting on an individualized educational plan (IEP) with all concerned. Overwhelmed by the length of the journey that you and Kelly must take together, you realize you need to make some important decisions: The first is what to teach.

Deciding What to Teach

When we decide to go on a vacation, the first thing we plan is our destination. Similarly, the Pyramid Approach to Education reminds us that our initial step in educational planning is to choose our destination. It helps for us to step back and pose this kind of long-range question before trying to answer for the here and now.

The Long-Range Goals of Education

One good way to begin is by asking ourselves, Why do schools exist in the first place? What is the purpose of public education? What does Kelly need to learn before her educational support runs out at age 21?

Getting a Job.   Often we hear that students should become contributing members of our society. For that, they need to be employed. Consequently, we teach skills to students while they are in school to improve their chances of getting and keeping a good job after graduating. We do not teach reading and math simply to be able to say that a child can read and compute but because these skills eventually should help lead to successful employment.

Living Independently.   What else do parents typically anticipate once their children reach 21 or so? We have asked this question of hundreds of parents everywhere. The resounding answer is that their children live elsewhere independently. In other words, parents hope schools will provide their children with the skills that will enable them to live outside their parents' home by the time they are adults.

     The long-term goals of education for children with autism or other severe developmental disabilities are no different from those for all students: helping them get a good job and be able to live away from their parents. The Pyramid Approach shares the same long-range goals for those it reaches. It is not any specific reading, writing, or mathematical level students might achieve but, rather, whether their skills are sufficient to help them become and remain as independent as possible.

Choosing Objectives

Having reminded ourselves of the long-range perspective, now the question becomes, How do we get from here to there? Our next step, then, is to focus in on the stepping-stones along the way. As we will see, more than one path can get us there.

Select Developmentally Appropriate Objectives

A common goal-setting strategy begins by comparing the current abilities of the student against skills mastered by typical age mates. Selection begins with those skills that are missing relative to peers. This developmental perspective suggests that if a child is five years old but does things more characteristic of a three-year-old, then one should begin teaching typical four-year-old skills.

     Making reasonable choices depends on how informed you are. Therefore, one of the first things to do is to find out about what typically developing children of the same age as your students are able to do. Such information can be very valuable. It can help guide what is and is not reasonable to expect of a child. For example, how would you respond to someone who says he wants his three-year-old developmentally delayed son independently to select his own clothes each day, to dress alone, and to put his soiled clothes into the hamper? Just about everyone one would point out that this expectation is far too high for any three-year-old.

This developmental perspective also encourages teachers and parents to be familiar with characteristic sequences in skill development in broad areas such as fine—and large-grained motor, communicative, conceptual, social, affective, sensory, and other skills. These will be useful as general guidelines but not necessarily as the sole basis for choosing curriculum content items because we realize how unsuitable it is to try to teach every age-appropriate skill to a youngster deficient in many.

Being informed about the usual sequence in which skills develop within a particular area also may guide our goal selection. Children at very young ages pick up and hold items differently from the way they do once they gain certain digital strength and coordination. We would not view a two-year-old's clenching a spoon in his fist as an error but would expect a 10-year-old's fingering position to be more age appropriate.

Identify Areas of Strengths and Weaknesses.   Use a checklist to inventory each student's performance across key areas. The developmental profiles of many children with disabilities are relatively "flat" across skill areas. That is, a child with a one-year delay in communication frequently will show a similar one-year delay in other ability areas. Such patterns tempt us to conclude that a student's performance in one area reflects his performance in other areas. However, students with autism or related pervasive disabilities often fail to follow this pattern. The developmental profiles of these children often show sharp peaks and valleys across skill areas. While their mean delay may be substantial in some, say, in subtle social skills, in others, like art, reading, or music, they may possess skills comparable to or even beyond those of their peers. Therefore, assessing abilities in each general skill area is important for every child.

When you look across performance areas, identify relative strengths and weaknesses. That is, although compared to peers a student may show delays in all areas, each child is likely to be more proficient in some than in others. Take advantage of both strengths and weaknesses when selecting goals. Obvious weaknesses readily lead us to choose objectives in areas where the student's delays are most severe.

By also focusing attention on a student's relative strengths, you can minimize the ongoing sense of failure the student would experience were instructional efforts limited only to critical weaknesses. Building on strengths leads to high rates of success and reinforcement. In fact, one effective strategy is to begin instruction not as you would be tempted—with the next level—but back one or two levels, where success virtually is guaranteed. The momentum of doing well and receiving appropriate reinforcement will carry both student and teacher along, readying them for greater challenges beyond. Furthermore, your focus on strengths is likely to coincide with activities the child enjoys, providing a motivational avenue to new skills. If your student has a "talent" for drawing, begin with a drawing exercise and then gradually shift it over to a writing task. Other children may have different strengths, such as singing, physical skills, or the ability to use pictorial representations drawn by others. The point is that knowing a student's relative strengths allows you to take advantage of these strengths to teach for success.

Promote Pivotal Developmental Skills.   Given whatever needs to be accomplished within the remaining available time and resources, teaching students with special needs is always a contest in efficiency. From the infinite number of possible instructional objectives, we need to choose those that will give us the "biggest bang for the buck." Certain clusters of "pivotal" skills serve as tools for mastering many other objectives. You could teach a child to clap his hands, or to touch his nose, or to tap his head as if these were three separate lessons. More effective would be to teach the child to imitate simple body actions, imitate object selection, and imitate object use. Then you would have a powerful strategy to rapidly develop new skills. Thus, generalized imitation functions as a pivotal skill. Other such skills could include attending to general instructional cues, orienting to one's name, effectively reaching for and picking up objects, and requesting desired items. Children who lack these kinds of pivotal skills are at a great disadvantage when it comes to more advanced learning.

Consider Student's Chronological Age When Choosing Instructional Objectives.   Applying a developmental perspective intuitively makes a great deal of sense, but sometimes, as the gap between the student's age and developmental level increases, we need to consider other factors. For example, if our student is 18 years old but is assessed as performing similarly to typically developing three-year-olds, then a strict adherence to the developmental model would suggest that we should work on skills appropriate for three-year-olds. Such reasoning easily can lead to providing this teenager with the kinds of activities and educational toys preschoolers enjoy. If you have ever watched a teen-ager or adult playing with pegboards or stringing large wooden beads, however, you probably have felt as uneasy as we have. In responding to this concern, many practitioners maintain that we should use age-appropriate materials in our teaching. The materials (including toys) that teenagers use should be the same as those used by typically developing peers.

One difficulty here lies in locating age-appropriate materials the student can successfully manipulate or play with appropriately. Another is that while we may succeed in locating such articles—maybe chess pieces instead of pegs or a basketball rather than a large rubber ball—we have to ask ourselves just how functional the activity is for the student, especially given time constraints.

Given that the student's skills already are delayed, time becomes an important issue. We need to begin to make some difficult choices, selecting the most critical ones from the large pool of possible instructional objectives. Should we concentrate on teaching age-appropriate social skills to a 15-year-old, or do we need to focus on enabling him to develop abilities that will be most beneficial to him in an adult-oriented world? An example may help clarify this point. People often have expressed to us their desire to teach their high school–aged students with severe challenges to be able join their age-mates for lunch in the cafeteria. Suppose, though, that a particular student seems frightened in crowded situations. How necessary would it be to teach this student the skills to eat his meals in a large communal setting? To decide, you might ask yourself, "When you have traveled to another city, have you ever asked a friend to take you out to the local high school for lunch?" Let's face it: After we graduate high school, most of us would be delighted never to have to eat in a school cafeteria again. Apparently, that skill is of time-limited value.[1] If we consider future needs, would not it be preferable to teach our 15-year-old to eat lunch in a break area among a small group of adults? That will serve him throughout his working life.

Another concern about using a developmental approach is that chronological age may be used inappropriately to explain behavior. "Oh, he's just in that stage—you know—the terrible twos!" In this case, the age of the child is viewed as a cause of his actions. Still one more issue is that teachers and parents overrely on age to choose objectives. If I want to choose a skill to teach my three-year old, I simply have to look at what other three-year-olds are doing and teach these same skills. If my student learns the skill—coloring, watching a video—then he is "acting" like a three-year-old. This reasoning risks overlooking the behavioral sequences that a developing child learns along the way, depending too heavily on the age at which certain behaviors typically appear.

For example, you are working with a six-year-old child who knows about 100 spoken words. Use of a checklist indicates that the child cannot name several convenience stores. Therefore, you set up a lesson to teach the child to appropriately answer the question, "Can you name some convenience stores?" After many trials, the child learns to respond, "Seven-Eleven, WaWa,

---

[1]It should be noted that our culture sets the context for how appropriate and time related a particular skill is. For example, in a kibbutz in Israel, the full community does eat main meals together. Thus, in such a setting, learning to eat cafeteria style would be viewed as a life-long skill.

MiniMarket." It seems like she has learned the lesson. However, then you ask, "What's a store?" and the child simply repeats the list. This child has never bought anything in a convenience store. In this case, a skill was taught that actually is functional only if other skills are present—skills related to shopping, familiarity with one's neighborhood, and so on. Developing meaningful, practical skills depends more on those the student has learned previously than strictly on age.

When teachers select objectives solely on the basis of a developmental assessment or some other inventory (i.e., "knows own address," "names five items to eat"), they are, in essence, "teaching to the test." A teacher may notice that a child cannot respond to a particular test question and then decide to teach the answer to that particular test item. However, items in developmental assessment tests are designed to sample from a much larger array of children's skills because it would be impractical to probe for every one of them. By limiting teaching to just that one test skill, a teacher would be violating the very basis on which the test was created. Furthermore, the test question was part of the assessment precisely because we assume that children are not drilled to learn the answer.

Choosing Functional Objectives

Is there another perspective beyond the developmental one that will help us select objectives? One alternative is to focus attention on skills a person needs to function in our society. How can we identify these functions?

Earlier, we noted that the long-term goal of an education was to enable students to be successfully employed and to live as independently as feasible. Therefore, even though we provide educational services within a school or classroom setting, part of our ultimate goal involves skills that must be applied outside of school—in the community and home settings. Therefore, the objectives we select also need to reflect the path we wish to take in those directions. Objectives need to be primarily functional to fulfill these important purposes; purposes that will afford students timely, frequent reinforcement here and now and later in their future jobs and homes.

Deciding Whether a Goal Is Functional.   "If the student doesn't do it, who will?" This question is one that Lou Brown and his colleagues[2] pose

---

[2] L. Brown, J. Nietupski, and S. Hamre-Nietupski, The Criterion of Ultimate Functioning and Public School Services for Severely Handicapped Students, in M. Thomas, ed., Hey, Don't Forget about Me: Education's Investment in the Severely, Profoundly, and Multiply Handicapped (Reston, VA: Council for Exceptional Children, 1976), pp. 2–15.

when they want to decide whether an objective is functional. Brown noted an important difference between activities begun by students that we adults would be compelled to complete for them and those not essential for the student's progress. For example, if a girl cannot feed herself, will someone else feed her? Of course. If a young boy cannot dress himself, someone surely will do that for him. Notice also that there are many auxiliary skills associated with these important ones. Eating cannot happen unless someone buys the food, unpacks it, and prepares it. Then someone needs to set the table, clean up the dishes, and so forth. These would all be viewed as functional activities because either the child learns to accomplish these independently or someone else will need to do it for her. Similarly, dressing appropriately requires that someone will need to buy, clean, and put the clothes away.

Contrast these types of activities with an objective like teaching size, shape, or color by enabling a student to fit items into their proper slots in a form board. If a child did not fit all the pieces into a four-shape form board by the end of lesson time, how essential would it be for the teacher to replace all the pieces before being able to progress to the next activity? Is this the most functional way to teach such skills?

Using Functional Activities as Vehicles for Teaching Other Skills

An especially meaningful way to teach students to think (i.e., cognitive skills), to interact with others, and to build their physical and communicative abilities is to set instruction within a functional context. So, rather than instructing a student about colors and shapes solely by using colored circles and blocks, we would find more meaningful materials and activities. In the process of organizing the clean laundry to put it away, we might teach a student to sort different items of clothing, shirts, socks, pants, or underwear by what they are used for or by their color or shape. Or you might teach him to separate the light from the dark clothes or group them by type of fabric in preparation for washing. While learning to put away toys, a child can be guided to arrange them by use, color, form, size, or number. (Later in the book we present various techniques for carrying out this instruction.)

How can we assure ourselves that we are covering the full range of necessary functional skills for any given student? In contrast with the developmental approach, where we looked for "underlying" skills and partitioned our objectives according to their form ("cognitive" versus motor skills—gross or fine), here we stress the importance of functional activities. We organize our objectives by asking what the student will need to be able to do within the various facets of daily life and classifying them into environmental or skill-based domains according to their common function. Critical environments include areas associated with living at home, at school, in the community and at work.

Critical broad skills that may be needed across environments include recreation and leisure skills as well as social and communication skills. First we address issues connected with environmental domains.

Functional Skills within the School

Within a school setting, we are used to planning to teach academic skills. Federal, state, and local educational agencies are responsible for specifying curriculum content students are supposed to learn through elementary, middle, and high school years. In general, such curriculum content emphasizes reading, writing, and arithmetic, along with specific factual information, such as history, art and music appreciation, and so on. Why have these skills been selected? Do we teach these skills merely to be able to say, "Johnny can read at a fourth-grade level?" No. It is because for the great majority of students, progress in these skills will contribute significantly to their success in earning a living and living as independently as possible. It will be possible for some special needs students to participate in exactly the same curriculum as that designed for the general population. However, if it is not reasonable to aim to teach a student the same curriculum content, we must still keep in mind that our lessons ultimately should help each student function more successfully in the world beyond school.

When we consider the skills that students need to succeed in school, we quickly see that academic tasks are only part of the story. Students with special needs are expected to engage in the same categories of activities as those within regular education settings. These include following individual and group instructions, taking turns, moving around the classroom and the school (e.g., going to gym, the nurse's office, the main office, the art room, and elsewhere), and being able, when appropriate to remain within identified areas (e.g., a play area, a classroom, or a line). Note that while regular academic objectives can be included within this domain, they are not the only focus. Rather, we consider all skills that students need to successfully manage themselves in school.

Functional Skills within the Home

The skills that everyone needs to be able to live successfully in a home environment can be clustered within a "domestic domain." Functional skills within this domain would include activities related to eating (storing, preparing food, eating, cleaning up, washing dishes, and putting away utensils), dressing (getting dressed, washing, sorting clothes, and folding and putting away clothes), grooming (washing, combing and/or brushing, and brushing teeth), cleaning (sweeping, mopping, vacuuming, and dusting), and recreation/leisure (playing with toys and games, watching television, and listening to music).

Why should a classroom teacher be concerned about the skills that students need to learn to use at home? Take the parents' perspective. Would you as a parent be pleased to learn that your child had learned to read and write but could do so only within the confines of the classroom? Undoubtedly not. Therefore, skills taught in the classroom must be able to be used within the home. Similarly, unless students learn skills for living successfully outside the parents' home, they will not be able to fully participate in our society. Although parents will have more natural opportunities to teach their children domestic skills, teachers and other educational professionals tend to have more instructional expertise for accomplishing this long-term goal. Of course, parents can learn the same teaching tools as used by successful teachers.

As we noted earlier, the age of the child will impact the degree of independence we may reasonably expect. For example, we can anticipate that a four-year-old boy can learn to help set the table, but the materials used, such as plastic cups and napkins instead of the full set of fine china, should reflect his age. Subsequently, we will discuss how important it is to teach even young children to be actively involved in many routines within the home—in part because the more they can accomplish, the greater the greater the opportunity for setting a variety of communication goals.

Functional Skills within the Community

Assuming that students are to function effectively within their local and wider communities, teachers within the regular education systems focus considerable effort on teaching students about the "real world"—the world beyond the classroom. The same is true of students with special needs. We may need to modify our methods for our special students but not that long-term objective. Because most schools lack sufficient resources to bring their students in contact with the broader experiences the world might offer, teachers arrange instead to convey the world to the students through media like books, newspapers, magazines, films, videos, slide shows, computers, the Internet and so on.

Where does "the community" begin? Fundamentally, "the students' community" is everywhere they might spend time now or later outside their home or primary classroom. Initially, children need to learn to move around all areas of the school and later to function effectively in parks, playgrounds, shops, libraries, health care settings, transportation, and the many other places youngsters make use of outside of school.

Even very young students, including preschoolers[3] need community-based training. Even if teachers routinely do not take preschoolers out of the

---

[3]A. Bondy, and L. Frost, The Delaware Autistic Program, in S. Harris and J. Handleman, eds., Preschool Programs for Children with Autism (Austin, TX: PRO-ED, 1994), pp. 37–54.

school building, such training is warranted with children with special needs because parents often face problems with these children when they venture outside their homes. For instance, many parents of preschool children with autism have reported difficulties when attempting to take their child to the store, medical or dental offices, places of worship, or the homes of neighbors, friends, or relatives. One family we know reported that they went shopping at 2:00 A.M. because previous attempts to take their son into supermarkets at more usual hours had proven embarrassing and futile. This was the only time they could be assured that their child would be asleep. The boy's school team decided that teaching this three-year-old to use socially acceptable manners while visiting common community settings would relieve the entire family's major problems and permit them a more normal lifestyle.

Safe Pedestrian and Transportation.   skills also fall within community-based domains. Most children will need to learn how to wait for the green light, use a crosswalk, and behave appropriately in a car: using seat belts and operating windows and doors properly. Different rules apply to riding on a school bus; others to using public transportation like buses, subways, or trains. In these latter cases, socially acceptable ways of interacting with other travelers become especially critical.

Community Recreational Settings.   offer important opportunities for skill development. Whether at a sports event, film, picnic, or other amusement, students need to be prepared to participate in such activities without interfering with the enjoyment of others. Explore your community to see what recreational facilities are available and tie some objectives to those.

Are there ways that we can subdivide the potentially vast realm of the community? One is to look at how we interact with its various elements.[4] For example, we act as consumers of products in some locations, such as stores, restaurants, and recreational facilities, while in other locations we are assisted by different service providers (e.g., banks, post offices, libraries, movie theaters, and sporting events). Quite different types of objectives need to be set for those two different categories.

Finally, when selecting a community-based objective, we need to consider our main purpose. Is it to teach the student a set of skills or to meet our own needs as consumers? If our goal is to teach a community skill, then we should not simultaneously plan to use the setting for our own personal needs. That is, if the teachers' or parents' aim is to teach a child to shop in a grocery

---

[4]D. Squittiere, and A. Bondy, Autistic Students as Consumers and Providers of Community Service: Implementing Community-Based Training within a Public School System (paper presented at The Association for Behavior Analysis Convention, Philadelphia, PA, May 1998).

store, then the adults should not plan to do their own shopping at the same time. Should a temper tantrum suddenly erupt, they would want the freedom to be able to leave, not feel bound to remain because they have not finished purchasing all the items on their lists[5]

Functional Job Skills

Given that one of the school's principal functions is to help students develop and practice job skills to enable them to obtain and retain satisfactory employment, many decisions must be made about what objectives to set, when, where, and how. Many of the general developmentally and functionally related objectives, like core academic subjects, social skills, and so on, can be tied to eventual successful employment. Additionally, there are those particular to specific jobs, including using tools and materials and performing tasks correctly in their appropriate sequence. Just as an auto mechanic must know what tool needs to be used with what parts in what order, a schoolteacher how to handle audiovisual equipment when teaching academic subjects, and professional ball players how to handle the ball, our students need to master the specifics of their own trades. Still, long before providing work materials to our students, there are a great many skills that can be addressed involving more age-appropriate materials.

Generic Work Skills. Some features are common among most jobs, despite dissimilarities between particular ones. Included here are the ability to arrive and depart on time, to follow specific instructions, and to practice basic social skills, like being appropriately attired, meeting fundamental hygienic standards, saying "Good morning" and "Good evening" and "Please" and "Thank you, " cleaning up one's work space, refraining from distracting others, and so on.

How correctly a job is done is of paramount importance. Suppose that a candidate for a mail-advertising job were able to fold a brochure neatly sometimes but not every time. His potential employer might insist on no more than a 1-percent error rate. She probably also would be interested in the total number of times the applicant was capable of repeating the process within a given time period (its rate), for example, filling 100 envelopes per hour. What if the worker could meet that standard but was capable of doing the job for only one hour per day? As his teacher, you might have to refine the objective to include a minimum time requirement of six hours per day, five days a week. Finally, we learn that the job requires that the employee work among five other

---

[5]A. S. Bondy, and K. Battaglini, A Public School for Children with Autism and Severe Handicaps, in S. Christenson and J. Conoley, eds.; Home School Collaboration (Silver Springs, MD: National Association of School Psychologists, 1992), pp. 423–41).

employees, sharing the same supervisor. Being able to work effectively only under one-to-one supervision, with no one else present, would be insufficient. The training objective would need to be clarified to include those kinds of specifications.

The previous example illustrates several among many potentially important task dimensions that we ought to consider when setting instructional objectives:

(1) Frequency or number: A minimum number of work units to be completed
(2) Rate: The minimum number of repetitions per time block
(3) Accuracy: The minimum proportion of perfect performances to the total number or the maximum error rate allowed
(4) Duration: The minimum length of time the work must continue
(5) Social/communicative elements: Social standards to be met at work
(6) Supervisory conditions: The ratio of workers to supervisors

Can we teach these general skills without working on actual vocational material? That is, must an 18-year-old student use actual job materials to begin to gain the kinds of skills just listed? Suppose that we were to change the situation to a much younger child learning to put away his blocks. Just as being able to fill a single envelope would be unsatisfactory, were this boy to put away one block properly, we hardly would conclude that he had mastered the skill. More likely, we would feel content only if he put away many blocks (number) within a set amount of time (rate) without making too many mistakes, such as putting the square blocks with the round blocks (accuracy), throughout the entire cleanup time (duration) surrounded by other children (social/communicative) and with the teacher standing far from the child and next to the doorway (supervisory). As we can see, each of the factors we have identified as important for job success can be identified in teaching younger children far simpler skills. Similarly, wherever possible, we can and should include such elements within activities at school and home (cleaning one's room, setting the table, doing the laundry, and so on).

Within the Pyramid Approach, we promote working on these general vocational skills long before beginning to teach the student how to manipulate real work materials. Furthermore, it is important to recognize that these changes gradually will accumulate over a number of years. Therefore, good record keeping, in the form of carefully documented changes in these various facets of doing a good job, is very important. Such information will permit new annual teaching teams (whether IEP or vocational) to be able to set realistic goals based on prior student progress. Next, we turn to critical skill clusters that often cross environmental domains.

Recreational and Leisure Skills

Leisure and recreational skills form a domain that spans multiple activities and environments. Although the particular recreation/leisure activities in which we engage at home often differ from those in community settings, presumably both are fun (i.e., reinforcing), relaxing, and socially acceptable. For example, in our home, recreation or leisure activities might include watching television, listening to music, reading books and magazines, playing cards and board games, and small-area sports such as Ping-Pong or pool. We may be less concerned with wider social aspects. In the community, different rules apply. How we conduct ourselves while watching a movie may differ from the way we watch television; listening to music at a dance involves different skills from listening to music with a headset, and playing baseball demands following many more procedural and social rules than playing Ping-Pong.

We need to consider especially teaching recreation/leisure activities for transition times or long waiting periods because those times are especially challenging. Remember that we all tend to self-stimulate more when we have nothing to do—biting our nails, bouncing our legs, or playing with our hair. In fact, in our culture, under circumstances when waiting often is necessary, books, magazines, music, video displays, and other stimuli often are supplied. When visiting the doctor's or the dentist's office, many of us anticipate the possibility of a delay and make adequate provision by bringing along something to do in the interim—a book to read or our laptop computer. Similarly, we must make certain that our students can entertain themselves in socially acceptable ways while waiting for the next activity or en route to their destinations. Being capable of reading a magazine, playing with an electronic or handheld toy, listening to music over a personal stereo player, or similar skills will serve our students well while using public transportation to travel about the community.

Solo and group, simple and complex, and brief and extended recreational and leisure activities are apparently an essential aspect of everyone's lives—young children, adolescents, and adults. Our students need to learn and practice these skills at home, at school, during breaks on the job, and while being transported about and making use of services and facilities in the community.

Social and Communicative Objectives

Given the characteristic social and communicative difficulties of children with autism and related conditions, designing objectives focused on promoting these skills is especially important. Instructional teams need to identify not only which skills should be taught but also the conditions under which these skills should and should not be displayed. For example, because Kelly does not greet people appropriately, the team stipulates that skill as an important instructional objective. "Being able to greet people," though, is stated too vaguely because social convention dictates when, where, and how greeting others is acceptable or not. The team needs to determine the way Kelly's peers hail one another or adults in school and elsewhere. They discover that they say "Hi" or some equivalent in these situations:

- At school when their classmates enter a room, when joining others at the cafeteria table, or in other informal groupings.
- When other children or adults say "Hi" to each other.
- When they do not respond to another's greetings while the teacher or another person in authority is addressing the class.
- In the community when a shopkeeper, salesperson, receptionist, or person in charge (doctor, bus driver, and so on) greets them first. They do not initiate or respond to greetings from strangers in malls, parks, movie theaters, and other public areas.
- There are others. Can you add a few?

In this realm especially, we see how important it is to specify objectives in sufficient detail that all the crucial conditions and restrictions are included. Clustering these skills within an IEP may be helpful to the team members as a way of ensuring that all critical skills are addressed. However, although these skills may be combined within the same IEP domain, we should not assume that all would be taught the same way.

General Considerations in Using Functional Objectives

Before finalizing a set of functional objectives, you need to take stock of the resources that are or will be available to you for achieving each. Also important is considering how suitably they will lend themselves to generalization or transfer across situations or responses and how useful they will be as conduits to other skill categories.

What Materials Should We Use?

Detailing the various times, places, and other conditions in our objectives can help us select instructional materials wisely. That is, when we construct our lesson, we should consider the long-term use of the skill, including generalization across time, place, people, and materials. Many teachers err by choosing their instructional materials prematurely. Here is an example:

Assume that an assessment has indicated that a four-year-old student does not "know" her colors. Based on this, the teacher writes an objective: "Mary will learn to identify five colors." Because the teacher has not considered the long-range purpose of knowing colors, she chooses colored paper circles (or blocks or similar simple objects). She conducts all lessons individually with Mary at a small desk. Maybe the teacher places the circles before the child and, using a prompting strategy, instructs her to "touch red." However, at another time of day, this teacher may be instructing the youngster in the bathroom how to brush her teeth. Because eight similar soft-bristle toothbrushes of different colors hang on the wall, the best cue for the child to distinguish her own toothbrush from the others is by its color. Yet, despite learning to distinguish paper circles by their color, Mary seems completely unable to use the "color" skill in the bathroom. Here many would be tempted to ascribe the problem to the child—"Mary has failed to generalize her color skills to toothbrushes"—when in reality the instruction was less than optimal.

Now the teacher would have to teach the entire lesson over with the toothbrushes because brushing one's teeth is an essential functional activity, while choosing the correctly colored paper served purely to teach that lesson and no other purpose. Would the quality of the child's life change markedly if she were unable to touch the red paper circle but could pick her own toothbrush from the group? Had future needs been considered and detailed in the objective, such extra effort could have been avoided. (Chapter 7 contains helpful information on how to design lessons to promote transfer of skills from function to function, time to time, place to place, and material to material.)

Why do so many of us choose to start a lesson on colors by labeling colored paper shapes? Maybe because it is easy to prepare such materials. While that certainly is understandable, throughout this book we hope to challenge teachers to consider their choices of materials with care, basing them on their likely effectiveness rather than on how easy they are to obtain or prepare. One way to avoid this kind of trap is to ask questions like "Who benefits from the lesson?" or "How has the child benefited from this lesson?" Such questions will help you choose which objectives to teach first. In the lesson involving teaching the child to respond to "touch red," what is the outcome from the child's point of view? When the child responds correctly, we will praise the child, "Good job! Way to go! Nice touching red!" Is such praise truly reinforcing to all students? We could try to boost the power of the reinforcer by using some type of token-reward system, but we are still the one arranging to provide some reward for appropriate performance. Are there other types of reinforcers that can be more effectively integrated into this lesson? That is, are there lessons associated with color in which the reward is built in?

What we can see in these examples is that when we want to teach a skill, such as "colors," we should first determine how color is (or should be) important to the child. This determination may take some time, as different children will have different preferences. We may decide to create situations in which color is important, as in teaching a child to find his favorite toy hidden inside a red box. When we think about Mary as a four-year-old, we can consider where color is important to children of this age. Notice that some lessons may not be age appropriate, as in teaching her to walk versus stop at green and red traffic lights (we do not expect any four-year-old to walk around the neighborhood independently). In searching for important items for four-year-olds associated with color, we may find that, besides candy, various toys, clothes, drinks, or utensils are relevant. What we must now do is find materials for which color is important but is also the only distinguishing feature. That is, we could not effectively teach Mary to request a red ball from a blue ball if the red ball is also bigger than the blue ball (or striped differently and so on). Obviously, gathering such materials will involve more effort than simply cutting out circles of colored paper, but our increased initial effort will more than pay off by reducing the total amount of time we will spend on teaching this lesson. In part, this issue is associated with selecting effective reinforcers, but it also is pertinent to the topic of which lessons we should begin to teach.

In our work with Mary, we have noticed that when offered a handful of Skittles, she always selects the red ones. What is her action telling us? First, it tells us that she 'knows' how to discriminate colors. She is very careful in her selection of the candy. Second, we now know that "red" is associated with a powerful reinforcer. Can this information influence how we teach this lesson? We can teach her to request her favorite candy (via speech, PECS, or some other modality). When she requests "red candy," what will be the reinforcer? Of course, it is simply the candy, though we will be sure to add our praise as well. Which lesson will the teacher find more interesting: "touch red" or teaching Mary to request something important? Of course, other children may be more interested in their favorite red toy, shirt, ball, or whatever.

Preparing for Generalization and Discrimination

When choosing objectives, being very precise and detailed about our instructional objectives helps us avoid falling into a couple of common traps. One is assuming that when we teach students something at one time and place, they naturally will transfer that skill to other relevant times or places (technically, the assumption is that the behavior will generalize spontaneously). For instance, if Mary learns how to ask to join in a circle game in the playground at school, she will use the same skills to ask to join other children playing in the park. The other is that the student will not automatically transfer the skill when circumstances dictate otherwise (technically, discriminate). Although Mary has learned to accompany her to a different part of the school at the invitation of the communication specialist, she will not go along with just any stranger who approaches her in the mall. Like so many other situations in life, investing up front, in this case by being as detailed as necessary about specifying instructional objectives, will pay off in the future.

Goal Selection and Generalization. Later we will review in depth methods for promoting generalization of skills. At this point, however, we wish to emphasize that your plans for generalization need to be taken into account while you are selecting and planning curriculum. Choosing single skills without regard to how they relate to other skills, settings, people, and so on is neither very effective nor efficient in the long term because you would have to reteach the skill under each of those other circumstances. Planning teams, therefore, should map the various forms that they hope generalization will take before they begin to train any specific skills. This is why we caution you to include long-term planning in the very earliest stages of identifying what to teach.

Criteria of the Next Environment

Typically, we tend to focus on the present when considering what is functional for children to learn—where they go to school, where they live, where in the community they go, and so on. A while ago, though, we noted how important keeping the big picture in view can be by asking what our students will need to be able to do when they leave school. Is there an intermediate point between our hopes for the future and our lessons for today? That is, what are our next steps, and how large should they be?

One tactic is to investigate the student's next environment and match it against what we know about his present environment. For example, if a child currently is in kindergarten, it will be helpful to know what is expected of typical first graders. Will the children be expected to sit in chairs at individual desks quite different from the classroom arrangement for kindergarten? What songs does the first-grade teacher usually teach the children to sing? Must the children have to line up at the doorway and wait for several minutes? Although these routines may not currently be expected of the kindergarten class, rather than waiting for the child to enter first grade, it may be possible to begin teaching the necessary skills before the end of kindergarten. Here, though, we want to be cautious about stretching too far because that could lead to the child becoming confused or the teacher wasting her efforts by teaching meaningless lessons. Attempting to teach a kindergartner second-grade skills can be an exercise in futility for the child and a time waster for the teacher.

The same concept of planning for the next environment also needs to be considered for adolescents and other older students. For example, if we are informed about the location of a job-training site for a trainee, it would be very helpful to find out about typical routines, such as where employees take a break or eat lunch and where employees typically meet and interact during the workday. We have found that some work locations have break areas very different from any available in a school. By knowing how it was configured at a work site, we were able to simulate the break area within the school. Students then could practice taking a break or eating lunch in the type of environment into which they would soon move. Already familiar with the expectations and routines associated with the workplace, by the time they began going to work, the students' transition from school to work went smoothly.

Summary

As so often happens, advance planning really pays off when it comes to instruction. Yet deciding what to teach our students is no easy matter because there is so much for them to learn, and the time available to teach them is finite. Planning ahead by choosing those instructional objectives of greatest importance for our students is the most reasonable way to proceed. If we remind ourselves that the long-range goals of education are to enable the student to get a job and live independently, we can match any tentative objective against those qualities.

Whenever possible, objectives should be as developmentally appropriate as feasible, especially those pivotal to learning other, related skills. Most critically, the academic, personal, communicative, and social skills we hope to teach in school, at home, on the job, and in the community need to be as functional as possible. These then have a better chance of maintaining over time and fulfilling important purposes in the student's life.

When we select and detail our objectives, considering in advance how the skill is to generalize will prove most cost-effective because it will allow us to avoid reteaching the skill from scratch under varied circumstances. Beyond obtaining essential materials, referring to the circumstances of the next environment into which the student will progress as a guidepost also should enable an efficient and smooth transition.

Chapter 3 What to Teach: Functional Objectives

To	*Read*
Develop an effective Individualized Educational Plan	Chapter 8, Develop a Balanced Program in Janzen, J. E., Understanding the Nature of Autism. In J. E. Janzen (1996). *Understanding the nature of autism.* San Antonio, TX: Therapy Skill Builders: A division of The Psychological Corporation.
Select teaching programs to match chosen objectives	Taylor, B. S. & McDonough, K. A. Selecting teaching programs. In: In Maurice, C., Green, G. & Luce, S. (Eds.) Behavioral intervention for young children with autism. Austin, TX: Pro-Ed, 63–194.

Decide what to teach how to teach it	Harris, S. L. & Weiss, M. J. (1998). What to teach and how to teach it. In Harris, S. L., & Weiss, M. J. (1998). Right from the start: Behavioral interventions for young children with autism: A guide for parents and professionals. Bethesda, MD: Woodbine House, 79–112.
Choose what to teach and how to teach it; an older version	Lovaas, O. I. (1981). *Teaching developmentally disabled children: The Me Book.* Austin, TX: Pro-Ed.
Select targets for change	Chapter 3; Cooper, J. O., Heron, T. E. & Heward, W. L. (1987). *Applied behavior analysis.* Englewood Cliffs, NJ: Prentice Hall. Mager, R. F. (1975). *Preparing instructional objectives,* 2nd ed. Belmont, CA: Pitman.
Ethically decide whether and how to select goals and objectives	Chapters 2, 3 & 4 in Sulzer-Azaroff, B. & Mayer, G. R. (1991). Behavior analysis for lasting change. Atlanta: Wadsworth Group: Thompson, 15–54. Sulzer-Azaroff, B. & Reese, E. P. (1982). *Applying behavior analysis.* New York: Holt, Rinehart & Winston.

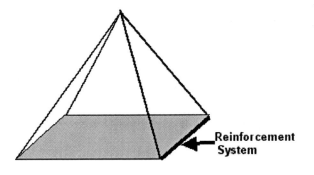

Reinforcement
System

4

Powerful Reinforcement Systems

Holding a favorite juice box in one hand and a thin straw in the other, Stacey tries to push the straw through the small circle of aluminum foil on the top. Finally, she succeeds and gleefully starts to drink the juice. Tony has a puzzle before him and is holding the last piece in his hands. He manipulates the puzzle piece, and it finally falls into place. He beams proudly as he shows the finished puzzle to his teacher, who pats him on his shoulder, saying, "Well done, Tony!" Charlotte goes outside for a walk with her umbrella tucked under her arm. Within minutes, it begins to rain. She opens up her umbrella and continues her walk. What does each of these scenarios have in common? They all demonstrate reinforcement at work.

In Chapter 2, we reviewed the basic principles of applied behavior analysis and described how behavior analysts study how both antecedents and consequences influence particular actions. Stacey's handling of the straw led to the consequence of her being able to drink the juice. The probability of her repeating the technique of inserting straws into other juice boxes increased thereby. Manipulating the puzzle piece led Tony's teacher to provide the social attention he treasures, virtually ensuring that he will try to put more puzzle pieces into puzzles. Raising her umbrella kept the rain from soaking Charlotte's hair, increasing the probability that she would take her umbrella with her in similar situations. In each case, the consequences of an action resulted in a greater probability of the children's repeating the same action. We now know that these types of consequences are called *reinforcers*. In these examples, we can see the two main types of reinforcers—positive, like receiving added juice or praise, and negative (removed or subtracted), as in stopping rain from soaking our heads, the sound of the alarm clock's buzzer, or a baby's crying.

Accentuating Positive Reinforcement

Although both applying and removing certain consequences can reinforce the actions that lead to these changes, choosing positive over negative consequences is more ethically defensible and effective in the long run. Yes, in teaching a lesson we could encourage a child to work harder to avoid our scolding, but that is using coercion, not education, as a teaching process.[1] Although any instructional procedure, including positive reinforcement, can produce some unwanted side effects, whenever possible it is best to avoid negative reinforcement, punishment, and extinction. Those latter, aversive methods tend to evoke aggression, escape, and a variety of other reactions that can get in the way of productive learning. Therefore, in this chapter we emphasize most heavily the why's and how's of using positive reinforcement effectively.

Identifying Student-Centered Reinforcers

Reinforcers powerful enough to motivate the effort that learning requires vary from person to person. Doing your homework on this subject will be worth the investment, though, because you will see your students learn better, faster, and more durably as a result.

A Natural Solution

Many of our own actions are part of a natural sequence, or **chain,** of events. We prepare our food, then eat; groom and dress ourselves, then go out; earn money, then spend it; and turn the key in the ignition, put the car into gear, press the accelerator, and go, eventually reaching our destination. We open a door and go outside and go to the refrigerator and get something we like to eat. Similarly, when our students apparently enjoy doing or getting something, those events will function as reinforcers. These natural consequences provide an excellent teaching opportunity. When you block access to that event temporarily, you now can teach the next essential element of the

---

[1]Sidman, M. discusses this topic in Coercion and Its Fallout (Boston: Authors Cooperative Inc., 1989).

sequence. Marcus runs to the door, but his teacher blocks the doorway and uses the incident as an opportunity to teach Mark to request opening the door. When Mark makes the request, his reinforcer is getting to go outside.

Let us look at another example. Suppose that a little girl, Anna, has learned to dress herself. Now you want to teach her to tie her shoelaces. For most youngsters this is a very difficult skill,[2] requiring strong motivation. You know that powerful reinforcers will be essential. You have a choice: Anna loves M&Ms and she also enjoys going out to the playground, especially when she is told that you are going to push her on the swing. Which would you choose?

If you seek a natural solution, you will take the latter course of action. Why? M&Ms are artificial and may not always be around. Anna's efforts might become dependent on your presence and seeing M&Ms; also, the candy might lose its appeal after a while, and Anna will diminish her efforts. You want to resort to those contrived reinforcers only when strong natural consequences are unavailable.

Reinforcers Incidental to Activities of Daily Living

A person's day is full of **incidental teaching** opportunities. Being able to eat the food right afterward naturally reinforces setting the table or making sandwiches. Spoken or signaled (with pictures or gestures) words or phrases could function in a similar way. Place the peanut butter jar just out of reach so that the student must request it. If number concepts are of concern, place the napkins on a shelf and ask the student to say or show the number she needs. We might say that these consequences fit the **context** of the lesson.

High-Rate Behaviors

In the event that you are having a difficult time identifying sufficient reinforcing opportunities of this kind for someone (yourself included), observe the individual throughout the day. Take note of the things he or she approaches, requests, or spends lots of time doing. Is it watching television, leafing through magazines, running around, playing with or holding a favored object, or socializing? Interpose instruction at a point just prior to those preferred, or high-rate, activities. You will be capitalizing on a behavioral principle known as the **Premack principle,** which states that access to high-frequency behaviors can serve as reinforcers for lower-frequency behaviors.

---

[2]In Chapter 7 we discuss keeping the size of the teaching objective adequately challenging to encourage progress but small or simple enough so that it can be fairly readily achieved.

Locating Functional Reinforcers

By definition, a reinforcer is functional. It increases the rate of the behavior it follows. Most of the time, the reinforcers maintaining a behavior seem fairly apparent. We shop for food to have the ingredients to prepare and then eat and work at our jobs to earn the money that allows us to buy food and other necessary and optional items. We work to stay in shape, to be healthy and attractive to others and ourselves.

Sometimes, though, the reinforcers supporting a behavior are difficult to figure out. Why does Aunt Cora complain so much? Is it because complaining gets a reaction and any attention is better than none? Perhaps you have a student with a history of displaying dangerous behavioral eccentricities, such as severe aggression or self-injury. Maybe you have attempted already to determine the function that those behaviors serve for the student. Do they allow escape from the task, or do they produce assistance, affection, or attention? Whichever is the case, those very same consequences have a good chance of being effective when used as consequences for learning productively. Give the student a way to request those items: ask verbally if possible or use a card, picture, or gesture and deliver the item following successful progress in the task at hand.

When we observe behaviors that are very persistent, even in the face of our best efforts to eliminate them, you can bet that some very powerful motivators are at work. In Chapter 6, you will see that the most effective interventions begin by determining the function of the behavior—by asking why the student is engaging in this action. As with any behavior, reinforcing consequences play a major role both now and in the past. Some students hit their heads for attention or to obtain help or gain access to something they want. Others may hit their heads to get away from hard work or noisy environments. These same consequences can be used for educational purposes—to teach more socially acceptable tactics, like calmly requesting attention or help, or asking for a break or for a moment of peace and quiet. How such lessons can be incorporated into a plan to deal with problem behaviors will be clarified in Chapter 6.

Inquire.   Similarly, if you are searching for other powerful reinforcers to apply in a particular teaching situation, do not overlook the obvious. Ask your students to say or signal what they like or want, either directly or by means of a survey, questionnaire, or checklist. In cases where a child has limited communication skills, teachers can interview parents or other teachers for this kind of information. Frequently, but not always, the answer will be accurate. What do we do, though, when our students say they want to do or have something but then fail to work hard enough for it? Sometimes a child may find something reinforcing at home but show no interest for the same item at school. Therefore, whatever we are told about a student's preferences, to verify our hunches, we must move to direct observation.

Offer Choices.   Similar to inquiring is to assess for reinforcers by offering choices. Present two objects, such as two toys, sets of materials, or activities. See which one the student reaches for or points to first. Allow the student briefly to enjoy that reinforcer, then say, "My turn." Remove the item. Then present two other choices and repeat as before. Continue this process several times until you have a set of preferred objects or symbols. Eliminate those not chosen, then pair two of the formerly preferred items. See which one of the new pairs the student prefers. Repeat with the other selected items, each time eliminating the one that was not chosen this time. By this process of elimination, ultimately you will have discovered the child's number one choice. As a bonus, you also may find that students who have the opportunity to choose their own reinforcers engage in fewer problem behaviors.[3] For children with reliable picture or symbol selection skills, you may want to use such symbols to offer the choices.

Making the Most of Reinforcers

In any given situation, some reinforcers may work more powerfully than others. Scientists have invested a good deal of effort over the years attempting to unravel the mystery of what accounts for these differences. Today we know that a person's history of learning or conditioning has much to do with them. What happens when those historical experiences blend with current circumstances also is becoming clearer. The more teachers understand the way people learn and change, the better they can maximize the power of reinforcers and, as a consequence, the outcome of the lesson.

The Origins of Reinforcers

Some reinforcers are tied to the person's physical survival, such as food, fluids, warmth and so on. These **primary,** or **unconditioned, reinforcers** are effective without parents or teachers needing to take any special actions. They appear to work the first time the individual encounters them. Other reinforcers become effective only because they occur close together in time: Sunshine and a blue sky signify an absence of rain, and a smile on daddy's face often is followed by a treat or pleasurable event like being hoisted on his shoulders and being paraded around the room. Parents or teachers often arrange these kinds of pairings as an aspect of their formal teaching: A good paper earns the student a star and praise from teacher and parents. These

---

[3]See K. Dyer, G. Dunlap, and V. Winterling, Effects of Choice-Making on the Serious Problem Behaviors of Students with Severe Handicaps, Journal of Applied Behavior Analysis 23 (1990): 515–524.

secondary, learned, or **conditioned reinforcers,** such as praise and money, are effective only because they were paired in time with a reinforcer already powerful for the person. We work hard for money because of all the reinforcing items that money can buy us.

At any given time, circumstances like deprivation and satiation can influence the effectiveness of both primary and secondary reinforcers. A student who has not eaten all day is likely to be highly motivated to learn how to make a pizza. However, a student who has just eaten a few slices of pizza probably will feel relatively sated with food. He then may put out less effort to learn a new set of words during the pizza preparation activity. Deprivation can even make a difference with conditioned reinforcers, though perhaps to a lesser extent. Anna probably will work harder on her shoe tying if she has been cooped up in the house for a couple of days and really wanted to go outside. Fortunately, people do not satiate as rapidly on recreational activities, social events, praise, recognition, affection, and other sorts of secondary reinforcers. That is why frequently praising progress can be helpful.

Reinforcers Are Relative

Do you recall your own childhood experiences of going to a toy or candy store where so many options were offered that you were unable to settle on a satisfactory choice? How about the three- or five-ring circus? Where did you concentrate your attention? You would hardly notice and certainly not make any concerted effort to pay attention to still one more option. By contrast, do you remember days when it was so unpleasant outside that you began to feel stir crazy? Almost any novel event would have been appealing.

To make the most of a potential reinforcer, then, evaluate its relative value at that time and place. The effectiveness of any one reinforcer relates to the availability of other reinforcers. Therefore, to increase the effectiveness of a reinforcer, you have two choices. You can boost the power of the reinforcer or minimize the availability of alternatives. For some students this means arranging a significant reduction in environmental distractions, while for others alternative stimuli may be kept to a reasonable level, as long as they are not overly intrusive. On the other hand, make sure that the reinforcers you do use are sufficiently powerful to retain their potency during the instructional sequence or be prepared with a sufficient array of different reinforcers to support continued effort.

Establishing Events

As in the case of the relative number of available reinforcing opportunities, special events may establish the very same item or event as a stronger or weaker reinforcer (or even a punisher). Your first candy bar or favorite beverage may taste terrific, but the tenth could make you ill. We already have seen instances of **establishing events**[4] or operations: When the person was deprived of a given reinforcer for a time, it became more powerful; when it was freely available for a long time or other stronger reinforcing opportunities were available, it became less potent. Among numerous possibilities, other examples of establishing operations might include the following:

- Providing salty food or encouraging vigorous exercise (changes the value of liquids)
- Providing brief access to items or activities or the opportunity to watch someone else enjoy that item or activity
- Exposing someone to a rhythmic beat in the background to enhance the likelihood of dancing
- Allowing an enticing aroma to waft into the room to enhance a food's attraction

You even can transform a potentially unpleasant event into a reinforcer by applying these strategies. Typically, Harry gets very upset when the gym period is over and he must return to his classroom. To avoid his frequent tantrums, his teacher comes up with a clever solution. Before she announces the end of gym, she asks Harry, who enjoys listening to music, which one of his favorite tapes he would like to listen to back in the classroom. Being aware that he will be able to listen to his preferred tape now establishes leaving the gym as major signal to the availability of a reinforcer. His teacher has changed the focus from a negative one—what he is about to lose (gym)—to a positive one—what he is about to gain (music).

Timing of Reinforcement

The sooner reinforcement happens following a behavior, the more powerful the effect. Just as we adults appreciate getting the good things in life as rapidly as possible, the same is true of students. Wouldn't you like your next raise right now rather than having to wait until the next calendar year? Don't you wish you could attend right away that basketball, football, or soccer game or the play or movie now scheduled for a month away?

The issue, though, is not only one of preference; it is one of instructional effectiveness. Behavioral scientists have found that immediate reinforcement is much more powerful than delayed reinforcement. In fact, if reinforcement

---

[4]Jack Michael used the term establishing operation while elaborating on the distinction between discriminative and motivational functions of stimuli (Journal of the Experimental Analysis of Behavior 37 [1982]: 149–55).

is delayed too long, learning can be severely jeopardized. What is too long a delay? Surprisingly, especially for new skills, delays more than even half a second can substantially reduce the effectiveness of the reinforcer.

How can teachers ensure that a reinforcer can be provided that quickly? We might be tempted to put food or drink directly into the child's mouth. However, not only does this look unappealing, but it also is not as effective as other strategies. Fortunately, we need not be limited to providing only primary reinforcers within the critical half a second. As an alternative, we can use secondary reinforcers, such as praise (e.g., "Way to go!" "Great!" or "Yes!"), instead. Of course, if you want to use such consequences, you must be sure they are truly reinforcing before you start the lesson.

"Certainly," you might reasonably protest, "we do learn to wait for our reinforcers: We save our money, put our children's needs ahead of our own, avoid getting trapped into enticing entanglements, schedule, and plan." However, that takes the right kind of reinforcement history, one in which we have learned to tolerate longer and longer delays in order to benefit the most in the long run. Youngsters and people faced with special challenges typically lack that sort of fortunate history. If they are to learn as efficiently as possible, they must attain their reinforcers immediately after each successful effort.

Earlier we noted a preference for tasks that have natural consequences, like peeling a banana, then eating the inside. In such lessons, task completion results in immediate access to the reinforcer. Not every activity has a naturally reinforcing consequence, though. When we are hired to wash dishes in the restaurant, we get paid when we have finished our job. However, while a student is learning to wash dishes, there are many steps to be acquired before mastering the entire sequence. What reinforcers should teachers provide while the lesson is taking place—that is, within the task? Along with social reinforcers, they can use a variety of other, more concrete secondary reinforcers, such as points or tokens to mark progress through the task. Over time, all within-task secondary reinforcers should be removed, while natural reinforcers for completing the task are left intact.

As we recognized earlier, learning to tolerate reinforcement delay is essential to socially acceptable behavior. Given a gradual increase in the level or complexity of the instructional objective, this will occur as a matter of course. Alternatively, consider introducing gradually longer and longer delays between the response and the more powerful reinforcement while in the meantime substituting weaker, more natural social consequences, such as praise, recognition, and feedback, to bridge the gap and assist the student to tolerate the delay.

Other Strategies to Boost Reinforcer Effectiveness

Many factors can influence the reinforcing effectiveness or potency of an item or event. **Novelty** itself can be reinforcing for some children: seeing a new toy in the classroom, being offered a new candy, or having a new shirt to wear. Reinforcer **variation** can be a powerful tool to heighten reinforcer effectiveness. It may help limit access to certain toys or games for planned periods so that their reintroduction gains the student's immediate attention. Do not offer everything you have at once. Plan to create variation and even novelty by rotating toys, treats, books, and other interesting items. Providing the same reinforcer constantly and rapidly often leads to satiation. **Choice** and **control** over reinforcer selection can raise the value of rewards selected. Giving children control over choosing may be an indirect way of influencing their actions. "It's bedtime! Do you want a glass of juice or water?" The child can choose what to drink but not whether or not to go to bed. That is not an option.

Using Powerful Reinforcers to Promote Learning

When, where, how, and how many reinforcers of what kind you arrange for your students to receive can affect how rapidly they learn and how long that learning lasts. Teachers need to be clear about the purpose of their lessons so that they can make the most suitable plans.

Frequency and Distribution of Reinforcers: Learning Versus Sustaining Change

Is it best for teachers to deliver a reinforcer immediately following every single appropriate response or to limit the number of reinforcers they distribute? That depends. If students are trying to learn to do something new and especially challenging, the more frequently they receive reinforcers, the better. For new, challenging tasks, in the beginning, arrange things to permit every single successful effort to produce a rich and powerful reinforcer. When reinforcement is scheduled to occur every time a behavior is emitted, we use the technical label **continuous schedule of reinforcement (CRF).**

You may be concerned, and rightly so, that continually receiving a reinforcer will cause it to begin to lose its value. Certainly, this would happen if the reinforcer were food, like fruit, candy, or an activity that involved much time or effort, such as shooting baskets in the gym. Fortunately, a few options are available to avoid such satiation, including the following:

- Soon begin to limit the size or amount of each individual reinforcer to just enough to sustain the student's continued effort: one or two raisins instead of a handful or a short section of a tape instead of the whole song
- Offer choices and switch to a different reinforcer
- Begin gradually to lessen how often you deliver the reinforcer (thin the schedule) so that instead of continuous it now is intermittent

Probably the most effective schedule would be one that varies about a given average number of occurrences, such as roughly every three times. The technical term for this sort of schedule is **variable ratio (VR).** These schedules tend to promote high, steady performance rates, as the example in Box 4.1 indicates. The thing to avoid in using intermittent schedules is thinning

---

Box 4.1   Intermittent Schedules and the Real World

With an intermittent schedule, only some, but not all, of the responses of concern are reinforced. This strategy may sound complicated, but it is also one of the oldest strategies around. Gambling relies on this principle, and those who run casinos are masters at controlling variable ratio reinforcement schedules. If you want to watch the impact that such schedules have on persistent behavior, just watch people operating a slot machine for hours on end.

---

them too rapidly. Begin to suspect that the schedule needs to be adjusted back to a richer level when the student's efforts begin to pale. Otherwise, change the activity, the reinforcer, or the schedule.

Should you conclude that the student is tiring of the activity, before ending it present a previously mastered task and heavily reinforce its successful completion. That enables you and the student to end up on a successful note and makes returning to the task later on more appealing. Other strategies include the following:

- Substitute a token instead. A token is like an IOU. It can be exchanged for the actual reinforcer at a later time. Most of us are familiar with bus or subway tokens. Money is a token, as is a check or certificate exchangeable for a prize.[5]
- Gradually match the schedule of reinforcement to that of the real world. If the task is doing an assembly or service job, aim toward the standard compensation for that task. In assessing natural community settings, consider multiple sources of reinforcement. For example, in addition to working for our paychecks, we all take a break every couple of hours and find something to drink or snack on. So, too, should our students have the same opportunities for the types of rewards we all seek. If an academic response is needed, try to approximate the requirements of a regular classroom (e.g., 10 spelling words for the test).

---

[5]The Pyramid Educational Products offers as a product a token system appropriate for students with delayed development.

- Pair natural consequences with the currently effective reinforcers, gradually thinning the latter while retaining the former. Similarly, if students are to succeed in a broader environment, their behavior must ultimately be controlled by natural consequences. Social behaviors tend to elicit reciprocal responses: A "Hi" for a "Hi" or a "Bye" for a "Bye." Classroom learning leads to comments from the teacher, grades, and report cards.

Teaching without Prompting

Most of us think of teaching as giving clear instructions to students. Is it possible to teach without the use of instructions or prompts? Consider the dilemma of someone given the responsibility of teaching a pet pigeon or porpoise to perform a trick. We will not be able to tell the pet what to do. Physical prompts may be impossible—imagine trying to take the head of a pigeon and pushing it to peck a small disk on a panel. Would the pigeon tolerate this? If we want to teach a porpoise to jump several feet out of the water, it will not help to try to model the trick, either. When watching people who are highly skilled animal trainers, we see that reinforcement is the best tool available when they want to teach new actions. With the porpoise, the instructor often uses a conditioned reinforcer, such as a clicker or whistle, to reward any movement out of the water.[6] Gradually, the porpoise will need to jump higher and higher to earn the reinforcer. This process starts with what the learner currently can do and rewarding small changes in the direction of the action we are trying to develop—a process known as **shaping.** In more technical terms, shaping is reinforcing successive approximations toward the ultimate objective.

Of course, although our children are hardly pets, we do face a similar problem in that our instructions and prompts may be meaningless to the child when we start to teach. The systematic use of reinforcers will permit us to shape behaviors toward more useful and functional skills even as we develop more traditional instructional strategies.

In addition to shaping new forms of behaviors, we can alter the form of existing behaviors via the same process. Joe can reliably throw a ball three feet. His teacher now stands three and a half feet from Joe and patiently waits for a throw long enough to reach him. When the ball does reach him, he praises Joe excitedly and profusely. Over the next several trials, Joe routinely throws the ball all the way. Now his teacher once more stretches things by standing four feet away. Some of Joe's throws fall short, but some reach him, and these are followed by enthusiastic praise. The teacher is using reinforcement to shape Joe's throwing over greater and greater distances.

---

[6]For numerous other examples, read Karen Pryor's book Don't Shoot the Dog! The New Art of Teaching and Training (New York: Bantam Books, 1996).

Sometimes a learning objective is so complicated that we are forced to delay reinforcement to such an extent that it loses its effectiveness. Try teaching a three-year-old to tie her shoe, or a nonverbal child to make a request in a full sentence or us to embroider a tablecloth. Success is so remote as to make it virtually unattainable. The opportunity for reinforcement is lost, and effort ceases.

The solution is to break the task down into achievable yet challenging parts. In such tasks, provided the segment is achievable, reinforcement can be immediate as well as frequent. Challenging implies that because the person has not yet fully mastered the task, room for progress remains. Once the part is close to being fully mastered, the response requirement can be adjusted by increasing its complexity or difficulty via shaping.

Differential Reinforcement: A Little Here Means a Lot There

Patience is an important aspect of shaping. When Joe's teacher used shaping to increase the distance Joe threw the ball, he had a difficult choice—how much farther should he move away? The lesson began with Joe throwing the ball three feet, and then his teacher moved six inches farther. What now was the consequence to throws that went only three feet? While they used to result in reinforcement, now they only bounced at the teacher's feet. In order to promote new behavior, the teacher had to withhold reinforcing behaviors that Joe could already accomplish and wait to see whether the new criteria could be met.

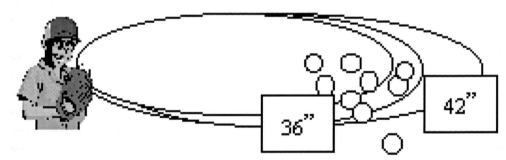

Figure 4.1   Differentially Reinforcing Increasingly Longer Throws

It is impossible to say precisely how far Joe's teacher should move. We know that if he moved 25 feet away, none of Joe's throws would ever reach him. Yet if he moved only one millimeter, stretching the throw by one foot would almost take forever. Therefore, the key is making a change in the reinforcer criterion that is likely to occur within the natural variation in all the actions of concern (see Figure 4-1). Suppose that Joe threw the ball the designated distance of three feet when he and his teacher were that far apart but that some of the throws fell short and some landed farther away. When they stood 42 inches apart, Joe succeeded more than he failed but did better at 40 inches. His teacher would have the choice of dropping back to a 40-inch distance or keeping at the same level until successes were more consistent. (No one does exactly the same thing over and over.) Patience will be required of Joe's teacher while waiting for that slightly longer throw. Withholding reinforcement from one behavior in reserve for another is called **differential reinforcement.**

Differential reinforcement can be part of a strategy in which the student cannot lose. For example, Sarah wants Sean to use an entire phrase when he asks for something, such as "I want a cookie." At the same time, she is trying to teach Sean to be polite by saying, "Please." If Sean says, "I want a cookie," Sarah will reinforce the use of the full phrase by giving him a cookie. But if he says, "I want a cookie, please!" not only will he get a cookie, but she will heap praise on him and may even give him several cookies. Both statements work to get Sean a cookie, but one earns him more (i.e., a different quantity of reinforcers).

Helping Teachers Make the Most of Reinforcement

Effective teaching requires providing high rates of reinforcement to each student. Teachers are reinforcing new skills, new combinations, and some alternatives to problematic actions such as "I like how you raised your hand instead of calling out!" How frequently reinforcement is needed is related to how often both new actions and problematic behaviors are occurring. It would not be unusual in a preschool classroom for the children to need one reinforcer per minute to promote adequate learning. In light of all the other things that must take place, the reality of life in the classroom makes it remarkably difficult for teachers to attend to the need to deliver high and sustained rates of reinforcement. Teachers are taking data, consulting with other staff, dealing with immediate crises, responding to the demands of administrators, and so on. It is not practical to expect them to remember to look up at the wall clock every minute or so. How can a teacher set a minimum rate of reinforcement for all students and stick to it?

One solution is to help teachers with one of several automatic reminders. For example, they can set a timer and each time it rings praise those students engaged in appropriate actions. A more sophisticated system involves the use of audiotapes that contain a set of tones that sound on a variable interval basis around a set period: 1, 2, 3, 5, 7, 9, or 15 minutes.[7] These audiotapes can be used either continuously or primarily during busy times when the teacher's attention tends to be required elsewhere, as during chaotic transitions, group time, or even free play. When a two-minute tape is used, it ensures that at least every two minutes throughout the activity, teachers will be reminded to scan each student to see whether some action is deserving of reward. Of course, teachers can, and frequently should, provide more than the minimum reinforcement. In Chapter 6, we describe the use of such audiotapes within an intervention effort.

Putting It All Together: Let's Make a Deal!

Teachers want their students to learn, and, as we have seen, learning means changing behavior. In our society, students come to school—because they must. These relatively small people come into a situation where more powerful people want something from them. What other relationship does that sound like? Parent and child for one. Boss and employee for another. Our bosses want us to do something—the job—for them. Why should we do the job—just to please the boss? No, we work for the boss only when we know what we will get for doing the job—the reinforcer for completing our work. We would almost never accept employment in a situation in which we did not know in advance what we would get from the job. In fact, we diligently prepare a contract containing a great deal of critical information before we start the job. That is, before agreeing to work for our boss, we negotiate a deal.

What does a well-designed deal include? Probably, we want to know how much we will get paid, the pay schedule, and information about benefits—especially our vacation days. Just about everyone knows about these aspects before agreeing to accept a job. Now think about how we often interact with our students. How many of us greet our students and then immediately tell them to get to work? We would not tolerate being treated in the same way by any potential boss who pronounced, "I want you to get to work," and offered nothing more about what you may expect in return later on. In the Pyramid Approach, we believe that we should interact with our students just as we would like to be treated in a similar situation. What we set up in our interactions with our boss should resemble what we do in our interactions with our students (even though here our relative "power" position has changed).

Therefore, when a teacher wants a student to learn something, just as when a boss wants an employee to do a job, the first thing to determine is the reinforcer—what the student wants to get or do. Once the teacher knows what the student wants, then the teacher can make a deal in which the student gets the desired outcome after learning the lesson. Furthermore, remember that just as you—even with your accomplished verbal skills—insist

---

[7]Pyramid Educational Products, Inc., offers as a product a set of Audio Reinforcer Reminder Tapes (ARRT) appropriate for students with delayed development.

on having your reinforcers listed in a written contract, so too it is reasonable for every student to have a visual or tangible representation of the deals set with their teachers.

What information should be part of this deal? The student should know what the reinforcer is, how much work is needed to earn it, and when (and how many) breaks—just like a vacation days—will be available. Over time, the nature of the deal may change. The teacher will require more work or more complicated work for the same outcome, but the contract should not disappear. Would you let your boss tear up your contract after a couple of years?

One way to create a visual representation of the reinforcer to come is to use a type of **token system.** Start by finding out what the student wants in a particular situation. Place a visual symbol, like a three-dimensional object, a picture, or a written word, on a card that represents the contract. For example, initially the card may display "I'm working for——" printed on it. It contains only a single open circle. Ask the student do a very simple task—one she already has mastered. As soon as she has completed it, immediately give her a token in the form of something small and age appropriate. Teach her to place the token on the open circle. Since there is only one circle, the deal is now complete; that is, the student has placed a token on all empty circles. Teach the student to hand in (or cash in) the tokens and immediately give her the reinforcing item. Over time, gradually add open circles onto the card until there are five circles. You might be able to include more than five circles with older students (see Figure 4.2 for an example). Gradually increasing the work the student is required to do to earn each token is like applying the principle described earlier: thinning the schedule of reinforcement.

This type of visual reinforcement system contains information about what the student is working for, how much work is needed, and when the reinforcer will be earned. You may want to add a visual symbol for "break" to this sys-tem (see Chapter 5 for a description of how to teach this skill). The student may even want to "renegotiate" the deal in the midst of a lesson; that is, perhaps she changed her mind about what she really wants.

A second option is for the teacher to use a picture of a ball that a child wants to play with and have the child earn the picture before receiving the ball. Then the teacher can cut the picture into pieces and have the child earn parts of the picture and gradually put it together like a puzzle. When all the parts are earned and the puzzle is complete, the student trades it in for the corresponding item.

No Reinforcer, No Lesson!

What should teachers do when they cannot determine an immediate reinforcer for a student? If the schedule says, "Set the table," should the teacher compel the student to perform the task? The Pyramid Approach adheres to a simple rule: no reinforcer, no lesson. If a teacher insists that a student set the table when no reinforcer is available for the student, the teacher is using his or her size or power to take advantage of the student. That is coercion, not education.

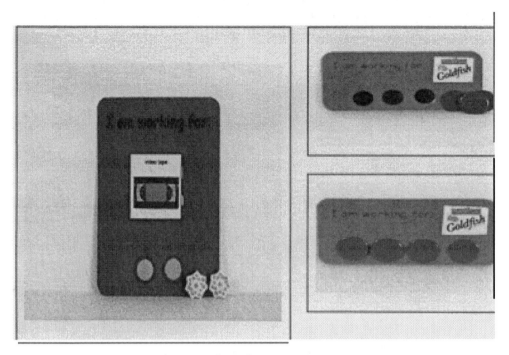

Figure 4-2   Token Boards With Various Response Requirements

Does every lesson need a token system? No. Every lesson does need a reinforcer, but remember that the best reinforcers are those that are natural to the setting or context. Teachers try to design lessons that are fun to do or that result in a sense of accomplishment for the student. However, just as many adult jobs require repetition, so do many lessons. In such circumstances, it is easy to forget the point of the task in the absence of visual reminders of what is the goal. Constantly prompting students to pay attention and get back to work is just a way of nagging, not a well-documented successful teaching strategy. If a student's attention drifts, reminders about the potential reinforcer should be sufficient to get the child to attend to how to earn it.

When you work with a student on a token system, you will be very tempted to take away tokens for inappropriate behaviors. Throughout this book, the emphasis of The Pyramid Approach will always be on using reinforcers to promote positive changes in learning. If the tokens were earned for learning a skill but an inappropriate behavior arises, develop a separate system to deal with those behaviors you are trying to reduce or eliminate. Chapter 6 provides many potential solutions.

Summary

We need to use reinforcement effectively for our students to succeed. We want to accentuate the positive by using reinforcers that are powerful for our students. Although this is easier said than done, behavior analysts have discovered a number of ways to help us find and use reinforcers.

The first and best way to learn what is reinforcing for a student is to identify events and objects natural to the situation. We can observe many reinforcers that are incidental to the student's preferred activities. Other methods include asking (by using any effective modality) what they want to work for or offering them choices between several things they would like to do or get. Unconditioned reinforcers, like water when thirsty, food when hungry, or relief from pain or discomfort, can be especially powerful. The value of conditioned reinforcers is different from person to person and time to time, depending on an individual's experiences. The more we know about our students, the easier it should be to find promising reinforcers. Sometimes, introducing new or different items or activities makes those reinforcers temporarily more powerful. Usually we see the most long-lasting results when we first routinely give reinforcers immediately after the student does what we are looking for; then we begin to systematically delay or skip giving those reinforcers from time to time.

When students do not know how to do what we expect, there is no opportunity for reinforcement. One way to deal with this situation is to shape the behavior by reinforcing actions that resemble our goal more and more closely and withholding reinforcement for actions that are not gradual improvements. This combination permits learning to progress without teachers prompting or correcting too often. Negotiating clear "deals" with our students at the beginning of a lesson allows everyone to know what to expect when they do their part. These deals can gradually be made more and more challenging, requiring increasing student effort and "tolerance for delay." A well-designed token system can be a very powerful additional tool because it allows teachers to include each of the factors that make reinforcement powerful. Everyone wins when reinforcement operates effectively. Students learn, while teachers, freed from needing to resort to coercion, can enjoy seeing the progress their pupils are making.

Suggested Readings and Viewings

To	*Read*
Use reinforcement effectively in general	The sections on increasing and maintaining behavior in Cooper, J. O., Heron, T. E. & Heward, W. L. (1987). Applied behavior analysis. Englewood Cliffs, NJ: Prentice Hall. Sulzer-Azaroff, B. & Mayer, G. R. (1991). Behavioranalysis for lasting change. Atlanta: Wadsworth Group: Thompson.

Apply behavior analysis with children with autism	Ghezzi, P. M., Williams, W. L. & Carr, J. E. (1999). Autism: Behavior analytic perspectives. Reno, NV: Context Press.
Make the most of your reinforcement procedures through variation	Egel, A.L. (1981). Reinforcer variation: Implications for motivating developmentally disabled children. Journal of Applied Behavior Analysis, 14, 345–350.
Through choice	Dyer, K., Dunlap, G. & Winterline, V. (1990). Effects of choice-making on the serious behaviors of students with severe handicaps. Journal of Applied Behavior Analysis, 23, 515–524.
Practice increasing behavior	Chapter 5: Operant procedures I: Increasing behavior. In Sulzer-Azaroff, B. & Reese, E.P. (1982). *Applying behavior analysis.* New York: Holt, Rinehart & Winston.
Gain an everyday understanding of how to increase and change behavior in general	Pryor, K. (1999). Don't shoot the dog. New York: Bantam Books.
Survey current research on reinforcement in applied settings	American Journal on Mental Retardation Analysis and Intervention in Developmental Disabilities Journal of Abnormal Psychology Journal of Autism and Developmental Disorders Journal of Applied Behavior Analysis Journal of the Association for Persons with Severe Handicaps Research in Developmental Disabilities

To	**Do**
Use a token system	Order a Visual Reinforcement System from Pyramid Educational Products Inc., 5C Garfield Way, Newark, DE 19713 (or use their display as a guide to developing your own).

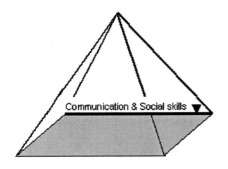

5

Communication and Social Skills

A cup of milk tips over. Little Isabella, a typically developing 18-month-old, stops what she is doing, looks at her mother, and begins to point back and forth between the spreading pool of milk and her mother. She has not yet learned to talk in whole words but her mother certainly understands what Isabella means. Examples similar to this one remind us that communication does not always involve speaking. Still, the question remains: What is communication? How does it differ from other categories of behavior?

What Is Communication?

To help clarify what is unique about communication, consider a situation in which none takes place. Silvester walks into his kitchen, where his father is sitting unnoticed, and heads straight to the refrigerator. He opens the door and takes out a can of soda. He pops the lid and drinks it. Is this an example of communication? No. Silvester simply acted on objects in the environment (the refrigerator, the soda can, and so on), and a rewarding experience, drinking the soda, followed. These actions would not have changed if his father were absent from the room—that is, getting his reinforcer did not depend on the help or involvement of another person.

Conduct directed solely toward the physical environment and leading to rewarding outcomes is not communication. Now, you may feel uncomfortable with this assertion. After all, as the father watches his son, he may well conclude

71

Figure 5.1   Noncommunicative Sequence of Behavior

that the boy wants to drink something. That is, by watching what his son does, the father can interpret what those actions may mean (Figure 5.1). Being able to interpret someone's behavior does not mean that the action is communicative. Explaining someone else's behavior does not change the nature of that behavior. Something more is required beyond a simple action affecting something in the environment for it to be labeled "communication."

Now consider a different scenario. A young girl walks into the kitchen, sees her mother and says, "I want soda!" Her mother gets up, walks to the refrigerator, opens the door, takes out a can of soda, and hands it to her daughter. The daughter quickly drinks the soda. First, notice that the girl obtains the same thing that the boy did: soda to drink. However, this episode does involve communication because the girl acted toward her mother rather than some physical object, like a refrigerator. So, communication requires (1) at least two people and (2) that one person direct a behavior toward another person. In this case, the girl directed her behavior toward her mother (Figure 5.2).

What is the role of the recipient of communication, that is, the audience? In our example, the mother's role was to mediate her daughter's reinforcement by delivering what the child wanted: the soda. The situation illustrates communication because it involves behavior directed to another person, who then provides some reinforcing outcome to the person doing the communicating. In this illustration, since the outcome was something the girl asked for, we will call this form of communication a **request.**[1]

Is there only one type of reward for communication? In our example, the outcome for the girl was something material or concrete. In another case, consider a toddler sitting in his high chair in the living room. Looking out the window, he suddenly says to his mother, "Truck! Truck! Truck!" What does he want? How likely is it that he wants his mother to go outside and get him the truck? Not very. As we continue to observe, his mother replies, "Yes, dear, that's another truck!" Clearly, the boy wants his mother's attention; for her to acknowledge what he is seeing. He is rewarded by the social response from

---

[1]B. F. Skinner (*Verbal Behavior* [Englewood Cliffs, NJ: Prentice Hall, 1957]) termed this type of behavior a "mand," created from the words demand and command.

Daughter's behavior

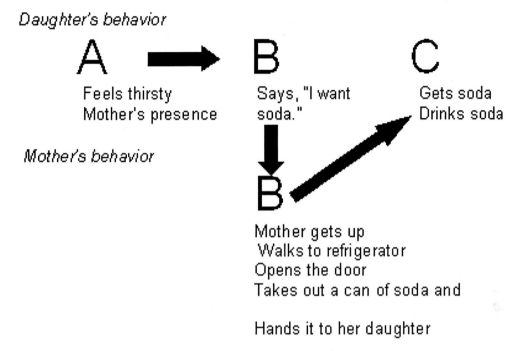

Mother's behavior

Figure 5.2   Communicative Behavior

his mother: the attention, her praise, and her apparent enjoyment in conversing with him. His communication does not get him anything material, like the soda the young girl requested. Instead, he **commented** to his mother, who provided him with a social reward.[2]

We can now define functional communication as follows: Functional communication involves behavior (defined in form by the community) directed to another person who in turn provides related direct or social rewards.

Why Do We Communicate?

As we see, we can divide these most basic purposes (or functions) of communication into two categories: requests and comments. Therefore, when our lesson is to focus on communication, our first job will be to consider what purpose the communicative act will serve for the child (i.e., what reinforcer it will produce). Before beginning, we need to know a lot about the child because this may influence the specific goals and methods of our lesson. For example, if a very young child has the classic characteristics of autism, we might predict that social rewards

---

[2]Skinner, in Verbal Behavior, pointed out that the function of this type of comment is educational; that is, it is provided to teach the child the names of various things. His technical name for this category of communicating by labeling is a "tact."

would not to be very effective for her. So, initially, instead of targeting communicative skills that serve primarily a commenting function, she would be better off if we taught her how to request the things we know she likes to do or have.

Choosing Communicative Skills to Teach

Communicating effectively consists of a fairly complicated set of skills. Teaching students with communication deficits need not be overwhelming, though, because we now have some idea about where to begin. Of course, other factors strongly influence which specific kinds of communicative skills we might teach our students at any given time. Among these are the following:

- The function of the communicative act
- Teaching for generalization
- Potentially effective modalities
- Addressing the most basic and critical communicative receptive and expressive functions
- "Talking" about emotions
- Interacting with others in a socially acceptable way.

Specify the Function of the Communicative Act

In Chapter 2, we stressed that we must look at conditions that exist prior to a behavior as well as its consequences. How, then, do we analyze the A-B-Cs of given communication episodes? Lori is standing in her classroom waiting for her students to return from recess. She is eating from a bowl of popcorn. Sarah walks into the room, sees Lori and the popcorn, and immediately says, "Popcorn!" Lori gives Sarah some popcorn. Soon, Shawn walks into the room. He walks over to the bowl of popcorn and starts to reach for some; Lori keeps the popcorn out of reach, patiently waiting for him to communicate. He remains silent until she asks, "What do you want?" He immediately says, "Popcorn!" She gives him some popcorn. Nathan walks into the room and goes over to the bowl of popcorn. Silently he reaches for some. When Lori asks him what he wants, he remains silent. She finally says, "Say 'popcorn.'" He immediately says, "Popcorn!" and she gives him some to eat.

Notice some similarities across children. Each one said "popcorn" and got some to eat. However, we recognize that each child actually did something slightly different from the others. Sarah **initiated**—she saw something she wanted, she saw someone to communicate with, and she spontaneously said something. Shawn said "popcorn" only after Lori provided a **prompt** or a **cue.** Nathan spoke the word only when Lori provided a specific type of prompt—that is, she **modeled** the word "popcorn," which he then **imitated.**

Communication Is Bidirectional

So far, the focus has been on teaching children to communicate with us. However, it is also important to teach children to understand what we are trying to communicate to them. Teachers often ask simple questions, like "What's your name?" or "Where is your pencil?" or give instructions such as "Go to gym!" "Line up!" or "Take out your crayons!" They expect that their pupils will learn to express themselves and to understand what others are attempting to communicate. Unfortunately, these two skills do not automatically develop hand in hand or simultaneously. Just as we ourselves may understand particular "10-dollar words" but never use them in ordinary conversation, we all have known children who obviously can understand a spoken word but are not capable of saying it. That is, John may be able to respond correctly when told to get a spoon, but when he needs a spoon to eat his ice cream, he may not be able to say the word. On the other hand, people who study language development have found that very young children who are just beginning to talk may be able to say a particular word but not respond correctly when that same word is used within an instruction. Therefore, speaking a word and understanding that word spoken by someone else are learned independently. As language develops, children eventually do learn to generalize across these two types of skills.

To review, before teaching children to communicate about a particular word or phrase (e.g., the word "popcorn"), we need to identify its intended functions. This list could include teaching them to do the following:

- Initiate "popcorn" when they want popcorn
- Say "popcorn" spontaneously when they see it
- Imitate the word "popcorn"
- Say "popcorn" in response to questions
- Get popcorn when presented with an array of food items and an instruction to take some popcorn

. . . and all these lessons, just for the single word "popcorn!"

Is Talking Always Communicative?

Are there reasons to speak that do not involve communication? Remember, communicative acts must be directed toward another person.[3] We may hear

---

[3]We typically separate the roles of communicator and communicative partner. Skinner, in *Verbal Behavior*, used the terms "speaker" and "listener" though he made it clear that the analogy pertained to any modality of communicative interacting. He also pointed out instances in which an individual can perform both roles; that is, in some instances, I can talk to myself just as I would to someone else. However, in this chapter we will keep things simple and separate the two roles.

a lovely song and sing it to enjoy its delightful sound. It could even be in a foreign language, and we may not understand its literal meaning. Sometimes we sing in the shower just for the pleasure of hearing our resonant voices. Singing of that sort would not meet our definition of communicative. It is not uncommon for some children with autism and related developmental disabilities to repeat words, phrases, television or radio jingles, or even entire dialogues from videotapes without any apparent understanding of what they are saying. Their words do not appear to be directed toward other people. As likely to repeat the words or phrases alone as in the presence of an audience, these children probably derive some reinforcement from their utterances different from what communication typically yields. Therefore, when we assess a child's ability to communicate, we must go beyond a description of the words the child can say to analyzing the function it serves.

Don't Just Hope for Generalization—Teach It

Wouldn't it ease our task as teachers if each of these three types of behaviors automatically spread, or **generalized,** from one to the other? Unfortunately, as research in child development and in learning has shown us, we must not assume that such generalization will occur spontaneously. That is, just because a child can imitate a spoken word or respond correctly to a prompt does not guarantee that the youngster will be able to use that same word spontaneously as either a request or a comment. In the early stages, typically developing children tend to acquire each of these types of communication skills separately. Eventually, at some later point in their development, most do learn to generalize their new vocabulary across the various skill categories. However, in the early stages of teaching children with communication deficits, we will have to arrange to teach each of these three classes independently and design specific plans to foster generalization.

Choose a Communicative Modality

Imagine your mouth taped shut. Would you still be able to communicate? Although speech is impossible, other forms are available to you. For example, you might gesture to get people to understand what you want or what you want them to do. If you knew how to sign, you could communicate very effectively with someone else who also understood sign language. Given paper and writing implements, you could write your message to someone who can read. If you were a competent artist, you could draw pictures of objects and actions. If you could not draw but had access to pictures and visual symbols, you could manipulate those. (Of course, even with all these options, you still would prefer to reach up and pull off the tape.)

Each of these examples illustrates a different communication modality. Each can work effectively alone or in combination with others. In choosing which forms to teach, we need to assess the child's current skills and different rates of learning via one or more of those modes, along with the comprehension and expressive skills of his or her local and broader audience. This selection process requires a fairly thorough assessment of the individual's communicative skills. Our assessment may reveal that although the child can imitate certain sounds, she cannot initiate requests. Our primary goal, then, needs to be to teach her to communicate functionally, while our secondary goal should be to teach the child to speak. We recognize that successful communication is a more important initial goal than speaking. Of course, if we can accomplish both—shifting from one mode to the other—all the better.

What Is PECS?

The Picture Exchange Communication System (PECS)[4] is a system illustrating the promotion of communication skills independent of speech. The training sequence in PECS begins by teaching children to initiate communication by giving an adult a picture (or other visual symbol) of something desired held by the adult. The system moves through a set sequence of phases to teach simple sentence structure, using attributes within requests, and finally how to comment. The phases within PECS consist of the following:

- Phase I: Initiating requests
- Phase II: Expanding persistence and spontaneity
- Phase III: Discrimination of symbols
- Phase IV: Sentence structure for requests
- Phase Ivb: Use of attributes within sentence structure
- Phase V: Respond to "What do you want?"
- Phase VI: Comment in response to questions and spontaneous comments

The PECS was developed by Lori Frost and Andy Bondy in the Delaware Autistic Program. The system aims to teach children (and adults) with communication impairments to rapidly acquire socially initiated functional communication skills. The system begins by teaching the exchange of single visual symbols for desired items and proceeds to teach more complex communication structures as well as additional communicative functions. While PECS was developed with children with autism, it can be effectively used with individuals with a wide array of communicative difficulties.

4A. Bondy, and L. Frost, "The Picture-Exchange Communication System," Focus on Autistic Behavior 9 (1994): 1–19.

The first phase of training takes advantage of the wants and desires of an individual. The training protocol uniquely specifies the use of two trainers: one to entice and the other to physically prompt. This strategy minimizes the chance of the development of prompt dependency. To further ensure spontaneity, no verbal prompts are used during this critical phase. Thus, PECS users first learn to initiate an approach to someone else rather than waiting for a prompt from a communicative partner. As soon as a reliable exchange is evidenced, the user is taught during the second phase to generalize this skill to other people, motivators, distance to partners, distance to the pictures, environments, and so on.

The third phase of training focuses attention on selecting specific symbols associated with specific wants and needs. While some children readily acquire the ability to discriminate between pictures, others need to be taught this skill. Training protocols involve a variety of strategies developed within the field of Applied Behavior Analysis (ABA) and include specific strategies associated with error correction.

The fourth phase involves teaching users to build a simple sentence using the icon "I want." From here, the PECS protocol diverges into two paths. One path leads to expanding vocabulary by teaching users to include various attributes in their simple sentence constructions—for example, "I want *big* cookie" or "I want *red* crayon." Lessons involving such attributes are far more motivating than learning these same concepts within a receptive mode—for example, "Touch the *big* circle" or "Point to the *red* circle."

The other path leads to the fifth phase of training, in which users are taught to respond to the direct question, "What do you want?" At this point, it is important to ascertain that the user can both respond to this question and request spontaneously when warranted.

The final phase of training involves teaching users to comment, first in response to direct questions (e.g., "What do you see?" "What to you hear?" or "What is it?") and then spontaneously.

The use of PECS has lead to rapid functional communication with young children. The use of PECS by children with autism under the age of five for at least one year has been associated with a large proportion of children acquiring speech. Other benefits include reductions in behavior management problems, increased social approach, and increased peer interactions. (See references at end of this chapter.)

Select Critical Communication Skills

Alberto approaches his teacher and frantically tugs her arm. When she does not move because she does not understand what he wants, he begins to bite his arm and slap his face. Minerva's teacher tells her to do a job. Minerva drops to the floor and begins hitting her head on the tiles. Dominick is putting on his coat to go outside to play when his teacher approaches him, saying, "It's raining outside. We can't go out until it stops raining." Dominick stares at her for a moment and then punches his head.

All these children obviously are upset with their situations. Alberto wants to get something, Minerva wants not to do something, and Dominick appears not to understand that if he waits for a while, he will be able to get what he wants. It is essential for these students to learn to communicate calmly their wants and needs by becoming competent in using particular basic critical functional communication skills. What are those critical skills?

Critical Productive Skills.   One set of critical skills deals with productive (or expressive) communication, that is, skills the child uses to communicate effectively with others. These include such important functions as the following:
   (1) Asking for powerful reinforcers (including materials, activities, and events)
   (2) Asking for help
   (3) Asking for a break
   (4) Answering "yes" or "no" to "Do you want————?"

These skills are so crucial because if the person cannot calmly and effectively communicate to get what he wants or needs, then he most likely will try other ways to obtain those outcomes. When Alberto wanted something important like a cookie, after his approach to the teacher failed, he became upset.

Asking for help is universally important. Every one of us has experienced situations in which we needed to depend on someone other than ourselves to solve a problem, like repairing our automobiles, piloting our plane home, or performing a surgical procedure essential for our survival. A child may be unable to reach a toy displayed on a high shelf, open her favorite cereal box, push her straw into the juice box, or open a heavy door. Unless the child is able to request a helping hand, a tantrum could result. At that point, an observer might realize the nature of the problem and be tempted to approach the frenzied youngster, reminding her, "You need to ask for help!" Even if the child did stop and ask for help, following the prompt, what would we predict would happen the next time the child needs assistance? There is a good chance she again will start to cry, leading someone to prompt her, and the entire cycle repeats itself, as shown in Figure 5.3. The solution is to teach the child to ask for help before a tantrum begins.

Asking for a break as a form of relief also is critically important. We all have experienced situations in which the demand is so great, long, or difficult that it has fatigued us. In these cases, we may request time to recuperate, recognizing that after our break, we will return to work. Certainly we adults negotiate our vacation days when contracting to do a new job, knowing that

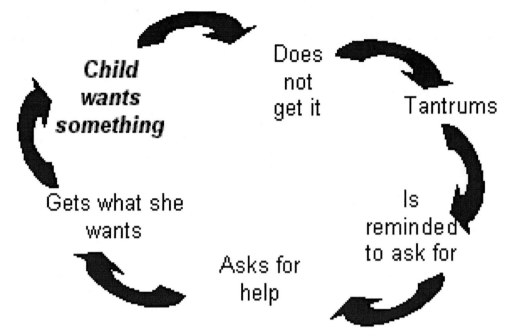

Figure 5.3   A Vicious Cycle for Getting Help

periodically we need to get away from tedious routines. Similarly, children also need to have a calm way to ask for a break, and we must teach them how. As with learning to ask for help, the key will be for the child to ask for a break prior to escalating into an emotional outburst.

Being able to affirm or reject offers from other people also is an essential skill for surviving. Billy hates pickles—their very smell makes him gag. Walter walks over to Billy and offers him a pickle. How will Billy react? In large part, it depends on Billy's communication skills. He may be able to say, "No thanks!" However, if he cannot communicate, he still will convey his disgust—maybe dramatically in some unpleasant way. If, on the other hand, Walter shows Billy something the boy likes and Billy cannot calmly communicate "yes," he might just grab the item, an outcome reasonably safe for both of them.

Notice that answering "yes" or "no" to an offer is functionally different from responding "yes" or "no" to a question like "Is this an X?" When we say "yes" to "Do you want a cookie?" we get a cookie. The utility of this kind of affirmation is similar to that of a request; it is a critical functional skill. When a youngster answers "yes" to "Is this a cookie?" he does not get the cookie. Instead, the teacher says, "You're right! It is a cookie!" Here the function is similar to that of a comment. Thus, two different lessons are needed, the first of which is especially critical.

Critical Receptive Skills.   A second set of critical communication skills is concerned with a person's ability to understand important messages from other people. These receptive skills include the following:

(1) Functional instruction/direction following (to auditory and visual cues/prompts)
(2) Transitioning from one activity to another
(3) Waiting patiently
(4) Schedule following

These particular skills are viewed as essential because failure to understand the message could be dangerous or distressing. Contrast a teacher shouting, "Move! There's a car coming!" with "What is this called?" while holding up an apple or with someone saying, "Hello!" In the first instance, failure to respond correctly could be life threatening, whereas nothing critical would result from not following the others.

Following Directions: Children's general well-being, though, demands that they learn to follow directions. The most reasonable way to accomplish this is to teach direction following that leads to functional outcomes. The teacher should design lessons in which naturally reinforcing consequences follow the directions. "Go to the door" should lead to going out the door and "Go to the refrigerator" should lead to opening it and getting something good to eat or drink. Attributes like colors can be made functional by using the name within an instruction important to the child, as in "Your favorite toy is in the red box."

Sometimes we give directions because they help *us* in some way. Dad may be thirsty and would like to ask his daughter to please bring him a soda. He realizes that he can get his drink only if his daughter understands what he said. So he considers teaching her that skill, but how would his daughter gain from the interaction? Presumably, her father would thank her or maybe give her a smile or a hug. However, we should recall that not all children with disabilities find smiles or hugs very motivating. When they do not, it is better to begin to teach the students to follow directions that will produce some reinforcement for them rather than benefiting the instructor.

Just as people use various modalities to convey their messages, they need to be able to receive and understand communication that others send in different ways. Beyond the essential ability to understand when we talk to them, to be a productive member of our society, children must learn to respond appropriately to messages conveyed in other forms. For example, drivers must adjust their reactions to different traffic signs, lights, and lines painted on the road independent of any spoken cues. We assemble toys or furniture by relying solely on diagrams to guide our actions, especially when the suppliers serve an international clientele. Although we can competently use speech and are able to read and write, frequently we find ourselves in situations where we must rely on information conveyed in visual form. Regardless of whether *they* speak, sign, or use pictures to express themselves, we must plan also to teach students to respond appropriately to a range of pictorial, written, and spoken instructions.

Transitioning from One Activity to Another: A student has a major temper tantrum on arriving at school. You firmly take him to class. After 20 minutes or so, he calms down and plays with a toy. Then you approach him and say, "It's time for gym!" He immediately starts to cry and scream. Firmly, you take him to gym, where he continues to cry for another 15 minutes before settling down to play with a ball. Then you walk over and say, "It's time to go back to class!" His tantrum picks up where it left off earlier. Following each transition throughout the day, this cycle replays itself.

What is happening here, and why do we list transitions under receptive skills?

Probably the child did not recognize that another reinforcing activity will begin shortly. Instances of this nature are not as rare as we might think. Transition times tend to be problematic because they signal not only what is next but also the termination of an ongoing, presumably reinforcing activity as well as a delay until the next one begins. These are the times when students are most likely to get into trouble, inflicting damage or attacking others or even themselves. Part of this reaction has to do with the delay issues we just discussed. However, a significant part of the youngster's maladaptive response to transitions is **elicited** by the loss of the current reinforcer.[5] What can we do about it?

The kinds of visual scheduling cues we described earlier may help but often are insufficient. While the symbols inform students about the upcoming activity, they may not provide enough information about the next reinforcer. This element is crucial, as the transition signals the loss of the current reinforcer. Is there a way to ease the situation by communicating more directly about the child's focus? Rather than describing the next activity, the teacher can signal the next reinforcer. One tactic is to use props. While the child is playing with blocks in the classroom, the teacher can approach with a ball used only in the gym. When the child is playing with a ball in gym and the teacher wants him to return to the classroom for snack time, she could highlight the reinforcer first by saying or showing something familiar about the snack before informing the child about the necessary transition. In each situation, to obtain the next reinforcer, the child must change activities. This strategy shifts the emphasis from what the child must *give up* to

---

[5]See Chapter 6 for a complete description of this behavioral function.

what the child will *get*. So, when dealing with transitions, focus on communicating about the child's primary concerns: reinforcers.

Waiting Patiently: Dominick, you recall, punched himself in the head when he misunderstood the instruction "Wait." Waiting is unpleasant for everyone because it means that the anticipated reinforcing event is being delayed. Even we adults probably can do a little better in the patience department (as our mothers constantly reminded us). What are we trying to communicate to someone when we say, "Wait"? A complex message: "I know what you want, and you are going to get it, but not for a while." What factors do we need to consider teaching this difficult but crucial message?

The first step in teaching patience is to determine what the child wants. Then we must consider whether we can control the delivery of that reinforcer. We would not choose to teach patience in a setting like a fast-food restaurant at lunchtime because we could not be certain about exactly how long we would need to wait before getting our food. A better choice would be to begin the lesson when we have prepared the lunch ourselves and it is ready to be served. Then allowing access to the reinforcing items is completely under our control.

The next important factor in this lesson is controlling how long the child has to wait. The general strategy is to begin with an interval so brief that the child cannot fail to be successful. Then we gradually stretch the waiting period. As we expand the length of the intervals, if the student fails to wait calmly, then we might slightly shorten the waiting interval for the next few teaching opportunities. Next, just as the yellow traffic light signals that we should get ready to stop at the upcoming red light, we should consider adding a visual cue to help the child succeed with this task. A bright pictorial or written "wait" signal, along with a visual representation of the item the child is waiting for, may help him better tolerate the delay.

Finally, we should prepare alternative reinforcing activities for the child to do during the waiting period. What did *you* do the last time you sat in the waiting room before you were called in to be examined by the doctor? Because they know that all of us hate to do nothing while we wait, doctors supply their patients with magazines, books, or toys. Clever parents, teachers, and camp counselors teach their students to sing songs, skim books, or play games during the interval to keep them out of trouble. Therefore, as the intervals for waiting are stretched by the teacher, students should be taught how to stay out of trouble by occupying their time (see Figure 5.4).

Figure 5.4   A Visual Cue
to Wait for Lunch

Figure 5.5   A Pictorial Schedule

Following a Schedule: How do you keep track of all the important things you need to do today, this week, or this month? Perhaps you use some type of date book to help you organize your activities instead of depending on memorizing when you are supposed to be doing what. Children also like to know what is expected of them and when those activities should occur. Therefore, we should teach them to refer to visual reminder systems (similar to the one shown in Figure 5.5 that we use) to cue them about their future schedule of activities.[6] Those with good reading comprehension can depend on written words just as adults do. Students who are unable to understand text can learn to refer to schedules depicted by images and objects instead, especially when those symbols previously have been included successfully within their instruction-following routines.

Communicating about Emotions

Many parents and teachers think that it is very important to teach children to express their own feelings and emotions. To better understand how we can teach children to communicate about their emotions, consider how typically developing children appear to learn this skill. Billy's mom is seated on the park bench watching her two-year-old son, Billy, trying to climb onto the slide. The toddler falls and scrapes his knee on the sidewalk. Billy's knee is bleeding, and he is crying. His mother runs and comforts him, "Wow, you poor boy. I bet that hurts!" In this scenario, Billy's mom used information about (1) the **context** (i.e., she saw him fall and bleeding) and (2) his **affective display** (i.e., she saw him crying) to label how he is feeling. On other occasions, when his mother saw Billy laughing and giggling while devouring an ice cream cone or when his

---

[6]Instructions for designing schedules are included in L. Frost and A. Bondy, The Picture Exchange Communication System (2nd ed.) (Newark DE: Pyramid Educational Consultants, Inc., 2000).

uncle swung him high into the air, she commented to Billy about how happy he was feeling. In short, others were teaching Billy to learn to communicate about how he was feeling by using situational and affective cues to label his feelings. Later, if Billy fell on his elbow, he might say to himself, "Gee, my elbow feels like my knee did when mom said that hurt!" He now runs to his mother and says, "Elbow hurts!" Similarly, when he tastes a delicious candy or laughs when his mom tickles him, he tells her he is happy. Especially when the emotions are negative, describing one's feelings in words may be preferable to acting them out. Saying, "It makes me feel bad when you say that" is far better than a child shouting, screaming, and flailing out when her parents say something that distresses her.

Billy's statement about his feelings is a form of comment; that is, he is describing something happening inside himself. Children typically learn to comment about external things before they can describe events inside themselves. When we want to teach children to comment about their feelings, we will need first to determine that they already can comment about common things in their environments, or we may find ourselves spinning our wheels. It is safe to assume that when he talks about the way his knee feels, Billy already has learned to comment about things surrounding him, such as about toys, furniture, and his family.

Teaching children with autism how to label their emotions can present a special challenge, especially if they do not cry, laugh, or otherwise express affect as their contemporaries typically do. Joey burns his hand on the stovetop. Although he pulls his hand away immediately and strenuously avoids touching the stovetop again, he does not cry. Catherine eats ice cream as vigorously as other children but neither smiles nor laughs. Few cues are available to their teachers and parents to guide them to label the child's feelings. Lacking those affective cues, they are less likely to label for the children their feelings. Do these children have feelings? Absolutely. Joey avoids the stovetop, henceforth and Catherine will reach for more ice cream when given the opportunity. Communicating effectively about emotions is not the same as having the emotion.

How can we arrange to teach children like Joey and Catherine to tell us about their feelings? The teacher must be fairly certain of their current status before naming the feeling for the youngster. Doing this is a lot easier for positive affect because teachers need only to pile on those reinforcers known to be effective with that youngster after withholding them for a while. Labels of negative feelings, like sad, angry, and hurt, are harder to teach because intentionally arranging for unpleasant situations is very touchy. Teachers generally would not want to provoke unpleasant feelings and indeed are responsible for doing everything possible to prevent students from getting hurt. Therefore, they need to be prepared to seize the opportunities when they present themselves naturally.

Under circumstances when a typically developing child would be expected to display a negative reaction, whenever possible the teacher should interrupt whatever else is happening, label the appropriate emotion, and encourage the student to do the same. Gradually the teacher should diminish the prompts guiding the child's verbal labeling (see Chapter 8 for additional details about fading prompts). One major dilemma presents itself if the opportunity to teach a child to label his discomfort does not present itself often enough. Are there, then, ever situations in which it might be defensible intentionally to arrange conditions to ensure that the child will experience negative feelings, such as taking things away from him abruptly or permitting him to suffer a minor discomfort rather than preventing it? That solution raises obvious ethical concerns that are best discussed openly among teachers, parents, and community representatives.

Communicating Skillfully in Social Circumstances

Several communicative skills appear to be crucial for initiating and sustaining productive social relations with other people. Among these are making eye-contact, greetings, and maintaining and terminating interactions.

Eye Contact.   Children with autism often are at a disadvantage in cultures where making and maintaining eye contact is considered essential to polite communication because many lack this skill. In fact, teachers frequently find themselves cuing the child to look at them, whether it actually is specified in the child's educational plan or not. However, they may overlook the **reciprocal function** of eye contact: A young girl's mother answers the telephone. In need of help, while her mother is conversing, she calls out, "Mom!" but her mother ignores her. The girl then begins to tug at her mother's apron, then on her sleeves and shoulders, and finally she grasps her mother's face, turns it toward herself, and shouts, "Mother!" In this situation, the girl understood that unless her mother was looking at her, there was no point in trying to communicate her needs. Thus, at an early age, typically developing children learn the importance of both looking at others and having others look at them. Consequently, when we want to teach children lacking those skills about eye contact, we need to be certain to address both initiating and eliciting eye contact from others.

Greetings.   Greeting one another appropriately also is important in society. If the youngster fails to return our "Hi" or wave, we conclude she is rude. However, learning this skill is deceptively complex. It is one thing to learn to imitate someone else's greeting. Learning to initiate a greeting is much more difficult, especially because there are subtleties to when, where, and how to greet under what particular circumstances. Furthermore, children need to initiate a greeting when they enter a room occupied by one or more people as well as when someone else enters their room. Finally, children must learn to greet only once within an interaction because repeatedly saying "Hi" is considered impolite.

Communicating within Social Interactions.   Conversational or play interactions include four distinct components. How we respond when someone approaches us is one set of skills. For example, approaching Justine, Phillip may say, "Let's play ball" or he might ask, "Did you watch the *Power Rangers* last night?" An appropriate response in the first situation would be for Justine to join Phillip in a ball game; in the second to begin talking about *Power Rangers.* A different set of skills is involved in teaching a child to approach others. That is, we also have to teach Phillip how to approach Justine. Some children may approach by formally communicating in speech or sign or with pictures or by offering a simple object (e.g., Phillip brings Justine a ball). Often many children seem to find it easier to learn to respond to social approaches than to initiate them.

Once a child has either initiated or responded to an initiation, other skills are needed to maintain the interaction by taking turns. When Phillip throws the ball to Justine, she should catch it and throw it back. Each needs to learn to take turns. When Phillip tells Justine about the *Power Ranger* show from the night before, she should continue discussing that topic.

The final interactive component, one often neglected, involves the skills essential for politely ending an interaction. Phillip may tire quickly of playing ball, but his peers might be unwilling to play with him again if he abruptly walks away in the midst of the activity. Social graces include comments such as "Hey, thanks for playing. I'm going to get a drink now!" or "Wow, my arms are tired. Let's take a break!" Justine may not enjoy watching or talking about *Power Rangers.* Still, rather than simply turning her back on Phillip, she could say, "Well, I didn't watch that show, but I did watch *The Simpsons.* Did you see that one?"

Assessing Your Student's Most Critical Communication Needs

As you can see, speaking is but one facet of communication. Other elements, like the way a student reacts to what others say, request, or do, can be equally if not even more important. Obviously, it would be impractical and inefficient to attempt every one of a student's communication objectives at the same time. As so often happens, we are most likely to achieve our best results when we know how things stand currently, where we are headed, and in what order we should address the challenge. A formal critical functional communication checklist is just the kind of instrument that teachers and parents should find especially helpful in sorting out what skills to teach, how, and when.

Table 5.1 displays a checklist containing many important skills. First, the instrument helps you to determine the characteristics of a child's current modes of behaving in terms of each important communicative function. For example, when the child wants something to eat, does he grab for things, point to items, take your hand to the item, or ask for it? Next, it asks you to judge whether the form of communication is appropriate for the youngster in that setting. After reviewing all the items on the checklist, you can arrange the skills in order of priority by asking which ones will be most important for the child to acquire first or modify, then next, and so on.[7]

Play

Play situations provide children with valuable opportunities to communicate. Although not the equivalent of communicating, the ability to play interactively certainly is essential if students' language is to develop at a reasonable pace. The mechanical requirements of play, such as how to manipulate toys and play materials, though, are distinct from the social components of play. While the manipulative skills may be taught independently of playful interactions, we need to be skillful in planning ways to enable the student to apply those skills within a social context.

Mechanical Requirements of Play.   In planning ways to foster interactive play, the teacher needs to decide the best route to follow. Is it better to provide the student with skills essential for playing in a particular way, or should teaching take place in groups from the start? If being able to manipulate toys and play materials is the ultimate objective, we might teach those skills separately from playful peer interactions. Assuming that the ultimate purpose, though, is to promote social play by teaching our student to use toys, like Legos®, modeling clay, or toy cars for props, we might begin our instruction in a setting that includes at least one other child. Then there are some play materials that require interaction from the beginning. Another person, for instance, has to be there to throw a ball if the child is to learn to play catch.

A reasonable way to choose toys is to include those that tap into the student's currently powerful reinforcers. For example, if we have noticed that a child likes to watch objects spinning around, like wheels on a toy car, a top in

---

[7]As students begin to progress, the functions of their communication can become increasingly complex. Eventually they may use their skills to solve new problems. See "Suggested Readings and Viewings" at the end of this chapter for more advanced sources.

Table 5.1   Critical Functional Communication Checklist

Name: Tony   Date: 5/14/00
DOB: 3/12/96   Age: 4-2

Skill	*Example*	*Appropriate?*
1. Request reinforcers		
edibles	Stands in front of cupboard and screams	No
toys	Climbs shelves to get toys on his own	No
activities	Brings mom to door to go outside	No
2. Request help/assistance	Tantrums when toys don't work	No
3. Request break	Tries to walk away from activity or tantrums	No
4. Reject	Tantrums	No
5. Affirm/accept	Takes offered items	Yes
6. Respond to "Wait"	Screams	No
7. Respond to directions		

Visual Directions

Orient to name being signaled	Does not orient	No
"Come here"	Complies if speaker shows reinforcer while gesturing	Yes
"Stop"	Complies if speaker blocks movement	Yes
"Sit down"	Complies if speaker shows reinforcer and chair	Yes
"Give it to me"	Tantrums if he's holding a preferred item	No
"Go get——" (familiar item)	Does not respond	No
"Go to" (familiar location)	Does not respond	No
"Put it back/down"	Does not respond	No
"Let's go/ Come with me"	Complies if mom shows keys to go in car	Yes

Oral Directions

Orient to name being called	Does not respond	No
"Come here"	Does not respond	No
"Stop"	Does not respond	No
"Sit down"	Does not respond	No
"Give it to me"	Does not respond	No
"Go get——" (familiar item)	Does not respond	No
"Go to" (familiar location)	Does not respond	No
"Put it back/down"	Does not respond	No
"Let's go/ Come with me"	Does not respond	No
8. Transition between activities	Tantrums unless he knows what next reinforcer is	No
9. Follow visual schedule	Never attempted	

motion, and so on, selecting toys with similar qualities should help motivate the child to learn to play with that toy. Children who do not often spontaneously look at pictures in books or magazines may not find putting a puzzle together highly motivating because they may fail to "see" the picture revealed by the completed puzzle.

Learning how to play with toys and other play materials, though, does not ensure that interactive social play skills will generalize automatically to social play. Instead, parents and teachers need specifically to plan ways to promote social play.

Social Play: Parallel, Interactive, and Imaginative. As they develop, children tend to move through various stages of play. Initially, very young children play alone, even when they use the same materials in the same place as their peers. Watch infants in a sandbox or at the beach. All use shovels to move sand around, but each remains an "isolated island unto herself." The children are said to be engaging in parallel play at this point.

As they begin to mature, you will notice the same youngsters building on each other's piles, asking for different tools, or making or following a suggested design. Now the children truly are interacting while playing. Interactive play also may advance to using props or costumes like hats, shoes, or fancy dresses to enable children to act out various pretend roles, such as police, doctors, cowboys, or cowgirls. Shovels and sand become props for make-believe baking, serving, and eating cookies. Costumes transform them into superheroes, moms and dads, teachers, cops and robbers, or cowboys and Indians.

You can teach children who lack these more advanced play skills by systematically shaping each of the essential elements (see Chapter 4). Do not assume that if you teach children to play with you a certain way, they will transfer that skill to play with peers; nor should you assume that you will be able to promote the child's rate of social play solely by reinforcing it yourself. In fact, you may have to carefully create a reinforcing social situation for such play skills by ensuring that their peers can provide meaningful rewards to the children with whom they are to interact. For instance, typically developing classmates of preschoolers with autism have been systematically trained to teach and reinforce their delayed peers for taking turns and engaging in pretend play.[8]

---

[8]See, for instance, K. Lifter, B. Sulzer-Azaroff, S. R. Anderson, and G. E. Cowdery, Teaching Play Activities to Preschool Children with Disabilities: The Importance of Developmental Considerations. Journal of Early Intervention 17, no. 2 (1993): 139–59.

Empathy and Sympathy: Reading Others' Emotions.   It is Friday night. Seventeen-year-old Alex has just received his driver's license and wants to borrow the family car. Going over the checkbook, his mother mutters angrily to herself. His father is calmly reading a magazine. Alex probably will choose to ask his father for the keys. As we grow up, we learn that people's feelings may impact on our chances of getting what we want or need. Of course, such material concerns are not the only reason we learn to read other people's emotions. If a girl sees her parents or teachers enthusiastically laughing and clapping their hands, she may join in and enjoy sharing their responses. If a boy sees his brother looking at a broken toy with a sad expression on his face and puts an arm around his brother's shoulders or offers some sympathetic words, his brother may thank him sincerely and his parents praise him for his compassion.

How do we teach children to become sensitive to other people's emotions? We could develop a lesson in the form of a simple receptive drill: "Point to the picture of the girl smiling." We even could teach a child to imitate someone else's emotional display: a smile, a frown, or an angry scowl. However, do these skills truly demonstrate the child's ability to understand what a smiling person is feeling? Do they go far enough, or do we need to ask how we can make knowing about someone else's feeling important to our students?

Labeling and imitating other people's emotions are only part of displaying empathy. Such a sophisticated skill involves many different ways of reacting to emotional signs—offering help to someone who looks frightened, smiling and laughing along with someone's joyful expressions, or providing assistance or sympathy to a person who looks unhappy.

As with other lessons involving communication and social skills, the use of visual cues (expressively or receptively) may aide in teaching these skills. Pictures or words may help a student "remember" to express their feelings through communication as opposed to more dramatic forms. Social Stories™ is a strategy that helps students review and rehearse potentially difficult interactions in a safe format before encountering the real situation.[9] With this strategy, students and teachers identify difficult social situations—responding to teasing, responding to or telling jokes, or determining how to tell someone to leave you alone—and then review potential alternative solutions. Pictures then are designed to help the student identify the scenario and review alternative choices. These options are initially practiced within controlled role-playing situations and then gradually introduced into real circumstances. This orientation permits the teacher to review common and unique complex social encounters for each student.

---

[9]See Carol Gray, Teaching Children with Autism to "Read" Social Situations, in K. Quill, ed., Teaching Children with Autism (New York: Delmar Publishers, 1995).

Summary

In and of itself, talking is not the essence of communication. Rather, communication involves directing behavior toward others, who characteristically respond in a reinforcing way by providing something material, paying attention, saying something in return, or in other forms. Without the use of language to make their wants and needs known, people are at a distinct disadvantage because they will use whatever works to obtain these outcomes, including harmful or distressing conduct.

Teachers and parents need to choose very carefully which communicative skills to teach by asking what functions these skill will meet, whether appropriately initiating or responding to someone else is involved, and where and when these skills should take place. The modality to be used and understood also needs to be carefully considered.

At the beginning phases of learning how to communicate, teachers need to consider several productive skills, like asking for powerful reinforcers, help, or a break or answering "yes" or "no." Also crucial are certain receptive skills, like following directions and schedules, waiting patiently, and transitioning from one activity to another.

To live effectively in our society, it is important for children to communicate in socially acceptable ways about their emotions, to make eye contact, to greet appropriately, and to participate in play groups by suitably initiating, maintaining, and departing from these groups. To interact with and gain from relationships with peers, children also need the essential mechanical and social skills demanded of play, including responding appropriately to others' emotions. We need to teach each of these skills systematically, using a mix of strategies and modalities that work currently while keeping an eye on future demands.

PECS related References

Bondy, A. & Frost, L. (1994) The Picture-Exchange Communication System. Focus on Autistic Behavior, 9, 1–19.

Bondy, A. & Frost, L. (1998). The Picture Exchange Communication System. Seminars in Speech and Language. 19, 373–389.

Bondy, A. & Frost, L. (in press). The Picture Exchange Communication System. Behavior Modification.

Charlop-Christy, M. H. (March 2001). Using PECS as functional communication training: Like water for chocolate. Paper presented at the 2nd annual PECS Expo, Philadelphia, PA.

Mirenda, P. & Erickson, K. (2000). Augmentative communication and literacy. In A. Wetherby & B. Prizant (Eds.), Autism Spectrum Disorders. Baltimore: Paul Brookes Pub. Co., pp. 333–367.

Schwartz, I., Garfinkle, A. & Bauer, J. (1998). The Picture Exchange Communication System: Communicative Outcomes for Young Children with Disabilities. Topics in Early Childhood Special Education, 18, 10–15.

Suggested Readings and Viewings

To	*Read*
Become familiar with verbal behavior from a behavior analytic perspective	Hayes, L. J. & Chase, P. N. (Eds.) (1991). *Dialogues on verbal behavior.* Reno, NV: Context Press. (A series of individually authored conceptual papers on language.) *Journal of Applied Behavior Analysis,* 1968 to present. (Presents behavior analytic research on many aspects of communicative behavior.) Skinner, B. F. (1957). *Verbal behavior.* Englewood Cliffs, NJ: Prentice-Hall, Inc. (Skinner's conceptual account of how verbal learning takes place, on a simple and complex level.) Sulzer-Azaroff, B. & Mayer, G. R. (1991). *Behavior analysis for lasting change.* Wadsworth Publishing. (Chapter on Communicative Behavior. Contains varied methods for teaching various classes of verbal or communicative behavior.)
Become familiar with the behavior analytic research in communication in developmental disabilities	Behavior Analysis in Developmental Disabilities. A reprint volume of research in developmental disabilities from the Journal of Applied Behavior Analysis, including language and numerous other topics.
Learn how to teach children lacking communication skills to use a Picture Exchange Communication System	Frost, L. & Bondy, A. (2000). *The Picture exchange communication system,* 2nd Edition. Newark, DE: Pyramid Educational consultants.

Learn how to teach children with developmental delays using sign	Sundberg, M. L. & Partington, J. W. (1998). *Teaching language to children with autism or other developmental disabilities.* Danville, CA: Behavior Analysts, Inc.
Learn how to teach social behavior and communication to children	Koegel, L. (1995). Communication and Language Interventions. In R. L. Koegel & L. K. Koegel. (Eds.) *Teaching children with autism.* Baltimore, MD: Brooks, 17–32. Hawkins, D. (1995). Spontaneous language use. In R. L. Koegel & L. K. Koegel (Eds). *Teaching children with autism.* Baltimore, MD: Brooks, 43–52. Frea, W. D. (1995). Social-communicative skills in higher functioning children with autism. In R. L. Koegel & L. K. Koegel. (Eds.) *Teaching children with autism.* Baltimore, MD: Brooks, 53–66. Lovaas, O. I. (1977). *The autistic child: Language development through behavior modification.* New York: Irvington. Maurice, C., Green, G. & Luce, S. (Eds.) Behavioral intervention for young children with autism. Austin, TX: Pro-Ed, Chapters 13 & 14. Quill, K. A. (2000). *Do-Watch-Listen-Say.* Baltimore, MD: Brooks.
Learn how to teach functional spoken language to those children with autism who can produce spoken words and phrases	Lovaas, O. I. (1981). *Teaching developmentally disabled children: The Me Book.* Austin, TX: Pro-Ed.
Teach independent behavior by means of activity schedules	McClannahan, L. E. & Krantz, P. J. (1999). *Activity schedules for children with autism.* Bethesda, MD: Woodbine House.
To	***Do***
Learn how to teach children lacking communication skills to	Attend a PECS workshop. For a schedule, contact the Pyramid Educational Consultants, Inc., 226 West Park Place,

use a Picture Exhcange Communication System	Suite 1, Newark, DE 19711. E-mail: Pyramid@pecs.com

To	***View***
Learn how to teach activity schedules at school and home, choice making, prompt fading and more	Princeton Child Development Tapes Princeton Child Development Institute, 300 Cold Soil Rd, Princeton, NJ 08540. E-mail: njpcdi@earthlink.net
Gain an overview of the potential advantages of the Picture Exchange Communication System	The Picture Exchange Communication System (PECS): A Videotape Overview Pyramid Educational Consultants, Inc., 226 West Park Place, Suite 1, Newark, DE 19711. E-mail: Pyramid@pecs.com

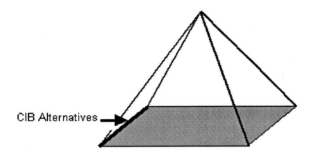

CIB Alternatives

6

Preventing and Reducing Contextually Inappropriate Behaviors

"Kill them," screams a youth. He shakes his fist, jumps up on a chair, grabs the person beside him, and pulls at his clothing.

A woman sits quietly, hands folded, head lowered, mumbling inaudibly.

A child moves her fingers rapidly up, down, and across one another, nonstop, for 20 minutes, completely ignoring everything else.

Are these inappropriate behaviors? Well, that depends.

In the first instance, if the youth did that in a restaurant or classroom, we might say "yes." However, suppose it happened during a football or soccer game? The behavior is perfectly acceptable; everyone else is doing something similar.

Lacking any additional information, your initial reaction to the description of the mumbling woman might be that she is suffering from some sort of mental illness. A few more clues about the context, though, could cause you to change your mind: a black book in her hand, an organ playing, everyone else doing the same thing, or a person clad in black standing on a raised platform. Of course—she is praying. This is totally acceptable in the context of a house of worship.

By now you are suspicious. Does the finger-flicking female have autism? Perhaps yes, if the behavior continues for hours on end with no functional outcome, but probably not, if the fingers are contacting ivory keys and producing scales or a beautiful melody.

Have you realized by now that it is not behavior per se that is inappropriate but, rather, that it is the context in which it occurs that matters? Almost any act you can think of could be inappropriate if it happened in the wrong place or at the wrong time, persisted too long, or was too weak or forceful. Recognizing this fact not only enables us to revise our assessment about what is acceptable or unacceptable conduct but also alters the way we go about addressing it. No longer, either, is the challenge insurmountable because instead of needing to eliminate a behavior, the task becomes one of changing when, where, and how often the action takes place. That is what this chapter is about. We will examine the kinds of contextually inappropriate behaviors we need to deal with, why they probably are happening, and what to do about them.

General Precautions

Acts of violence, property destruction and terrorism, unfortunately, are far more prevalent in our society than any of us wish them to be. Reducing and preventing them requires that we take every reasonable precaution to avoid their happening in our homes or organizations. Among these are the following:

- Developing and consistently applying policies relating to personnel practices, student and staff protection, health promotion, visitors, weapons, and so forth
- Promoting health by providing good nutrition, medical services, and opportunities for regular exercise
- Instituting stress-reducing methods for students and staff, including, among others, physical activities, comfortable physical environment, and relaxation exercises
- Minimizing a punitive and maximizing a positively reinforcing social ambience and instructional curriculum
- Organizing small-group or team activities in which cooperating on a task results in reinforcement for every member

Promoting the Well-Being of Students with Special Needs

Parents, teachers, and other providers of services to students with special challenges are no different than others. They are concerned with maintaining the wellness of those in their charge and of themselves. Regardless of the composition of the student body, the purpose of any school is to enable all students to learn and grow. Yet, unfortunately, individual students occasionally do things that interfere not only with their own learning and health but also with that of the others.

We are talking about harmful and socially obnoxious behaviors, like hurting oneself or others, destroying property, and disrupting others' ongoing activities with loud noises. Then there are attention-grabbing and socially unacceptable actions, like disrobing in public or interminably repeating strings of words, gestures, or songs. Although any of us might, under certain circumstances, spin a top, pull a string off a package, sing along with a favorite television commercial, curse, snap our fingers, and so on, when a person spends hours on end repeating those or other disturbing mannerisms, it becomes an issue to be addressed. Not only are the individuals themselves so engrossed in those activities that little else penetrates their awareness, but they also are interfering with the progress of others. When a team (e.g., the Individual Educational Planning or Overall Plan for Service team) deems it justifiable to treat directly an individual student's contextually inappropriate behavior pattern, we call the objective a **contextually inappropriate behavior (CIB) target.**[1] No matter how intrusive, aversive, or benign a strategy may be, as long as the purpose of the intervention is to reduce or eliminate a behavior, the focus behavior retains its label as a CIB.

The kinds of behaviors we have been describing are problems because they happen too frequently or too forcefully or often at the wrong time or place. Just knowing that reminds us that the student has been learning a good deal but of the wrong thing. The preferred solution is to promote more socially acceptable substitute behaviors by systematically applying behavioral principles as effectively as possible. These intervention procedures can vary considerably, though, depending on a number of factors, including the function of the CIBs, their resistance to change, the availability of more acceptable substitute behaviors, and the ability of the environment to support those alternatives.

Assessing the Function of the CIB

Behavior analysts accept the notion that conduct of any kind develops for a reason, not just by happenstance. This is true of all kinds of actions, including those that are adaptive, like caring for oneself, mastering learning tools, getting along with others, succeeding on the job, and so on, as well as those we

---

[1]The terminology and orientation to intervention described in this section follows the guidelines provided by state guidelines for the establishment of a Peer Review and Human Rights Committees for the Delaware Autistic Program. These behavior intervention targets include actions that are harmful to the child (i.e., self-injury), to other people (i.e., aggression), or to the environment (i.e., tantrums, property destruction, and so on) and that interfere with traditional educational approaches (i.e., self-stimulation, disruptive noise, and so on), either for the child or for other students or that may bring social sanctions against the child or caretakers (i.e., disrobing in public, speaking in a weird or bizarre manner, certain lengthy rituals, and so on).

are concerned with here: the contextually inappropriate ones. The reason is that somehow, somewhere, in the past, those behaviors either were reinforced—they got the individuals what they wanted at the time or rid them of what they did not want—or were elicited by the circumstances.

"I can see how a tantrum might produce reinforcement," you might protest, "but how could spinning an object, twirling a string, singing commercials, twiddling one's fingers endlessly, lashing out at people, or destroying things have done that?" Quite possibly the answer lies in some sort of pairing of the response with probably unintended or even accidental reinforcement. Do you know people who carry around a "lucky charm" or recite a phrase in the hope that it will ward off evil or enable them to win? We call these superstitious behaviors when we are convinced that one thing has nothing to do with the other. How did they evolve? In all likelihood through experience. Two events happened to coincide in time: the "superstitious" behavior and a powerful real or vicarious reinforcing consequence for the person. Because that kind of learning happens so swiftly, often it is difficult to determine what happened earlier to bring it about.

Inquiry of parents, teachers, and other caregivers might or might not provide some clues. Yet all is not lost if those original reinforcing conditions elude us. Recovering sufficient information from a person's past is not absolutely essential. What is crucial is finding out what events are maintaining them so that you can design methods for permitting the student to secure those same reinforcers in a more acceptable way. The objective is to determine the function of the unwanted behavior and teach the student preferable alternative ways to respond to duplicate that function. We refer to this strategy as the **functionally equivalent alternative behavior (FEAB) strategy.**

One way to search for the antecedents provoking or consequences maintaining the behavior pattern is to ask yourself or watch what tends to typically happen just prior to and following the behavior. Does the antecedent hint that occasionally it might gain the student what he appears to want or need? Is extra attention sometimes a consequence? Does the CIB gain the student access to preferred objects or events? Does it allow her to seal herself off from the rest of the demanding or distressing world or to keep unwanted contact at bay? If the consequences are apparent, you can use them to shape alternative responses. For example, withhold those consequences until you note the beginnings of a more acceptable alternative action and then deliver them on the spot.

A preferable, more ethically defensible way to discover the conditions maintaining an especially troubling CIB is to conduct a formal functional assessment.[2] Briefly, this method systematically supplies the individual with dif-

---

[2]For a detailed description of this method, see the following articles in the Journal of Applied Behavior Analysis: Carr and Durand, vol. 18 (1985): 111–26; Iwata et al., vol. 27 (1994): 197–209; Iwata et al., vol. 27 (1994): 215–240.

ferent classes of reinforcers to discover which are lawfully related to increases in the rate or intensity (forcefulness) of the behavior of concern. In a typical functional assessment, distinctive sessions are planned in which the client is:

(1) provided with some type of positive reinforcer (e.g., social attention, interactive engagement, material items, internally modulated events, and so on),

(2) allowed the opportunity to escape or avoid some type of consequence (e.g., of a social, material, or activity variety) as a function of engaging in the CIB, or

(3) observed to see whether the response is being elicited by specific or global antecedent events (e.g., pain, reinforcer removal or loss, dramatic reduction in the schedule of reinforcement, and so on).

Rates or intensity are measured for that session in an attempt to detect patterns revealing which of those consequences produces the largest increase in the CIB's rate. Often this assessment allows you to discover at least one stimulus that you now can apply or terminate to promote alternative acceptable behaviors. Of course, in the real world, CIBs are unlikely to be a function of only one set of factors, so it pays to continue to search for other supportive conditions in effect.

Identifying Functionally Equivalent Alternative Behaviors (FEABs)

Functional assessments are based on the assumption that behaviors do not take place within a "vacuum" but are related to factors in the student's external or internal environment. When we intervene, neither will those behaviors simply be eradicated and then replaced by behavioral voids. Instead, we must do the following:

- Anticipate that when a behavior intervention target is successfully minimized or entirely eliminated, other behaviors will take their place
- Plan the specific reactions and consequences to follow the occurrence of the CIB
- Identify more acceptable functionally equivalent alternative behaviors (FEABs)
- Set up an optimal reinforcement system for building those alternative behaviors

Comprehensive plans for behavior intervention must identify the FEAB before complex interventions are designed and implemented for the target behavior. Fundamental to the FEAB concept is the assumption that events in the environment (i.e., antecedents and consequences, broadly defined) shape and control each person's behaviors. If these environmental factors are not altered, even a strong attempt to suppress a CIB will fail over the long run. Why? Because the student's original wants and needs remain or return, and the target behavior has been the only way he has been able to fulfill it in the past. Thus, long-term improvement is unlikely.

Take care to distinguish between functionally equivalent and teacher-selected alternative responses. The FEAB is determined from the student's rather than the teacher's perspective. For example, if a child is screaming, the FEAB is not simply replacing it with silence, although that may be precisely what the teacher wants. The FEAB is dependent on why the child was screaming in the first place. Children who scream to get attention must be taught more appropriate (and, it is hoped, more effective) means of gaining attention. Although attempting to eliminate a behavior from a child's repertoire is reasonable, eliminating important reinforcers from the child's life is not, nor, as just suggested, is that likely to work. Instead, staff (or parents) and the child can "negotiate" when, where, and even how often to attain the reinforcer. Remember to use the "let's make a deal" strategies described in Chapter 4.

Many problematic behaviors gain the person access to some sort of reward, like a specific item or activity or someone's attention. In those situations, a reasonable plan is to teach the students to request the desired item calmly, preferably orally, or else through whatever socially acceptable modality they are capable of using—displaying a picture or written words, using a sign or gesture, or pushing a button. Perhaps the types of attention they are seeking vary according to a particular situation, as in the case of wanting recognition for their efforts versus needing assistance. In those cases, we would have to plan two distinct lessons, one to teach "How am I doing?" another for "I need help."[3]

Attention is not necessarily the sole reinforcer supporting all problematic behaviors. A young girl likes to run around the classroom, not for attention, but because it makes her feel good. Were the teacher to use some arbitrary reward for calm sitting or even punish running, it probably would not work because running remains a reinforcer and a readily accessible one at that. A better intervention would be to choose a FEAB that permits the child to run, but only on request and under conditions that would not seriously interfere with ongoing classroom routines. Alternatively, the teacher could determine when and how often the girl runs around the room and build running into the schedule accordingly. Again, the child still gets to run around the room, but the teacher gains some control over when and how much running will take place.

If escape or avoidance is the reinforcer maintaining a target response, a child could be taught a socially acceptable alternative, such as to request a break, signal a desire to leave the situation, or end a conversation. Each of

---

[3]E. G. Carr and V. M. Durand, Reducing Behavior Problems through Functional Communication Training, *Journal of Applied Behavior Analysis* 18 (1985): 111–26.

these would be FEABs to the original escape or avoidance target behavior. To teach this type of response, the teacher sets up a controlled situation that includes a relatively mild "dose" of what the student currently avoids. For example, if when presented with difficult work a student hits his classmates, the teacher could prepare a card that says "Break" on it and place it nearby. The teacher then would assign him a mildly difficult task, but not so complex as to generate an immediate tantrum. A second teacher would assist the boy to deliver the break card. On receiving the card, the first teacher would respond by guiding the youngster away from the work for a brief break. Over time, the second teacher's assistance could be faded, while the first teacher would begin to increase the difficulty associated with the demand.

Sometimes the same target behavior is being supported by an array of different consequences, such as relieving discomfort and gaining attention and food. Under those circumstances, promoting a single functionally equivalent response is more difficult. We need to:

(1) search harder for conditions, like insufficient rest, sleep, or food; internal or external irritants; or a recent loss of reinforcers or others that are establishing those varied consequences as reinforcers at the moment;
(2) relieve those conditions; and
(3) teach the student distinctively different functionally equivalent responses to replace the problematic one.

When Allison is suffering from an ear infection or has not had enough to eat or her teacher is trying to teach her a list of new, difficult words, she cries and whines. Unfortunately, detecting which one or combination is responsible for the crying is difficult. We need systematically to vary the suspected conditions, say, by having her examined by her pediatrician and providing her with pain-reducing mediation and watching what happens to the rate of crying and whining. If it drops, we then can suspect it was the pain of the ear infection. The FEAB for this circumstance might be to teach her to communicate "My ear hurts" orally, pictorially, or with a sentence strip or through sign language. Similarly, if the crying diminishes when she is fed, we would teach her a distinctive way to request something to eat. To test whether the academic demands are too stringent, we could try to give her easier work and see whether the crying stops. Then we know to teach her to ask for easier work or at least to intersperse or precede the more difficult assignments with less difficult ones.

Sometimes alleviating the stressful situation is beyond us—it just remains. It is hot in the house, and Allison wants to cool off. There is no air conditioner or fan or any way to take her to the pool or let her run under the sprinkler. In fact, mom is totally occupied bathing the baby and cannot help her older daughter. A FEAB for such circumstances is to provide Allison with an alternative way to express her frustration, perhaps by teaching her to describe her feelings, for instance, "I'm hot, "I'm angry," "I'm sad," "I'm scared," "I'm lonely," and so on. Although caregivers may not be able to eliminate the eliciting factor, they may be able more quickly to offer supportive comments and actions, such as listening, sharing their own feelings, offering some alternative activity (e.g., "I'm angry, too. Let's take a walk and talk about it"), or promising to deal with the issue as soon as the baby is down for her nap, and following through accordingly.

In many cases, a child wants something that cannot be delivered at the moment. The child misinterprets "You need to wait" as "No! Not now! Not ever!" and reacts by exploding in frustration. None of us lives in a world where all our desires can be instantly gratified. So, it is extremely important for our students to learn how to wait patiently. Everyone needs to have this skill reinforced repeatedly—toddler, child, adolescent, and adult—because there is always room for improvement in this area. Given sufficient teacher control over the reinforcer, the key elements of the lesson involve cuing the availability of a reinforcer and gradually increasing the size of the delay between the student's response and the teacher's delivery of the reinforcer. These strategies will be described in greater detail in Chapter 9.

Just as one set of events can induce a troublesome habit pattern and other conditions can maintain it, the same may be true of a single instance of a problematic behavior, like one tantrum. We need to keep this in mind when designing a CIB intervention plan because if we overlook both of those factors, we could inadvertently make matters worse. For example, a child may begin to tantrum in response to a teacher's even mildly stated demand to perform a "difficult" task—one associated with a low probability of reinforcement. Once the tantrum has begun, the teacher's reactions to the student may serve to positively reinforce the continuation of the tantrum. If we were to focus only on the role that the attention of the teacher plays in sustaining the tantrum, we might overlook what instigated the tantrum in the beginning: the difficulty of the work. By removing all attention, inadvertently we would be reinforcing beginning to tantrum because demands now would be removed. While we may choose to ignore the tantrum, we would also continue with some demands, preferably interspersed with some easier requests.

Manipulating Antecedents

If you are fortunate enough to be able to identify whatever antecedents reliably set off a CIB and if you can bring those antecedents under your control, you should be able to head off the CIB readily by avoiding using that stimulus. Parents are universally familiar with the way young children often react when told it is bedtime. Elsewhere, we have discussed how to rearrange antecedents to signal not the end of a reinforcing event but the beginning of a new one. A better ploy is to say, "As soon as you are in bed, I'll read you a story," and, of course, keep the promise.

Once one of us was acquainted with a boy we will call Peter, whose temper tantrum was reliably set off by someone asking him to "say" something, like "Peter, say 'car.'" We did notice that he would imitate our play activities, though, especially when we reinforced them with affection and praise. So we decided to build up and broaden his set of imitative skills to include sound effects. We would join him in manipulating cars and trucks, adding the roar of a truck or the siren of a fire engine, and he would imitate. Soon we sneaked into our dramatic play words like "come on" and "water." Inadvertently, Peter echoed what we modeled, and before long he was speaking aloud, without any need to direct him to speak along with the inevitable tantrums.

You also can arrange antecedent events like written or spoken phrases, signals, or other cues to promote behaviors incompatible with the inappropriate ones. It is important to make these antecedents clear while consistently pairing them with reinforcing consequences. In other words, keep your promises. "Let's work on your arithmetic workbook until the timer buzzes. Then we can stop and take a play or snack break." Carefully scheduling the timer to sound in less time than you know the student's attention span to last can establish the signal as a reliable cue that reinforcement in on its way. Later, over time, you can begin to stretch the time interval, seeing to it that the youngster works longer without needing to resort to a CIB as an escape tactic.

Differentially Reinforcing Acceptable Behaviors

The strategies we have just described require that we reinforce just the acceptable behaviors but not the others. When we concentrate on increasing some but not others, we are using a method called **differential reinforcement.** The more systematically we differentially reinforce, the more rapidly change will take place. This requires dispensing considerable reinforcement—much more than any the problem manages to garner—for the behavior we are attempting to promote. The right way is to "catch them being good." Yet this obvious solution is easier said than done. Parents and classroom teachers are beset by a multitude of responsibilities that require their intense concentration. Larger-group situations compound the difficulty even further, especially when a class includes several children, each of whom displays various problems. Maintaining the level of reinforcement teachers and parents must provide in order to promote ongoing improvement in students' behavior requires a well-crafted system.

Table 6.1   Differential Reinforcement Procedures

Procedure	Behavior(s) (Bs) Reinforced (R+)	Change over Time
DRO	Any other behavior	Gradually increases interval over sets
DROP	Any other behavior	Gradually increases intervals within a set
DRA	A specific alternative	Increases interval or increases B-to-R+ ratio
DRI	An incompatible alternative	Increases interval or increases B-to-R+ ratio
DRL	Lower rates of CIB	Increases time or reduces number within time

Several differential reinforcement techniques from which to choose are available (see Table 6.1). Some are based on a period of time passing during which the CIB has been absent. In that case, we are using **differential reinforcement of other behavior (DRO).** In this case we can choose to reinforce any behavior as long as it is not the target one. Ten minutes have gone by without Allison having a tantrum. She may happen to be working at a task, staring out the window, tying her shoe, rocking, or singing. Anything goes, as long as she is not engaged in a tantrum. By contrast, we can select one particular alternative behavior to reinforce or **differential reinforcement of alternative behavior (DRA).** For example, a boy can be called on only when he raises his hand but never when he shouts out. Or we could wait until the student expresses a behavior that is physically incompatible, or **differential reinforcement of incompatible behavior (DRI)** with the behavior we are attempting to discourage. For example, a girl slaps herself in the face whenever she walks down a hallway. The teacher could reward the child for carrying an object with two hands. As long as the girl has both hands on the object, they are not available to slap herself. The crucial element is to ensure that reinforcing consequences do not follow the CIB.[4] That is, the CIB must undergo extinction to whatever extent is feasible while the rate of reinforcement for other behaviors continues to increase.

Sometimes the problem behavior persists to such an extent that the acceptable alternative happens only once in a long while. In that case we can use a differential reinforcement of progressive interval procedure (DROP). We administer a small reward when the offensive target has been absent for a very brief period of time and correspondingly larger reinforcers as that time period lengthens. Use this progressive DRO technique, too, when you decide that a student's target behavior occurs so frequently that attempting to eradi-

---

[4]Mazaleski, J. L., Iwata, B. A., Volmer, T. R. (1993). Analysis of the reinforcement and extinction components in DRO contingencies with self-injury. *Journal of Applied Behavior Analysis, 26,* 143–156.

cate it completely would be unrealistic or when you conclude that completely eliminating a CIB may not be a fair long-term goal. Either of these would be acceptable, provided that it occurred just once in a while. A two-year-old child's temper tantrum is an example.

Should it be too much of a challenge to demand the complete absence of the target during a given a time interval, you can instead concentrate on gradually lowering its rate. In each of these cases, reinforcement is triggered when the number of times the CIB occurs falls below a given level within a time block. The child slaps herself 10 times a minute. Should the number of slaps drop to say eight times per minute, she would receive a reward. Be sure, though, to wait for a few moments during which the CIB is not ongoing to deliver the reinforcer, otherwise the connection CIB→Reinforcement will be reestablished. As the rate of the unacceptable behavior begins to fall, you can then tighten the rate requirement, say, to no more than six per minute and so on. Here you gradually are rewarding progress toward diminishing (not necessarily eliminating) the frequency of the CIB. The term that applies to this method of scheduling reinforcement only for responding at some preselected low rate is called **differential reinforcement of low rates (DRL).** The procedure focuses on gradual improvement, not immediate perfection.

Here is an illustration of a creative way a teacher applied a DRL method: To communicate to a student just how much screaming would be tolerated, the teacher provided the boy with a card containing 10 stickers. Every time the boy screamed, the teacher would calmly remove one sticker. If at least one sticker remained at the end of one hour, the boy could trade it in for some preferred item. Over time, as the boy consistently earned his rewards, the teacher began to reduce the number of stickers on the card. The card now contained only nine, then, assuming success, eventually dropped to eight, then seven, and so on. This procedure can help gradually to reduce the rate of the CIB without requiring its complete elimination right away.

Another variation is to remove more highly preferred reinforcers contingent on the CIB while less preferred reinforcers remain available. For example, one teacher placed on a shelf three of the student's most preferred toys where he could see but not reach them. One was his most favored, the second a little less, and the third the least preferred of the three. When the student engaged in the CIB, the teacher would remove the most preferred toy from the shelf, leaving the other two. If he engaged in the CIB again within the target period, she would remove the second favorite toy. In this manner, the student could see that while he may have lost the opportunity for the preferred toy, others remained available for him to access when he made appropriate improvements.

Combining strategies can be tempting, such as using the same token system to reward good academic performance as to remove tokens for CIBs.

More effective, though, is to have one system for good work (whether academic or involving any other performance criteria) and another for good behavior (such as a DRL for yelling).

Advantages and Disadvantages of Differential Reinforcement Procedures.

Each of these differential reinforcement systems has its advantages and disadvantages. However, staff need to incorporate some kind of differential reinforcement procedure within the daily program whenever a student regularly displays a severely inappropriate behavior. While differential reinforcement schedules would be expected to be most effective when CIBs are maintained by gaining for the student some type of reward, the procedures also serve to provide all students, including those whose problematic behaviors are controlled by escape/avoidance contingencies, with a context rich with reinforcement.

Practical Hints for Applying Differential Reinforcement Systems

Remember to Monitor the Absence of the CIB.   Do you recall being plagued by flies or mosquitoes at a recent picnic or outing? Noticing their presence required little effort. "If those creatures would only go away, I'd be so grateful," is what you probably were thinking. However, right now, unless you have just been out of doors, you probably have not given any thought to how wonderful the absence of those pests is. Just as we fail to notice the absence of irritants, like the fact that it is neither too hot nor too cold in the room, that we are not sick, or that no flies or mosquitoes are tormenting us at the moment, we are unlikely to notice the absence of a nuisance behavior. That is unfortunate because attempting to reduce a behavior by means of a differential reinforcement schedule requires that we take action when the target behavior is not taking place. Given the myriad of other demands on their time and attention, parents, educators, or caregivers may find it difficult to remember to differentially reinforcer the absence of the behavior. Fortunately, a number of timing and signaling devices are available to remind staff to adhere to the differential reinforcement plan.

Setting a kitchen timer or stopwatch to sound a tone every fixed or variable amount of time is one simple method. To encourage steadier good behavior, obscure the exact time when reinforcers will be delivered by using a variable-interval rather than the fixed-interval schedule. Here, you set the timer around a given average, like approximately every five minutes.

Teachers also can prepare a tape cassette with tones or beeps recorded at time intervals averaging around some set interval, such as 1, 2, 3, 5, 7, or 10 minutes. When a tone is sounded, staff momentarily stop and reward those

Behavioral Fly Trap

Figure 6.1   Behavioral Fly Trap

students whose behavior favorably conforms with the differential reinforcement contingency. Tapes can be programmed to combine two or more sets of tones associated with two or more variable intervals—a chime for Henrietta and a piano chord for Archie. When both sides of the cassette are automated this way, one can operate the cassette continuously throughout the day.

You can use a series of cassette-recorded signals like these also when systematically increasing the length of the interval over the course of the school year. You might begin with a tape containing signals for a DRO two-minute interval. When the student's responding reaches a predetermined level (e.g., 80 percent of the intervals are target free), following a rule to increase the intervals by no more than 50 percent, you might switch to a DRO three-minute interval. Now the student gradually receives fewer rewards for increasingly longer stretches of time intervals containing only appropriate behaviors. We have used this system with some adolescents with autism. At first, they were allowed a sip of soda within the classroom approximately every two minutes, provided that the problematic behavior had not occurred in the interim. Two years later, at the work site, the intervals were up to two hours, and the reward consisted of allowing the youth to buy and drink a can of soda.

React to the Contextually Inappropriate Behavior Directly.
Although we heavily favor promoting functional alternatives to contextually inappropriate behaviors as the primary approach, some CIBs are deemed by responsible parties to be so dangerous (producing tissue damage or injuring

others), destructive (breaking equipment, costly materials, or furniture), disruptive (commanding attention with exceedingly loud noises or seriously interfering with other's ongoing activities), or obnoxious (smearing feces or masturbating in public) that they must also be responded to directly. As with DRO and other reward-based systems, teachers, parents, and other caregivers must be consistent in the way they react.

An array of behavioral procedures is available, including presenting something the student clearly does not want at the time (punishment), such as an arduous work requirement or a reprimand, or withdrawing or terminating reinforcement for a time period (response cost or time-out from positive reinforcement). Such procedures also need to be applied with exquisite care because subtle differences in the way the procedures are applied—like how often, intensely, rapidly, with what cues, and so on—can speed up or delay short- and long-term success. The use of these strategies requires optimal personnel training and management.[5]

Additionally, considerable controversy has been and continues to be associated with these direct reductive strategies. In the first place, people's opinions differ about what constitutes acceptable and unacceptable behavior. Second, although some consider given treatments relatively benign, others see them as overly harsh, immoral, or otherwise inappropriate. Discussing at length the primary issues associated with the use of aversive or seemingly aversive procedures is beyond the scope of this chapter. Suffice it to say that the individual teacher should avoid unilaterally deciding how to proceed in attempting to eradicate a given behavior. This is a job properly delegated to a peer review and/or human rights committee composed of wise, respected, and informed professionals, parents, and other community representatives.

Furthermore, systematic review of direct reductive procedures should not be limited to those deemed "aversive." Interventions that appear "nonaversive" nevertheless may be detrimental or harmful, producing unwarranted negative side effects (cf., Balsam & Bondy, 1983), or be virtually ineffective.[6] For example, although rocking a 15-year-old boy with autism while feeding him with a bottle may not sound aversive or conform to someone's theory about what the youth needs, many would object strongly to such an intervention on ethical and/or humanitarian grounds.

Many local, state, and national educational and rehabilitation agencies have adopted ethical or peer review systems. In Delaware's public school program for students with autism, for instance, a system of review exists for all in-

---

[5]Sulzer-Azaroff, B. & Mayer, G. R. (1991). Behavior Analysis for Lasting Change. Ft. Worth, TX: Holt, Rinehart and Winston, Inc.
[6]Balsam, P. D. & Bondy, A. (1983) The negative side effects of reward. Journal of Applied Behavior Analysis, 16, 283–296.

terventions designed to reduce the rate, duration, or severity of a CIB among students with autism. All such interventions are defined as **behavior intervention procedures,** regardless of whether they contain intrusive or aversive components. A peer review and a human rights committee composed entirely of individuals not associated with the public school program annually review all potential CIB intervention procedures. These committees classify proposed procedures within one of three categories: (1) proceed with this intervention, (2) proceed with the intervention but report monthly data on student behavioral outcomes to the peer review committee or (3) use this procedure only after case-by-case review and approval by both committees. Often the very same procedure can vary from one to the next application only in terms of the size of the time interval, the number of reinforcers or repetitions of a work requirement, or some other parameter. When they do, how dense the reinforcers or how heavy or intense the penalties influences which of the categories applies. A very brief time-out (e.g., planned ignoring for five seconds) is quite different from isolating the students for 15 or 20 minutes. Therefore the former might be assigned to the first category, the latter to the third.

The particular intervention programs used in Delaware are based on effective interventions described in the applied literature. They include minimally intrusive procedures, including redirection, planned ignoring, mild verbal reprimand, briefly stopping an ongoing activity, as well as more intrusive procedures, such as isolated time-out and contingent exercise. Although no intervention is forbidden a priori, few highly controversial procedures have been used since these policies have been adopted.

Each intervention plan contains a generic description, a listing of behaviors commonly addressed by the intervention, and the parametric details needed to implement the procedure. For example, if a plan calls for a child to pick up blocks or toothpicks from the floor and put them into a box, then staff must detail how many blocks will be used, the degree of staff assistance, how long the intervention should last, how many staff may be necessary to complete the intervention, and other details.

Summary

In and of itself, any given behavior is neutral. Its context is what makes it inappropriate. Preventing or reducing the rates of contextually inappropriate behaviors requires a multifaceted approach, including the organization's taking general precautions and applying several specific methods for promoting students' well-being. Conducting a formal assessment to determine the function of the CIB is especially important because it often allows us to identify and apply a strategy to promote a more acceptable functionally equivalent alternative response. These alternative responses need to be viewed from the child's, not the teacher's or parents', perspectives and designed to yield the youngster what he or she wants or needs. Access to desired items, activities, attention, assistance, or escape from or avoidance of unwanted circumstances are typical examples. Just as they do to support any reinforcement program, antecedents like words, gestures, or signs can foster the change process.

Most essential, though, is the reinforcement program itself. In the case of CIB reduction, this involves two operations: ensuring that the acceptable behavior is powerfully reinforced while the unacceptable behavior is not. This differential reinforcement process may be conducted according to various schedules, depending on what specific behavior is the focus of change and when and how often reinforcement is to be accessed. Given the natural tendency of teachers, parents, and the rest of us to overlook gradual improvements, we have offered a number of tips for reminding ourselves to adhere to the selected reinforcement schedules.

There are times when CIBs are so dangerous, destructive, or socially inappropriate that they cannot be ignored and must be treated directly. Punishment, response cost, time-out, and other directly reductive methods need, along with the more benign ones, to be applied according to very clear standards, including oversight by a peer review or human rights committee. Along with ethical and humanitarian considerations, the approach must be decided on the basis of scientifically documented evidence of effectiveness with similar students.

Suggested Readings and Viewings

TO	*Read*
Learn about the role of punishment and coercion in society and our daily lives, the impact it has on those who apply it and those who receive it and how to change ourselves to make the world a better place.	Sidman, M. (1989). Coercion and its Fallout Boston, MA: Cooperative, Inc.
Learn how to conduct a functional analysis	The following articles in the Journal of Applied Behavior Analysis: Carr & Durand (1985), 18, 111–126; Iwata et al. (1994), 27, 197–209; Iwata et al. (1994), 27, 215–240.

Gain an overview scientifically documented programs to "promote effective change and reduce or prevent severe problems from occurring in the natural environment . . . P.4"

Koegel, L. K., Koegel, R. L., Kellegrew, D. & Mullen, K. (1996). Parent education for prevention and reduction of severe problem behaviors. In L. K. Koegel, R. L. Koegel & G. Dunlap (Eds.) Positive Behavioral Support: Including People with Difficult Behavior in the Community. Baltimore, MD: Paul Brooks Publishing Co., 3–30.

Mount an argument in behalf of early intervention with problem behavior and design a comprehensive treatment for children with serious behavior problems.

Dunlap, G. & Fox, L. (1996). Early intervention and serious problem behaviors. In L. K. Koegel, R. L. Koegel & G. Dunlap. (Eds). Positive behavioral support: Including people with difficult behavior in the community. Baltimore, MD: Paul Brooks Publishing Co., 31–50.

Attain an overview of current behavior analytic research in autism in the areas of disruptive and destructive and self-stimulatory behavior, language development and social skills.

Frea, W. D. & Vittemberg, G.L (2000). Behavioral interventions for children with autism. In J. Austin & J. E. Carr. (Eds.) *Handbook of Applied Behavior Analysis.* Reno, NV: Context Press, 247–273.

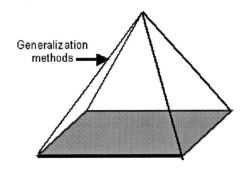

Generalization
methods

7

Generalization

It is 11:30 A.M. and Marie's mom, Wendy, is preparing 12-year-old Marie's lunch. Marie seems to be getting increasingly agitated, causing Wendy to race through the process. Meanwhile, Wendy is replaying in her head a conversation she has had with herself many times before. Her daughter is beginning to mature. What will happen when the child is a full-grown adult? Wendy wonders whether Marie will be able to feed herself and do what she needs to do to remain safe and healthy. How about when she, Wendy, ages and dies?

Wendy then thinks about the parents' meeting she attended last week. Among the points the speaker made is that it is reasonable to hope children with special needs eventually will become more self-sufficient. Today many do live away from their parents, with minimal guidance and support from social service agencies. They even can care for themselves in community living quarters. However, those young adults who have acquired some crucial communicative and activity-of-daily-living skills and are able to manage their emotions will lead far richer lives.

A few days later, Wendy meets with Marie's teacher to talk about how she might help Marie ask for food instead of grabbing for it or hurting herself. They discuss various alternative objectives. Will they teach her better ways to ask for food, ways to get it for herself, or both? They decide on the latter because that will serve all the purposes Wendy had identified: enabling Marie to ask for her food while becoming more self-sufficient at the same time.

There are many different kinds of lessons that Wendy could conduct to enable her daughter to achieve those objectives, but they decide to look toward the future. A good first step will be to teach Marie to prepare her own sandwiches—not just one kind but several. There will be different kinds of bread: white, rye, whole wheat; rolls, pita bread. Fillings, too, will vary: peanut and jelly; cheese and ham; later maybe even tuna salad.

At first the task seems awesome. So much is involved, including gathering the necessary utensils and ingredients, using them safely and correctly, and assembling the whole thing. Yet the teacher was wise in guiding Wendy to take this real-life approach, for a number of reasons:

(1) She knew that Marie liked to eat those particular sandwiches. The activity would contain its own natural reinforcement.

(2) Learning to make sandwiches would help Marie to become more self-sufficient.

(3) Teaching Marie to obtain her food in a less damaging and more socially acceptable way would be advantageous for all.

(4) By setting the lessons in the natural environment, Wendy could make good use of *incidental teaching.* This is a big advantage because it has an excellent chance for promoting increasingly complex, relevant, and general learning.

(5) By using varied ingredients, Marie would have to learn a variety of skills—not just one. These could come in handy for other purposes later on.

A few weeks later, one hour ahead of their usual weekend lunchtime, Wendy is supervising Marie in the sandwich-making operation. Velcro-backed pictures of ham and cheese, plus labels from the mayonnaise, peanut butter, and two kinds of jelly jars, are displayed on the cover of her PECS communication book. Similarly, pictures of dark and light bread are affixed to the breadbox. On the table is a breadboard and knife.

Wendy waits. Marie stands, flicking her fingers. Wendy touches her gently and says, "Let's make sandwiches," pointing to the breadbox. Marie gets a picture of white bread and hands it to her mother. Her mom exclaims "White bread!" and gives her daughter two slices. They continue with the process, until Marie has put together a reasonable peanut butter and jelly sandwich for herself. Eating it is the best part.

In the previous episode we can see the cleverness with which the lesson was designed. Not only did it permit Marie to learn to make choices, communicate, and perform a skill, but also set up a situation favoring *generalization* and *maintenance.* Marie would learn to make different kinds of sandwiches, and because she eats lunch daily, the skill would have a good chance of maintaining over time.

What Exactly Is Generalization?

Actually, there are two different kinds of generalization. One is called *stimulus generalization*. Stimulus generalization describes a situation in which a response learned under one set of circumstances occurs under a range of similar conditions, like with other people or materials, or at varied places or times. If after Wendy taught Marie to make her sandwich at home with white bread, the youngster were able to make different kinds of sandwiches in different locations, we would say that Marie's sandwich-making skills had generalized across those different stimulus situations.

The other category of generalization is *response generalization*.[1] With response generalization, it is not the situation or the circumstances that change, but the behavior itself that varies. In Marie's case, if after she learned to spread butter to make one sandwich, she also could make five new kinds of sandwiches within 10 minutes, we would say her skills have generalized to suit new demands.

Teachers need to plan for both stimulus and response generalization to design effective lessons. We often hope a new skill will generalize to other situations. We may teach children in a classroom to calculate the amount of change they should receive when making a purchase, with the intention that the students will transfer or generalize the skill to the real world. The same holds true for response generalization. We have finally taught our students to clean up their toys by themseoves after playtime. However, it now takes them 15 minutes to complete the task and so we hope they will learn to finish cleaning up within 5 minutes by the end of the year.

In some ways, generalization can be thought of as the opposite of discrimination, which broadly involves responding differently in different situations. (We will discuss more details about discrimination in Chapter 8.) Therefore, within each lesson we must determine how much generalization versus discrimination will be needed. Sometimes stimulus generalization is inappropriate. Treating pennies the same as dimes is a big mistake, so is wearing a nightgown out of doors. Shunning someone who is harmless but who resembles in one irrelevant way a person who has harmed us in the past is overgeneralizing, a form of prejudice. Likewise, with response generalization, some changes can be nonproductive. If a child usually whispers, we would want to teach the child to increase the loudness of her voice but we would not want it to increase to the point of constant shouting. Changes in one aspect of a response may lead to unwanted changes in other aspects. Marie may learn

---

[1]Some use the term response induction to describe this phenomenon.

to make sandwiches very quickly but if she always makes a mess, the overall situation has not improved.

The important point here is that before you plan a lesson, you need to re-fine the objectives to include how much of what kind of generalization you are hoping to achieve. You also want to be very clear about the opposite: what generalization you do not want to happen or what degree of discrimination you want to achieve. If you were about to have open-heart surgery, you would want your surgeon to be sufficiently flexible (response generalization) with her skills to work with distinctive cardiovascular systems like your own—that is, to discriminate one from the next.

As you can see, the two kinds of generalization are quite different. The question is what we are hoping to see happen. With stimulus generalization, we want the behavior to remain the same but we want it to occur with other conditions, people, places, and situations. With response generalization, we want to achieve variations in some aspect of the performance in terms of rate, duration, intensity, or similar properties. Accordingly, when we want to en-courage stimulus generalization, we need to teach the behavior under many situations, providing reinforcement when it happens under each of those con-ditions. For children to communicate effectively and use proper social skills, lessons should be relatively loose and flexible, with different people in different places and at different times of the day. On the contrary, if we do not

Term	Definition	Spread Effect	Examples of Wanted Change	Unwanted Change
Stimulus Generalization	Same act (behavior) occurs in other situations (Ss)	S_1 S_2 $S_3 \rightarrow B$ S_4 S_n	Whenever Marie sees a red traffic light, she stops, waits, and looks both ways.	Marie hugs whomever she meets.
Response Generalization	Same act begins to diversify	$B \rightarrow$ B_1 B_2 B_3 B_4 B_n	The firmness with which Marie spreads peanut butter (B) varies. She can push down strongly to form a thin layer or push down lightly to form a thick layer.	When Marie tries to open the sliding door, she varies the amount of pressure she uses, so sometimes the door opens and sometimes it does not.

want to see a behavior generalize, say hugging everyone in sight or shouting and running around in places like the library or during a ceremony, we have to carefully reinforce it *only* when, where, and with whom it should occur. In Chapters 8 and 9 we will describe issues and strategies related to *discrimination training* that will enable us to teach students the circumstances under which a behavior is and is not appropriate.

Considering Generalizations Right From the Start

You might wonder why we begin by teaching about generalization before teaching you how to plan a given lesson. Our earlier emphasis that reinforcement must be an integral part of a lesson before beginning is equally true of generalization. It must be considered in advance, instead of, as is our usual tendency, planning for it only after some level of performance has been achieved. For instance, we may proceed, without deept consideration, to have our students practice a skill in a quiet, separate area until they master it. Perhaps we assume that later will be soon enough to worry about how they will transfer their newly found abilities to the actual situations in which they will need to use them.

Unfortunately, in our eagerness to do something, we often wait far too long to begin planning for generalization. We may neglect anticipating when, where, and with whom the student ultimately will need to make use of the skill. Necessary supportive strategies are missing. For example, in conducting Phase I of the PECS, Donna has just successfully taught Denise to exchange a single picture for a piece of candy. The only person who Donna teaches Denise to give the picture to is Donna herself and no one else. They practice this exchange over a period of several weeks while remaining within arms reach of one another. What would probably happen at this point if Donna suddenly moved across the room from Denise? If Donna suddenly appeared with one of Denise's favorite toys instead of the candy? If they were out together in the community? If someone else were holding the candy? In each of these new conditions, Denise would most likely fail to communicate appropriately. Many would describe the situation as "Denise's failure to generalize."

From our perspective, the primary problem is not any failure on Denise's part but that generalization strategies have not been built into the lesson from the start. More often than not, generalization failures are due to the way teaching is structured, not to some deficiency in the learner. The way to avoid the kind of trap just described is to plan for generalization well before beginning a lesson; that is, before starting, we should know in the broadest sense exactly what is to be accomplished. With this long-term goal in mind, in this chapter we address generalization before sharing our perspective on how to design effective lessons.

Promoting Stimulus Generalization

As already mentioned, teachers and parents often assume that generalization will happen "spontaneously." If students learn in the classroom to exchange a picture of a ball for a real ball or the rules for organizing a paragraph, spelling a word, assembling a widget, or conducting a PECS training session, they should be able to apply the skill properly in real-life situations. Baer and Stokes (1977) have labeled this the "Train and Hope" approach to generalization. Unfortunately, training and hoping for spontaneous generalization frequently fails. This chapter focuses on ways to promote wanted generalization.[2] Conveniently, behavior analysts have learned many ways to promote appropriate generalizations across people, places, materials, and responses as well as how to maintain such changes across time. We summarize and illustrate those here:

1. Fully Describe the Various Response Qualities: Determine in advance the kind of response variation you wish to see transfer and maintain. Then you will know when to provide reinforcement and when to withhold it.

   A. Number of responses
   How many times should the response be repeated?

   Examples:

- I will do 10 push-ups.
- My teenaged daughter will learn 12 new Spanish words.
- Each sales representative will make 30 calls.
- The trainee should fill 200 envelopes.

   B. Rate
   How frequently should the response occur per unit of time?

   Examples:

- The trainee should fold 10 inserts a minute.
- I will work out three times a week.
- My four-year-old son will brush his teeth twice a day.
- Each sales representative will make 30 calls a day.

---

[2]By contrast, if the issue is avoiding overgeneralization, you should refer to the material on errorless learning and error correction.

C. Duration of responses
How long should a given behavior persist?

Examples:

- My workout will be 20 minutes long.
- Heather will participate in organized games on the playground for at least five minutes.
- The student should remain seated at the workbench for 15 minutes.
- The boss will spend 10 minutes a week out on the shop floor.

D. Complexity
How varied are the components of the response?

Examples:

- Does the student spend all his time folding enclosures, or does he prepare envelopes for mailing: folding the enclosure, slipping it into the envelope, and sealing and stamping the envelope?
- The workout routine consists of stretching, aerobics, and upper- and lower-body toning.
- There are 29 different steps included in the "Job Club" method for finding a job.[3]

E. Accuracy
How closely does the response conform to the definitions of a correct response?

Examples:

- Do all four corners overlap exactly? Does the student place the stamp in the upper-right-hand quadrant?
- Each of the 29 steps of the "Job Club" method match the description in the book, according to our checklists.
- Our sales staff follows the script for making an effective call.

F. Durability
How long should the skill be maintained?

Examples:

- Does the response, as described previously, persist for at least three months?
- If we were to return a year later, would we see the boss spend at least 10 minutes a day on the shop floor?

---

[3]N. H. Azrin, and V. B. Besalel, Finding a Job (Berkeley, CA: Ten Speed Press, 1982).

Stimulus Factors
• People • Environmental variations • Materials • Time

2. Assess The Environment: The next thing to do is to determine stimulus factors, such as with whom, where, with what, and when the given response and related responses should or should not occur. We do this to ensure that we have not overlooked some important detail. An example would be the student who is applying for a job following the proper steps with each potential employer, not only in simulated conditions but in actuality, by mail, over the telephone, and in person during normal working hours. By comparison, being able to act correctly in the classroom is of little value if behavior is out of control outside.

Assessing the environment also allows us to predict how likely it is that the behavior of concern will be reinforced and not punished. You may teach a student to fold inserts very meticulously, but this takes extra time that the hiring organization is unwilling to invest. Now you have a dilemma: teaching the person to operate more rapidly and perhaps less precisely or negotiating a different set of standards to be applied with your student. All this could have been avoided had details of the environment been investigated in advance.

3. Teach to Natural Reinforcers: Look at each of the settings and see who and what stands ready naturally to reinforce the response you are teaching. Train to those conditions. If you want to teach a youth how to shop, bring him to a store where a shopkeeper naturally would deliver an item on request. Find out who can be counted on to comply or make a big fuss about any new accomplishment. Maybe grandma and grandpa's house is the best place to teach requesting a video or how to set up the wading pool.

4. Teach Sequentially: In addition to any discrete-trial training, arrange to have as many of the people who will be present in the student's various natural settings teach the skill in those different places: the parents in the home, in the park, or at the beach; teachers in the classroom, hallways, cafeteria, or gymnasium; caregivers out in the community; or supervisors on the job. The more of these people who learn the Pyramid Approach to Education, the more rapidly and effectively change will occur.

5. Use Many Examples of the Same or Very Similar Responses: You might instruct a student to attach a picture into his own book to the object it represents, to a box containing the object, and to a daily schedule chart. You now recognize this form of responding the same way to different stimuli as stimulus generalization. Guide the student to affix pictures to a Velcro strip, stickers to a page in a scrapbook, or washable tattoos and band-aids to her own arm (both stimulus—the stickers, tattoo, and band-aids—and response generalization because the form of the response varies slightly).

6. Teach Loosely: Closely related is the approach that Stokes and Baer were referring to when they suggested training loosely. Other than the critical response, loosen the conditions under which teaching takes place. This means that if you are trying to teach someone to ask for a ball, vary the kinds of balls available: softballs, large rubber balls of different colors, footballs, small rubber balls, and so on. This prevents the student from attaching an irrelevant feature, like color or size, to the concept of ball. What you want is for him to use appropriate descriptive adjectives later on for the general class "balls" and to avoid requesting and receiving the exact same object every single time and showing frustration when that does not happen. This also is the reason we suggest that in teaching the PECS, you vary the teachers, their roles, the materials, and so on early in training.

7. Minimize Prompting: Prompt as little as necessary to evoke the response. As you do in teaching communication, pause between handing the learner the picture and assisting him. Count to 10; if you must, to avoid overprompting and making the student overly dependent on your assistance. Give him a chance to respond correctly without further help.

8. Promote High, Steady Rates of the Response: When a person expresses a particular response rapidly and smoothly, without pauses, it is more likely to generalize. Teach a child to put on his shoes, button his shirt, or brush his teeth without pausing before starting or while in progress. Then, when settings or times change, he will be more apt to practice those responses appropriately.

9. Spot Check for "Mastered" Skills: Mastering a response is not the same as retaining the response. A youngster may seem to be able precisely to follow her schedule for a day or two but then appear to have lost this ability. We need to probe by taking data periodically to see whether the newly acquired behavior is persisting intact or deteriorating and re-teach accordingly.

10. Fade Prompt Levels and Thin Reinforcement Schedules Unnoticeably: None of us is rewarded for every single effort we make. Our students need to be prepared for irregular payoffs and diminishing guidance. The best way is to lessen the prompts and reinforcers so gradually and irregularly that the student fails to notice the change.[4] One strategy is to have your students take turns with one another in groups of increasing sizes. This is a natural way for students to learn to tolerate delay and react under less intense guidance. Also,

---

[4]Psychophysics used the term just noticeable differences (JNDs) to describe the degree of change in a procedure below which the individual cannot sense any differences. Essentially, this is what we suggest you do when you diminish how heavily you prompt and how regularly and frequently you reinforce a response.

the prompts can shift from the artificial teacher-directed tell, show, and guide methods to those inherent in social situations as the other students model the correct response.

Promoting Response Generalization

As in teaching for stimulus generalization, you identify in advance permissible response variations for those circumstances. Then you teach toward those variations. The art teacher might encourage and reinforce the students' use of different kinds of brush strokes to obtain different effects. Children just learning to communicate could be given what they indicate they want, whether they make the request in the form of a picture, a sign, or a spoken or written word.

Often you also would adjust the methods and materials you use. If you were coaching an ice hockey team, you would be sure the players experience all the kinds of ice conditions they might be faced with: smooth, rough, wavy, and so on. Then you would teach them how to adapt their movements and rates of speed to those changing situations. Marie's mother would show her daughter how to press down on the butter harder than on the mayonnaise (but not too hard because the bread might tear apart, an error that then would need to be corrected). In these cases, you will note a combination of methods: teaching the student to differentiate one condition or material from another, then adapting the form of the response accordingly.

Strategies to Promote Changes in Response Rate

Frequently, teachers design lessons directed toward helping students learn a particular skill in the presence of particular environmental cues. To eliminate any ultimate dependence on prompts, teachers gradually shift from those that are highly contrived to those closer and closer to natural cues. When attempting to shift controlling stimuli, we suggest that teachers avoid presenting the same verbal (or other) prompts repeatedly and instead substitute a different prompt strategy of the type discussed in Chapter 8. Thus, when teaching a child to imitate saying a word, the teacher presents the stimulus once and waits a set period of time before adding another visual, physical, or gestural prompt. The teacher controls the pace of the lesson by beginning each trial with a distinct cue or prompt.

When our focus is on response generalization, though, our goal sometimes is related more to rate than to stimulus control per se. For example, suppose that our intent is for a child to run faster, not to have the child run when we say, "Run." The way we prompt students to run faster would be quite different from teaching toward other objectives. To illustrate, one adaptive physical education teacher's concern was to improve children's cardiovascular performance—to raise their heart rates and breathing levels—by teaching them to run longer and faster. He used many different verbal and physical prompts and aids. Whether students were running independently or in response to verbal prompts or were having their hands held throughout the run was not important. What did count was that they ran at a particular speed for a given length of time. The teacher's goal was not to achieve some type of stimulus control as in the objective "Given the instruction, 'run,' the child will run" but rather to have students reach some specific rate and duration.

Watch a coach working with her players in the weight room. She shouts encouragement to get players to try harder, go faster, and persist. The potential harmful effects of repeated verbal prompts are of little concern because achieving stimulus control over the responses is not the main objective.

Does coaching sometimes occur in the natural course of events, and can such cases help suggest different teaching strategies? We all have watched parents interact with their very young children beginning to babble. Parents tend to group their "prompts" into bursts and then pause. They do not just say, "Say 'ba,'" once and then pause for five seconds before repeating the single presentation. Instead, they repeat the stimulus—"ba, ba, ba, ba, *ba!*"—often with a rising inflection before pausing. Parents also use differential reinforcement in a way that guarantees the child's success. No matter what the child does, the parent pleasantly continues to model various sounds. Whenever the child responds in kind the parent provides more social reinforcement by way of changes in inflection, broader smiles, louder praise, claps, tickles, and so on. Should the parental modeling be construed as prompting, contrary to our suggestion that we avoid repeating verbal prompts? Or should the modeling be viewed as coaching (interspersing feedback and reinforcement among the prompts)? Our take on the matter is that because the parents are not trying to achieve stimulus control over specific responses, these repetitions are much more focused on encouraging a broad response class—any kind of vocal responding. Neither are the parents expecting their child to say a single "ba" or the child to repeat the same number of "ba's" as they modeled.

Good teachers act like coaches when their concern is promoting response generalization.[5] Watch effective coaches, and you will notice them

[5]For detailed descriptions of strategies that promote response fluency, see K. R. Johnson, and T. V. J. Lyang, Breaking the Structuralist Barrier: Literacy and Numeracy with Fluency, American Psychologist 47 (1992): 1475–90, and O. R. Lindsley, Precision Teaching: Discoveries and Effects, Journal of Applied Behavior Analysis 25 (1992): 51–57. For the influence of behavioral momentum, see F. C. Mace, et al., Behavioral Momentum in the Treatment of Noncompliance, Journal of Applied Behavior Analysis 21 (1988): 123–41.

using a procedure called **differential reinforcement of high rates (DRH).** They organize reinforcement to be set for delivery when the response is repeated a particular number of times within a given time limit. The youth stuffing fliers into envelopes earns his soda if he has finished at least 100 in an hour or less. The teacher praises his pupil's oral reading when the passage is read correctly in less than 30 seconds. The way to use this method is to build up the response-per-time-ratio requirement gradually, in small increments—30 per hour, then 40, 50, 60, and so on. If the student falters several times in a row, drop back a bit and later proceed more cautiously.

Another related strategy involves allowing the student to control the pace of a lesson. During a sight-word drill, the teacher controlled the pace of the lesson by handing the student the words one by one, asking the student to place a printed word on its corresponding object. Under those circumstances, he successfully placed 26 words in 45 minutes. We then rearranged the lesson by placing 10 objects on the table and handing the student all 10 printed words. He correctly placed the words on all 10 items in 40 seconds. Of course, had he made discrimination errors, the teacher would have had to respond appropriately, but by focusing on improving his rate, his performance was significantly smoother.

Summary

Just as learning about scuba diving only in a classroom would prepare us inadequately to try diving in the sea on our own, teaching our students in a classroom and then hoping that they will practice their newly learned skills whenever and wherever needed often turns out to have been overly optimistic. Instead, for any new skill we plan to teach, we need to have considered many factors. Are we seeking stimulus generalization, response generalization, or both? After answering that question, we then need to describe in detail the nature of the generalization we would like to see happen. Included in the list of elements are number, rate, duration, complexity, accuracy, durability of the response, and perhaps others. Next we need to assess the stimulus factors present in the environment to see whether we have described our instructional objectives in sufficient detail. Included in the list are people, environmental variations, materials, time, and so on. Ideally we need to determine what reinforcers are in place currently so that we can teach to these natural reinforcers. Then we can teach sequentially across these different environments, adjusting to the circumstances that vary from one to the next. The student's response pattern is more likely to be flexible and less rigid when we provide many different examples for a generic response. Similarly, loose training prevents students from attaching an irrelevant feature to the concept they are learning. Generalization over time (maintenance) is supported when we minimize prompting; intentionally promote high, steady rates of the response of interest; spot-check for the mastered skills, repairing if necessary with "booster shots" of training; fade any remaining prompts; and thin the schedules of reinforcement.

Response generalization also may not occur "spontaneously." When response variation is called for, we need to plan and conduct our teaching to take advantage of those differences, meeting the demands of the situation. Here we teach the student to distinguish between particular circumstances and adapt the form of the response to each one accordingly. Most important is that we do our best to plan in advance what these variations are and how to adjust to the diverse requirements necessary for appropriate behavioral generalization.

Suggested Readings and Viewings

To	*Read*
Understand the need for, choose and use methods for promoting generalization	Cooper, J. O., Heron, T. E., & Heward, W. L. (1987). Applied behavior analysis. Englewood Cliffs, NJ: Prentice Hall, Part 10. Sulzer-Azaroff, B. & Mayer, G. R. (1991). Behavior analysis for lasting change. Atlanta: Wadsworth Group: Thompson, Chapter 29.
Discover the various ways a response can generalize and how to promote or hinder this effect	Baer, D. M. & Stokes, T. F. (1977). Discriminating a generalization technology. In P. Mittler (Ed.) *Research to practice in mental retardation. Vol II: Education and training.* University Park Press, Baltimore: 331–336. Charlop-Christy, M. H. & Kelso, S. E. (1997). How to treat the child with autism. (Chapter 16) Claremont, CA: Claremont McKenna College, Chapter 16. Kirby, K. C., & Bickel, W. K. (1988). Toward an explicit analysis of generalization. The Behavior Analyst, 11, 115–129. Stokes, T. F. & Baer, D. M. (1977). An implicit technology of generalization. Journal of Applied Behavior Analysis, 10, 349–368.

	Stoke, T. F. & Osnes, P.G. (1989). An operant pursuit of generalization. Behavior Therapy, 20, 337–355.
Analyze the sources of the problem that stand in the way of children transferring newly acquired skills to novel situations	Cuvo, A. J. & Davis, P. K. (1998). Establishing and transferring stimulus control. In J. K. Luiselli & M. J.Cameron (Eds.) Antecedent control: Innovative approaches to behavioral support, Baltimore, MD: Paul Brooks Publishing Company, 347–369.
Experience vicariously ways that one family promoted their autistic child's generalization of new knowledge and skills	Chapter 21 in Maurice, K. (1993). *Let me hear your voice: A family's triumph over autism.* New York: Fawcett Columbine.
Arrange a classroom environment to support children's communication	Kaiser, A. P. & Hester, O. P. (1996). How everyday environments support children's communication. In L. K. Koegel, R. L. Koegel & G. Dunlap. (Eds.) Positive behavioral support: Including people with difficult behavior in the community. Baltimore, MD: Paul Brooks Publishing Co., 145–162.
See how some have organized the environment and taught students skills to manage their own behavior	See Janzen, J. E. (1996). Understanding the nature of autism. San Antonio, TX: Therapy Skill Builders. The chapters on Expanding Communication and Social Competence, Chapter 22, and Teaching Self-Control and Self-Management Strategies, Chapter 23 in Koegel, R. L., Koegel, L. K. & Parks, D. R. (1995). "Teach the individual" model of generalization. In R. L. Koegel & L. K. Koegel. (Eds.) Teaching children with autism. Baltimore, MD: Paul Brooks Publishing Co., 67–77.
Become familiar with a wide range of ways to support community	Koegel, R. L. Dunlap, G. (Eds.) Positive behavioral support: Including people with difficult behavior in the community.

integration	Baltimore, MD: Paul Brooks Publishing Co.
Locate sources describing methods to support socialization, including script following, peer mediation, incidental teaching and others	Refer to reference list in Krantz, P. J. (2000). Commentary: Interventions to facilitate socialization. Journal of Autism & Developmental Disorders, 30, 411–413.
Discover how teaching pivotal skills can contribute to children's development of social skills	Koegel, R. L. & Frea, W. D. (1993). Treatment of social behavior in autism through modification of pivotal skills. Journal of Applied Behavior Analysis, 26, 369–378.
Learn how to design and use activity schedules, a tactic for promoting independence, choice and social interaction among people with autism	McClannahan, L. E. & Krantz, P. J. (1999). *Activity schedules for children with autism: Teaching independent behavior.* Bethesda, MD: Woodbine House.
Become familiar with strategies that promote response fluency	Johnson, K. R. & Lyang, T. V. J. (1992). Breaking the structuralist barrier: Literacy and numeracy with fluency. American Psychologist, 47, 1475–1490. Lindsley, O. R. (1992). Precision teaching: Discoveries and effects. Journal of Applied Behavior Analysis, 25, 51–57
Appreciate the influence of behavioral momentum in promoting response maintenance	Mace, F. C. et al. (1988). Behavioral momentum in the treatment of noncompliance. Journal of Applied Behavior Analysis, 21, 123–141.
To	***View***
Learn more about teaching independence and choice	Teaching Independence and Choice. Princeton Child Development Institute, 300 Cold Soil Road, Princeton, NJ 08540.

Watch teaching students learn how to relax and use imagery

Groden, J., Cautela, J.R., LeVasseur, P., Groden, G. & Bausman, M. (1991). Breaking the barriers I: Relaxation techniques and Breaking the barriers II: Imagery procedure. Champaign, IL: Research Press.

To   ### *Do*

Practice programming for generalization and maintenance

Exercises in Sulzer-Azaroff, B. & Reese, E. P. (1982). Applying behavior analysis. New York: Holt, Rinehart & Winston, Chapter 7.

Teach a child or yourself to relax in new or difficult situations

Read and follow the instructions in Cautela, J. R. & Groden, J. (1978). Relaxation: A comprehensive manual for adults, children and children with special needs. Champaign, IL: Research Press.

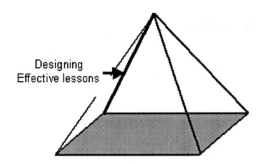

Designing
Effective lessons

8

Designing Effective Lessons

Although she cheerfully sorts her blocks in neat precise rows, five-year-old Alicia still does not talk. Instead, when she wants something beyond reach, she screams and tears at her clothing. Nor does she play with her brothers and sister or seem to notice who is in the room. Despite trying many different methods, her parents and teachers have seen Alicia make little progress in language or social development. Recently, while attending the child's Individual Educational Planning (IEP) meeting, they learned from her new teacher about the Pyramid Approach to Education. They can see how those methods may help Alicia: to begin to communicate more successfully; get along better with adults and children in school and at home; and begin to learn important academic skills like reading, writing, and arithmetic.

The teacher recognizes the importance of being systematic, though, and explains to Alicia's parents the value of well-designed lesson plans that describe the times, places, materials needed, teaching steps to take, and information to observe and record. Here we present the general game plan the teacher and parents will follow.

Preparatory Steps

Suppose that you and your family are invited for the first time to a colleague's house for a Sunday barbecue. Finding your way there will be much easier if you know the town, street, and house number and have access to a road map.

The same is true when you decide to develop a teaching strategy for each student you teach. If you are clear about where you are headed, you will get there more efficiently. So, before actually designing any lesson, begin by reviewing the objectives included in the students' individual educational plans. Then decide in what order to address those objectives, preparing instructional methods by adjusting the format and content of the lessons to each particular student.

Review Objectives

It might be tempting to begin teaching a particular lesson because it is timely, others in the group will be working on it, it is something you or someone else seems to want the child to learn at the time, or for some other reason. If, before beginning, you refer back to the objectives in the student's individual educational plan, you might save valuable time and effort. See whether the lesson matches the child's current needs. If it does, great. Otherwise, review the child's objectives to see how they can be woven most seamlessly into your teaching day.

Remember, too, that children differ in terms of how they can deal with various levels of complexity. Some need to proceed in very small, simple steps; others are capable of moving in larger, far more complicated ones. Even if you decide to teach three children in your group about Halloween pumpkins, one may be ready only to point to a pumpkin, so you target teaching him to indicate a pumpkin when other vegetables are present. Another can say "Pumpkin." You may want to teach that child to say "Jack-o'-lantern." The third is capable of describing it as the vegetable we use for making jack-o'-lanterns. You use the situation as an opportunity to teach her how to describe the process of creating the jack-o'-lantern.

Also, if, as suggested in Chapter 3, you have specified the dimensions of the instructional objectives, you and others will easily be able to tell when they have been reached. Together you then can celebrate the accomplishment.

Match Lessons to the Objective

Beyond allowing for individual differences, we also need to look at the objective itself to see what kind of a lesson would work best in any particular case. Sometimes an objective like teaching the child to ask for food lends itself very naturally to an event within the daily routine, such as snack time. Others need to be carefully arranged or contrived, such as teaching the child to write her name.

Later we will talk in more detail about three distinct types of lesson strategies that many have found to be especially appropriate for particular objectives; those involving basic actions (doing) as well as communicating (saying or responding to verbal instructions). For the present we just list them:

(1) Teacher-initiated **discrete trial** formats for lessons involving relatively direct instructions and simple responses
(2) Teacher-initiated **sequential**[1] lessons for skills that require a series of distinct smaller responses put together in a particular order
(3) **Student-initiated** lessons (including incidental lessons), suited to encouraging the child to initiate the action in response to naturally occurring cues from the physical (things) or social (people) environment.

Plan Ways to Incorporate and Apply Laws of Learning and Behavior Change

The Pyramid Approach's foundation in science distinguishes it from many other instructional approaches. The more we know about and use scientific principles of behavior, the better our lessons will work. Let us take a look at how this operates.

Learning. Learning involves systematic changes in behavior. These changes can involve (1) the acquisition of a new form of behavior, (2) behaviors occurring under new conditions, (3) new sequences of behaviors, and (4) new qualities associated with behaviors, such as how rapidly they are repeated or how long they continue. Teaching is doing things to support learning. In this case, typically two or more people are involved: the learner, whose behavior is to change, and the teacher, who behaves to support the change in the learner's behavior. Teaching happens before (in advance of, or antecedent to) and after (as a consequence of) the student's behavior.

Antecedents and Consequences. What are antecedents? Antecedents are things (stimuli) that come before a behavior that may influence whether the behavior takes place and how that behavior looks. A good way to view antecedents is as if they were like the props, sets, background music, and lighting for a play. Dim lights, a dark street, a bat flying overhead, and somber, discordant music prepares the audience for a mystery or dark drama; bright lights, cheerful colors, and sprightly music hints of a romance or comedy. In a similar way, antecedents signal something about what behavior "should" or "should not" follow because reinforcement is, in the former, or is not, in the latter, likely to follow as a consequence. In behavioral jargon, antecedents set the occasion for a particular response. Being presented with fleshy, seedy, farm produce, especially if it is sweet, should be an antecedent

---

[1] Technically, these would be labeled behavioral chains.

to the label "fruit." Instructions are supposed to be antecedents to teaching certain behaviors. Much of the work that teachers, teaching parents, and curriculum designers do is designing and arranging antecedents like text, pictures, audiovisuals, rules, instructions, and so on.

Different Kinds of Antecedents.   Technically an antecedent is a stimulus. The term *stimulus* has a long history in psychology and education. Most often it is associated with the phrase "stimulus-response," as when referring to certain reflexes. For example, often when we smell freshly baked bread, our mouths begin to water. If a pin sticks a baby, she immediately cries. These types of stimuli seem automatically to lead to particular reactions. If the name "Pavlov" rings a bell, it is probably because you remember that he studied how dogs would come to salivate at the sound of a bell. Pavlov noticed that if the sound of a bell reliably preceded placing food into a dog's mouth, the dog would begin to salivate at the sound of the bell, even when no food was immediately provided. This type of learning has been called classical conditioning, and in that case the antecedent stimulus is termed a conditioned stimulus. While such conditioning does play a large role in our emotional reactions, it seems to be less important to the acquisition and development of more complex skills, especially those related to social, communicative, and academic skills.

Consequences.   F. H. Thorndike first studied another type of learning early in the 20th century. He examined the impact of certain consequences on given behaviors. Later, B. F. Skinner refined those discoveries by observing that certain consequences, which as we now know he called "reinforcers," would increase the future probability of the response those consequences had followed. However, Skinner did not limit his analyses to just the impact of consequences on behavior. He also studied the influence of reinforcing consequences on the combination of particular events (or stimuli) that consistently preceded those reinforced actions—its antecedents—and the response. He and his colleagues discovered that when a particular stimulus reliably was paired with a particular behavior and that sequence was followed by a reinforcing outcome, then that behavior occurred more often in the presence of that stimulus. Such stimuli are called discriminative stimuli. It is important to understand that any object or event in the environment may become a discriminative stimulus. When such a stimulus has been created, we also say that the stimulus has gained stimulus control over the behavior with which it is associated.

Control by Discriminative Stimuli.   What is the nature of the control that discriminative stimuli exert over behavior? It is important to understand that such stimuli do not physically force a particular action to occur. Rather, think of them as signals that the particular action will lead to a particular outcome.

For example, consider the line painted down the center of a two-lane road. In the United States we have learned that keeping the car to the right of the line generally leads to reinforcement, that is, getting to our destination safely. The painted line does not physically force us to drive on its right side. We can drive on the left side of the road. In that case, however, we would be far less likely to arrive safely. Driving to the left of the line is *not* associated with reinforcement. Perhaps we learned this lesson when we were first taught to drive and our instructor scolded us for driving slightly to the left of or even on the line.

Antecedent Stimuli and Lesson Planning

Let us consider how understanding stimulus control will influence the way we teach our lessons. Assume that we want to teach Sarah to choose a spoon when we say, "Please get your spoon." We may start the lesson when Sarah has a bowl of cereal before her but no spoon. We then say, "Please get a spoon," and guide Sarah to get a spoon from a silverware tray containing only spoons. Quickly, she begins to retrieve a spoon each time we give her the instruction at breakfast time. Does Sarah really know what a spoon is? Can she discriminate it from a fork or a knife? In other words, has the word "spoon" gained stimulus control over Sarah's choosing spoons? One way to check would be to add forks to the silverware tray without any cues, like a bowl of cereal, before her. If we then ask Sarah on a number of different occasions to get a spoon and she comes back with the right utensil, we could move on to a more advanced lesson. By contrast, should she often select the wrong utensil, we would suspect that our verbal instructions lacked stimulus control over her choices. More likely, she had been responding to various accessory or contextual cues, such as the contents of the bowl or plate. Then we would need to design a lesson to teach her to respond correctly to our instructions. So, one of our rules of teaching will be always to test whether our intended discriminative stimuli truly is working by trying out other, nonrelated stimuli to see whether a student responds differently to them than to the cue we hope has taken control.

> Test the control exerted by an intended discriminative stimulus by displaying other similar stimuli and evaluating whether the response occurs only when it is supposed to but not otherwise.

Teaching Scientifically

Our survival, growth, and adaptation to society depend on stimulus control. What that means is that certain stimuli commonly cue our behavior. The flashing pedestrian signal tells us when it is safe to cross the street; the date stamped on a perishable product lets us know whether to buy and eat it; words on a page guide the way we assemble our lawn mower, our boss's expression indicates whether this is a good time to hit her up for a raise, and one set of positions of the hands on the clock cue us about when to go to bed, another when to catch our ride. Identifying these natural cues prior to teaching is essential if our instruction is to succeed efficiently. We include them as conditions in our objectives and teach toward that cue-response combination.

Enabling a student to behave reliably according to a given natural cue, like telling the time by the position of the clock's hands, though, is more easily said than done. To succeed with students who face special challenges, we need to use the best available in instructional technology; in this case a technology based on the science of human behavior. The guidelines we present in the following derive from that science.

Teach by Trial and Success

Baby Billy pulls himself up to a standing position, moves his wobbly leg forward, totters a bit, and flops back on to the floor. Maybe he will cry; maybe he will try again. Eventually he succeeds, and before long he is walking. Probably Billy learns to crawl, walk, feed himself, and many other skills through trial and error. However, suppose that he never succeeded after weeks or months of effort? Eventually, unless he received some assistance or formal training, he might give up trying. Because success is so essential to progress, the Pyramid Approach stresses the importance of designing instruction to maximize student success and minimize student errors.

Why do we intentionally try to bypass the "error" part? Because committing an error does not result in reinforcement and may even be punished. When that happens repeatedly, not only do students fail to learn, but, just as we are tempted to do when the vending machine swallows our dollar without delivering our selection, they can become aggressive or try to flee the situation.

Minimizing student errors, though, is not always easy. It may take a cleverly planned sequence of steps, often combined with a mix of natural cues and artificial prompts, to get the responses we are seeking. We may have to progress in very small steps, physically guide, or otherwise prompt the behavior by showing or telling the person what to do or exaggerating differences between the right and wrong antecedents. A complete description of how to deal with errors can be found in Chapter 10.

Shape for Success

Little Billy toddles over to the swing and stands there babbling. His mom responds by saying, "Oh Billy, you want to have a swing," as she lifts the child into the seat and pushes him. Mom pushes Billy each time he makes a sound that more and more closely approximates the word "up." Eventually he will say "Up" every time. Mom then can use the same method of reinforcing successive approximations to encourage Billy to build his vocabulary. "Up, swing," "Go up swing," "Please swing," and "Please up swing."

This method, called **shaping,** takes lots of patience, but the price is worth it. You can get the behavior you are hoping for without needing to resort to discipline. The trick is to make the required changes so small that only rarely does the student have to wait to obtain the reinforcer.

Beware of the teacher's trap, though. Our temptation is to tell, tell, and retell the student what to do instead of waiting patiently until that exact moment when the slight progress occurs. We need to remind ourselves that if, like the mother bird in the cartoon (see Figure 8.1) orally instructing the student did not work the first few times, it probably will not work any better the next several dozen times.[2] What does work is reinforcing progress and withholding reinforcement when there is none.

If need be, though, teachers can speed up the shaping process by adding prompts that are known to work effectively with that student under those circumstances. Having observed Billy's penchant for imitating his playmate Rory's behavior, Billy's mom could pick up and swing Rory when Rory says "Up." Billy imitates, and mom now can reinforce his progress. The following sections concentrate on establishing, using, and fading out various kinds of prompts.

Prompt for Success

Sometimes the more efficient way to obtain the behavior in the first place, as we just described, is to provide extra or artificial stimuli, such as spoken instructions, gestures, modeled demonstrations, or even physical assistance. Or in the case of teaching students to discriminate between visual stimuli, like the hands on a clock, numbers, letters, words, and pictures, we might highlight or exaggerate an aspect of the stimulus by making it bolder, brighter, larger, or more colorful. These extra elements are called **prompts.**

---

[2]Interestingly, this trap is by no means limited to teaching young children or students with special challenges. Even in business and industry, when workers fail to follow given procedures, such as adhering to given safety precautions, the natural tendency is to bring them back for retraining instead of the much more powerful technique of shaping their progress toward optimal performance.

Figure 8.1   Ineffective prompting

Natural Cues versus Prompts.   As we have seen, one of our main responsibilities is teaching children to respond correctly to important physical and social stimuli native to their environments. For example, to watch television, I need to learn which buttons to press; to make toast, I need to learn where to put the bread and what switches to push; to choose the right public bathroom, I need to learn the symbols related to male versus female; and, as noted earlier, to drive a car, I need to understand where to position the car relative to the lines on the road.

Often what other people do is part of the natural learning process. For example, children need to learn to put their things away when the teacher says, "Time to clean up"; to turn to the right page when told, "Everyone turn to page 10"; and to line up when the teacher says, "It stopped raining! Let's go outside and play!" In each example, the instructional stimuli are natural to the setting and will not necessarily need to be eliminated in the future. (Think how hazardous driving would be if all painted lines disappeared.) We will refer to discriminative stimuli that remain or are inherent in the environment as **natural cues.** As you might anticipate, if they are to function independently in that particular environment, students' behavior ultimately needs to be controlled by natural cues.

Unlike Billy, Rory is very good at imitating what he hears his parents say to him and is responsive to their gestures. If he whines for his dessert, his mom or dad will advise him to say "Please," and he does. If he wants to play his favorite video, they point to the receptacle and tell him to push it in. Eventually, though, Rory's parents hope that he will function independently of their help. If they fail to remove those prompts effectively, he may continue to rely on the prompt. In such cases, we say that the child's responding has become **prompt dependent.**

In fact, prompt dependency is seen so often, particularly among children with autism, that many have come to view this as a feature of the disability. Some people talk about prompt dependency as if it were a failure on the child's part—"He failed to generalize because he is so prompt dependent!" We are convinced that prompt dependency develops not through any deficiency in the student but as a result of the teacher's failure to plan and conduct lessons that successfully eliminate the prompt. It is not educationally sound to move students on to more advanced levels if they require a prompt before being able to perform a given response.

Formal Lesson Design

Within the Pyramid Approach, depending on the instructional objectives, available resources, and the student's entering skills, we structure the behavioral teaching guidelines into three categories of formal lessons: discrete trial, sequential, and student initiated. Let us look at each in more depth. Regardless of which lesson format anyone uses, it will be said to have done its job only when the student reliably responds to natural cues.

Discrete Trial Lessons

We plan discrete trial lessons to be short and simple. If lessons are too complicated, we break them down into their simple components and generally build repetition into the training. Soon you will see how this is accomplished.

What Is a Discrete Trial?   A discrete trial, according to Anderson, Taras, and Cannon,[3] consists of four parts: (1) the presentation by the trainer, (2) the student's response, (3) the consequence, and (4) a short pause between that consequence and the next trial. Typically, the point of each discrete trial lesson is to teach the child to respond appropriately to a simple verbal instruction. Such instructions are often referred to as the S^Ds. Remember, though, that not all such stimuli are verbal. That is, if someone were to ask, "What is the discriminative stimulus for this lesson?" it would not be correct to assume that "the stimulus" would have to be a verbal cue. Many lessons are designed

---

[3]S. R. Anderson, M. Taras, and B. O. Cannon Teaching New Skills to Children with Autism in C. Maurice, G. Green, and S. C. Luce, eds. Behavioral Interventions for Young Children with Autism (Austin, TX: PRO-ED, 1996, 181–94).

to teach appropriate responses to nonverbal social or physical-environmental cues, such as a fire bell or a "V" sign to quiet down.

Objectives Suited to Discrete Trial Lessons.   We can teach either verbal or nonverbal responses within a discrete trial format. For example, verbal responses are required by instructions such as "What is your name?" "What color is the ball?" "What is it?" "What number comes after two?" or "Say 'ball.'" On the other hand, we would anticipate nonverbal responses to instructions such as "Touch your nose," "Match the same," "Give me the car," or "Go to the door." As we discussed in more detail in Chapter 5, it is important to understand that even if a child can respond appropriately to the instruction "Give me the car," we should not necessarily expect the child to be able to ask for the car or even imitate the word "car."

Ensuring Student Attending.   When beginning a lesson, we want to be sure that the student is paying attention. In the beginning, we may need to use a general cue to attend, such as "Look at me" or "Get ready." Notice that these instructions specify something about being attentive. In form, they are not the same as when we say a child's name prior to asking him to do something (e.g., "Andy, please give me the spoon"). However, the function is the same; that is, each is a cue that essentially says, "Get ready to listen because the next thing I say will be important." If the child does not respond to the cue to pay attention, the teacher shapes that response by pausing until the child appears to be attentive (e.g., is making eye contact) or, if necessary at first, by gently physically guiding the child to "pay attention."[4]

Presenting Instructions.   How the teacher states the instruction is an important issue. We could say, "Beth, would you please reach over here and pick up the red ball and place it into my hand?" Many children will miss the essential information buried within this long statement. When introducing new terms, it is more effective to use simple statements, such as "Give me the ball." As the child learns to respond to the instruction, the teacher may adjust its form gradually to what the child would be expected to hear in the natural (non-teaching) environment ("Give it here," "Toss it to me," and so on). How narrowly or specially defined our instruction is will influence the child's ability to generalize it to other instructions and situations (see the section "Teach Loosely" in Chapter 7 for more details). For example, if we only use the phrase, "What's your address?" in this form for 12 months of training, the

---

[4]The fact that a student is looking at you is no guarantee that he actually is paying attention; looking at someone just tends to correlate with increased attention. The only way to really find out is to see what happens next, that is, whether the student responds appropriately to the stimuli you are presenting.

child may be unable to answer a parallel question, like "Where do you live?" or "What is the number of your house and the name of the street you live on?"

Presenting Consequences.   After giving the instruction, the teacher waits for the answer for at least five seconds and, if the child responds correctly, delivers praise. Sometimes when there is reason to believe that praise or other social rewards presently are not effective reinforcers for the child, the teacher pairs the praise with additional rewards, such as snacks or treats the youngster likes.

Using Prompts if Necessary.   If the child fails to react within the allotted time limit or responds incorrectly, the teacher says "No" or "Wrong," in a neutral, not in a harsh or punitive, tone. The reaction is meant to be informative and educational. (The specific way the teacher should react to the child's error will be discussed in more detail in Chapter 10.) In this case, the teacher next repeats the instruction and simultaneously adds a prompt likely to ensure a successful response. The type of prompt chosen varies according to the kind that regularly works with the student within that type of lesson.

Providing Opportunities for Repetition of the Correct Response.
So far, we have described the sequence within a single trial: present the instruction; wait for the student to respond; and provide an appropriate consequence. However, a successful single correct response is no guarantee the student has mastered the objective of the lesson. Therefore, the trial is repeated, but in what manner? There are several factors we must consider at this point (see Figure 8.2).

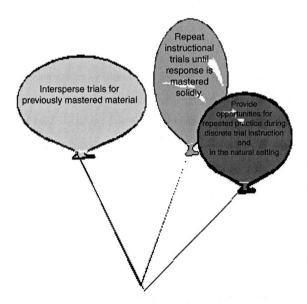

Figure 8.2   Tips for Successful Discrete Trial Instruction

Repeating Trials. A single success hardly guarantees learning. The trials need to be repeated, but not just haphazardly. We need to consider such factors as how long to wait between trials, how many trials to conduct, whether they should be repeated one right after the next or trials of a different kind interspersed, plus other details.

Frequently Posed Questions about Discrete Trial Teaching

1. How much time should pass between trials? The time between trials[5] generally is fairly short—a few seconds. The reason for using short intervals is to avoid the child becoming distracted by other stimuli in the immediate environment. However, over time, it will be important to stretch the length of the interval because simple instructions or other cues rarely are repeated in the real world.

2. How many trials should be carried out within a teaching session? Some lessons readily lend themselves to repeated trials. For example, putting spoons in the dishwasher often involves many spoons (and ultimately other utensils). Putting toys away, all socks of one color in one pile and all of another color in a different one, and the tall books on one shelf and the small books on another, all illustrate situations naturally calling for repeated trials. When repetitions are not necessarily inherent in the situation, choose a criterion for determining the number of trials to repeat before changing the lesson focus, say, when the child correctly responds correctly for four trials in a row or some similar criterion.

3. Should trials be repeated directly one after another (massed), or should they be interspersed within (distributed among) other activities? There is no simple formula for balancing massed versus distributed practice. In general, trials tend to be massed in the beginning and then become more distributed. However, overemphasizing massed practice significantly postpones the distributed work. This strategy, in turn, can delay introducing the skill within the more natural context and seriously interfere with generalization. Begin to apply the discrete trial in its natural context as soon as possible. Instead of sorting socks at the table, move to the wash basket next to the clothes dryer.

Finally, some discrete trial lessons do not lend themselves to massed or rapidly repeated trials. For example, when teaching a girl to say "Hi," it would not be effective to prompt her to say "Hi" for 10 or 20 massed trials. In fact, if this approach is used, when she leaves the teaching table and chair, she

---

[5]Those who appreciate the precision of technical jargon will refer to this as the intertrial interval.

Naturally Repeated Discrete Trials?

A parent related how at Halloween she designed a picture for her son, who used it to symbolize "Trick or Treat!" The boy toured the neighborhood with his friends, presenting the card to each neighbor answering the door. The rewards—candy and other treats—also fit the context naturally. Obviously, he went to many homes that night, repeating his simple request over and over again.

may not say "Hi" to anyone. Indeed, her responding may well have become dependent on the discriminative stimuli peculiar to the lesson, like sitting in a chair, repeating the instruction, and so on.

4. May we address more than one lesson within a session? Traditionally, discrete trials were rapidly repeated to help keep students engaged while minimizing any tendency for them to become distracted or to turn to self-stimulating. Today we question this assumption, opting instead to intersperse other instructional trials periodically within the session. Additionally, research[6] has shown that interspersing activities tends to improve the student's ongoing attention to the task.

In our discussion of reinforcement, we noted that surprise and novelty are usually reinforcing in and of themselves. Thus, adding trials for skills that students already have learned to a block of trials designed for a new lesson can be very effective. This mixture will help keep students attentive to your cues and prompts. Requesting previously

A Golden Rule for Lessons

One *new* lesson at a time!

mastered responses also will give you additional opportunities to reward them for successes, especially important at a time when they may be unsure of the correct new responses. Take care to avoid presenting two new lessons at the same time, as this will virtually guarantee high rates of errors, low rates of reinforcement, and consequently increased rates of disruptive behaviors.[7]

Sequential Lessons

Much of what we do in everyday life consists of routines composed of a complex of many simpler steps, as when we prepare meals, get dressed, clean the house, operate our VCRs and computers, groom ourselves, and play. As suggested earlier, skills of the sort we might instruct within a discrete trial format often need to be combined with others, typically in a particular order. If we change that order, we change the outcome—often not for the better. (Socks

---

[6]N. A. Neef, B. A. Iwata, and T. J. Page, The Effects of Interspersal Training versus High Density Reinforcement on Spelling Acquisition and Retention, Journal of Applied Behavior Analysis 13 (1980): 153–158.

[7]Adapted from K. Pryor, *Don't Shoot the Dog! The New Art of Teaching and Training.* New York: Bantam, 1999.

over our shoes may look cool but would not be very practical.) Consequently, when teaching such sequential skills, first consider what steps compose the sequence. This process is called a **task analysis.**

Designing Effective Task Analyses.   When teaching sets of sequential skills, the first thing is to identify each of the steps. Here is a sequence of steps, itself a task analysis, that you might follow when analyzing a task:

(1) Envision how you and others do that activity—an **armchair analysis.** Of course, if several people are working on the design, you may find that different people suggest slightly different ways of accomplishing things. For example, is it critical that the plates be put down before the glasses? One big advantage is that teachers usually know the skills themselves. The tricky part is accepting the idea that how we do a task may not be exactly the same as the way someone else does it, even though we both end up with good outcomes. Bob might put on his left shoe first, fold one loop of the lace, wrap the other behind the loop, and pull the first one through. Henry may put on his right shoe first, double loop the lace, and twist and tie them into a simple knot. Yet both walk out of their bedrooms without tripping. Must the salad fork be on the left of the dinner fork? Probably you will realize that there are various acceptable ways to sequence a task analysis for most complex behaviors.

(2) Watch a few experts performing the skill. Note each element. When you see differences in the content or order of components, discuss it with the others to decide which elements you absolutely have to retain and which can be optional.

(3) Sometimes published task analyses can be found in professional journals and books. A good place to begin is by checking for "task analyses" in the indexes of journals like the *Journal of Applied Behavior Analysis.*

(4) Consider the characteristics and abilities of the your students. You might need separate task analyses for two different students because of differences in their skills or other distinguishing features. For example, a task analysis designed to teach a seven-year-old to shop in a supermarket would be different than one for a 15-year-old. The sequence for a child who can read may be different than for one who depends on picture cues.

(5) Putting the task analysis to the test is essential. The only way to know whether what you have written is clear and effective is to use it and see how well it works.[8]

Task Analyses and Behavioral Chains.   Another term used to describe a complex response consisting of a sequence of steps is a behavioral chain. One property of chains is that each link, or response element in the chain is connected to both the link before and the link after it, as shown in Figure 8.3. Ultimately, in a smoothly executed chain, the step preceding each element functions as an discriminative stimulus for it; the link following as its (conditioned) reinforcer. The same applies to each of the components of a task analysis.

Turns on the water ➡ picks up the soap ➡ puts hands under t water ➡ rubs hands together ➡ rinses hands ➡ dries hands ➡ goes to lunch table ➡ eats lunch.

Figure 8.3   Washing Hands in Preparation for Lunch

Now, because each step is supposed to act as the effective discriminative stimulus for the next one, be very cautious about adding unnecessary prompts into the sequence. For example, it would be very tempting to add verbal prompts to each step. While teaching a child to wash hands, we could say, "Turn on the water, pick up the soap, put your hands under the water, rub your hands together, rinse your hands," and so on. However, as noted in our discussion of prompting, all prompts must be removed before independence is achieved. Although verbal prompts are easy for teachers to use, in practice, once the student begins to depend on them, they can be difficult to remove. Thus, in addition to determining the sequence of steps within the task analysis, it is important to identify which types of natural cues will be in place when the sequence is completely learned. To wash hands effectively, a child must learn how to manipulate soap, water, the faucet, and so on. Understanding spoken instructions is not a necessary aspect of washing hands. How to use prompts to teach the sequence of steps and permit the natural cues to become effective will be reviewed in Chapter 9. Figure 8.4 displays another task analysis: one for preparing a peanut butter and jelly sandwich.

Initiating the Sequence: In designing effective sequential lessons, consider how to begin the sequence. What is the natural cue for the activity? Sometimes, a verbal cue is appropriate. For example, a teacher announces to the group that playtime is over and that everyone should get ready for lunch (e.g., "It's time to wash hands"). The bus has just driven up, and mom says, "Time

---

[8]The Murdoch Center Program Library is a collection of almost 1,000 task analyses applicable to the habilitation of people with severe special needs (Murdoch Center Foundation, P.O. Box 92, Butner, NC 27509).

- Place breadboard on table
- Get knife from silverware drawer
- Get plate from cabinet
- Get package of bread from breadbox
- Place next to breadboard
- Get peanut butter jar from cabinet
- Place next to board
- Get jar of jelly from refrigerator
- Place next to breadboard
- Take two slices of bread
- Open the jar
- Place the cover beside the jar
- Use knife to get some peanut butter
- Spread the peanut butter on one slice of bread
- Add more peanut butter if parts of the bread not covered
- Wipe knife off on other piece of bread
- Close the peanut butter jar
- Open the jelly jar

- Place cover next to jar
- Use knife to take some jelly out of the jelly jar
- Spread jelly onto the second piece of bread
- Repeat if surface not completely covered
- Close jelly jar
- Turn over and place the side of the bread with the peanut butter on top of the other piece containing the jelly
- Cut the sandwich in half
- Put the sandwich on a plate
- Put peanut butter and jelly back where you got them
- Put the knife in the sink
- Sit down at the table with the sandwich in front of you
- Put a napkin in your lap
- Eat the sandwich
- Mmm!

Figure 8.4   Preparing a Peanut Butter and Jelly Sandwich

to dress to go outside." The music teacher says, "Here's my guitar" or "Now we can sing." Although it is tempting use those kinds of verbal cues, teachers try to encourage students to be more independent and thereby, over time, to be less reliant on an adult's directions. Thus, for any particular activity or element of a chain, assess whether verbal instructions can be dispensed with in favor of natural cues. For example, children ultimately should respond to fire bells and not someone telling them what to do after the fire bell sounds. Bringing out the guitar could just as well signal sitting on the rug in a circle as telling the group to gather. Seeing the bus drive up could cue getting dressed to go home and so on.

Reinforcement During Sequential Lessons: The types of reinforcers associated with a task should be considered when designing effective sequential lessons. As noted in our discussion of reinforcement, use reinforcers that fit the situation—those that are contextually relevant. Some of these rewards can be thought of as intrinsic to the activity. Many of us find something about throwing and catching a ball that is enjoyable, independent of social reinforcers. It just feels good.

On the other hand, some contextual reinforcers are connected to what happens following completion of an activity but not necessarily in between. For example, maybe a student does not care about the "feel" of tying his laces but loves to have his sneakers on when he runs around outside. Creating a relationship between completing something that is not naturally reinforcing and the resulting access to something that is naturally reinforcing opens up some interesting options. You could be direct and instruct, "Put on your sneakers," running the risk that the only time the child will put on his sneakers is when he is told to do so. However, at a time when the child's sneakers are off, you could say, "Hey, let's go outside!" At this point the child is likely to bolt for the door. Now, you could say, "Uh oh. We wear sneakers to go outside" (or some such similar reminder). What happens when the child has completed putting on his sneakers? Does he get M&Ms for nice lacing or being compliant with the demand? No, because praise and quick access to the door are all he needs. The type of reinforcer associated with a sequential lesson influences how the lesson is taught.

Table 8.1 provides a list of common sequential skills and potential contextual rewards (both intrinsic to the situation and related to natural outcomes). You may find it helpful to complete the table and add examples of skills you plan to teach.

For some activities, the assumed natural reinforcer for completing the task will occur long after its completion. For example, why do we brush our teeth? Presumably to prevent cavities. Manufacturers of toothpaste certainly know

Table 8.1   Common Contextual Skills and Intrinsic Rewards

Sequential Skill	Potential Intrinsic Reward	Potential Completion Reward
Washing hands	Sensory stimulation (feel, sound, sight, smell) of soap, water, rubbing hands	Access to meals/snacks, access to activity after cleaning dirty hands
Getting dressed	Feel or look of clothes	Access to next activity (smock leads to art, T-shirt leads to gym, coat leads to bus/outside)
Brushing teeth	Feel/taste of toothpaste/ toothbrush, water play	Access to next activity or meal, clean feel of mouth
Setting the table		
Putting away groceries		
Putting away plates and utensils		
Putting toys away		
Playing a game		
Washing laundry		

about manipulating immediate or intrinsic rewards. They add pleasant flavors to the toothpaste and reassure us that our breath will be kissing sweet right afterward. Such additions increase the probability that we will brush our teeth (and thus consume more, resulting in our buying more toothpaste). It also is true that sometimes when we finish brushing our teeth, we enjoy the clean feel of our teeth and mouth in general, but that probably is not a sensation we notice every time we brush.

We also are taught that brushing our teeth (sometimes with certain additives) will help prevent future dental problems. However, as all teachers and parents know, getting children (and even adults sometimes) to do something now, in anticipation of some far-off reward, is not easy. Therefore, arrange to deliver arbitrary reinforcers on the completion of activities lacking naturally reinforcing consequences. In this particular case, you might arrange a simple deal with the child by requiring that he brush his teeth after a snack but before going to the play area.

Finally, not every sequential lesson can be arranged to be intrinsically rewarding or result in naturally or immediately arranged outcomes. For example, what is the natural outcome for completing the stuffing of 100 envelopes with a newsletter for the neighborhood association? Perhaps a sense of civic pride would be sufficient for you. Suppose, though, that the task were for you to pack boxes of manufactured goods for a profit-making business. What would it probably take to motivate you to do this activity? Right, a reasonable amount of money. The advantage of using money or tokens is that we can exchange it for a variety of rewarding items some time later.

If you decide to dispense tokens during a complex task, watch that they do not disrupt the lesson. If the tokens distract the student, try placing them out of reach but in such a way that the student can detect each time he has received them. Pair the delivery with a sound or word (e.g., "Another chip" or "That's 16; four more to go"). Place it into a glass jar. Use pegs, puzzle pieces, or other objects that provide a visual cue that the token has been delivered. Display a number showing the amount earned or use some other method suited to the student.

Student-Initiated Lessons

Mindy clearly wants to eat some popcorn. She is standing in front of the bowl of popcorn. She even reaches into the bowl but says nothing to her teacher. Anne appears to want to watch her favorite videotape—she has the tape in her hands and is standing in front of the television set and the VCR but does not know how to put the tape in the machine or how to turn on the television. Tony has just asked his teacher for an apple, but the teacher wants him to indicate whether he wants the red or the green one. In each of these cases, the child has started a pattern of actions but is not able to bring them to completion or can do so only in a limited fashion. How, then, can we teach children successfully to initiate an action or to expand on skills they currently demonstrate? Will we be able to rely on the same teaching strategies needed to teach discrete trial and sequential lessons?

Discrete trial and sequential lessons are typically begun with an instruction, such as, "What's this?," "Clap your hands," or "Set the table." It is tempting to use a similar strategy to get a child to initiate. However, what would happen if a teacher said to a student, "You start the conversation with me—go ahead, start"? If the student starts to speak at that point, has the child started the interaction?

As we noted in our discussion of powerful reinforcers, we encourage using motivators that fit the context or are natural to the situation. Can we use this strategy to help children initiate and expand their behavior patterns? **Incidental teaching** is one well-researched strategy to expand children's skills by capitalizing on this idea. This strategy was first used with young children with impoverished speaking repertoires[9] but has since been extended to children with a variety of disabilities[10].

Your efforts to use incidental teaching should be more successful if you try to adhere to the following strategies:

(1) Observe the child's preferences: Rather than choosing what a child can earn within a lesson, observe what currently motivates the child. For example, a child is observed to reach for a truck while saying "Truck." Another child picks out all the red candies from a handful offered by the teacher. Incidental lessons start only when the teacher has observed what the child wants or is trying to accomplish.

(2) Use natural cues: The teacher manipulates various objects and events in the natural setting in order to entice the child to interact with something interesting. For example, the teacher places a group of toys just out of reach of the child or shows the child a preferred snack inside a closed clear container. Thus, rather than always using a direct strategy,

---

[9]B. Hart and T. R. Risley, Incidental Teaching of Language in the Preschool, Journal of Applied Behavior Analysis 8 (1975): 411–20.

[10]For example, V. Farmer-Dugan, Increasing Requests by Adults with Developmental Disabilities Using Incidental Teaching by Peers, *Journal of Applied Behavior Analysis* 27 (1994): 533–544, and S. G. McGee, C. Almeida, B. Sulzer-Azaroff, and R. S. Feldman, Promoting Reciprocal Interactions via Peer Incidental Teaching, *Journal of Applied Behavior Analysis* 25 (1992): 118–126.

like asking the child what he wants, the teacher modifies the physical environment, using an indirect strategy to attract the child's attention[11].

(3) Assess the child's current repertoire and choose an expansion to teach: The teacher carefully observes how the child currently attempts to obtain the desired outcome. For example, when shown a truck, Doris merely reaches for the truck without saying anything, while Lily says, "Truck," and Yosi says, "I want the truck." The goal with Doris is to communicate (in any effective modality) her desire for the object, while the goal for Lily is to add "I want" to her single word. Yosi's goal is to add color or size adjectives to his short sentence structure. Notice that the original approach to each child is the same but that the lesson changes in relation to the how the child responds.

(4) Take advantage of spontaneous opportunities: Another term for a teacher is an **instructor**—one who instructs. Thus, teachers often feel compelled to give instructions as a way to start each lesson. How can we teach without beginning with instructions? One way, as we have seen, is to take advantage of teaching opportunities as they arise across a day, including instances when the child initiates toward something. For example, while a group of students are playing at the sand table, one student begins to walk toward the art area. Rather than assuming that the child must play with sand, the teacher sees this as an opportunity to teach the child to communicate her desire to change activities. Likewise, a mother may be taking a walk with her son when he bends down to examine a squiggling worm. Instead of insisting on continuing with the walk, the mother comments about the worm and encourages her son to express his interest in a more mature fashion. In this way, teaching opportunities are not limited to when the teacher is ready to teach. Rather, teaching occurs when the student is ready to learn. This can happen almost any time. Like a good photographer, teachers are ready to "capture the moment" and create a minilesson on the spot.

(5) Do not predetermine the exact number of trials in a lesson: Teachers often set the number of trials or teaching opportunities within a particular lesson. For example, a teacher decides that she will put out six objects and teach the child to name each one 10 times. The same is often true for sequential lessons. A teacher asks a student to set the table with plates, forks, spoons, knives, and napkins for eight. Can we predeter-

---

[11]This strategy also has been described as contriving an establishing operation, a term described by J. Michael, Distinguishing between Discriminative and Motivational Functions of Stimuli, Journal of the Experimental Analysis of Behavior 37 (1982): 149–55.

mine the number of repetitions within incidental lessons or other types of self-initiated lessons? Adam likes to play with a ball. Can his teacher make Adam want to play with the ball exactly 20 times during the next hour? Of course not. Teachers must observe how strongly a child wants to play with an item and be ready to move on to a different lesson (or the same type of lesson with a different object) when the student's interest shifts. So, while a teacher will try to create many teaching opportunities within a set period of time, there is no way anyone can precisely determine how many such opportunities will take place.

(6) Manage the student's access to high-preference objects and activities: While predetermining the number of incidental teaching trials to hold is not realistic, you can arrange to increase the number of opportunities by limiting the amount of time the student maintains access to the item or event. Use a natural strategy: taking turns. After learners have obtained the reinforcing item (event), permit them to enjoy it for a period of time, then remove access, as people do when the "take turns." Shift to another video or program, allow another child a turn with the toy, or use some other reasonable strategy. Then, after a few minutes, display the reinforcer once again for another trial.

(7) Involve peers in the process, when possible: Provide the peer tutor with a set of toys or other items the student prefers. Teach the peer tutor to (1) wait for the student to initiate, (2) prompt the student to label the item, (3) turn the object over to the student, (4) praise the requesting, (5) allow the student to sample the reinforcer, (6) ask for a turn for himself, (7) play with the item himself for a short period, and (8) repeat the sequence.

Summary

Designing effective lessons depends on a number of important actions. We need to prepare carefully by reviewing to the objectives contained in the student's individual plan. Instruction designed to conform not to our intuitive feelings about how to proceed but instead to incorporate principles of effective learning and instruction is most likely to succeed. Fortunately, we are not forced to begin from scratch because many other instructional designers and teachers have paved the way for us. In fact today there exists a huge library of behavior-analytic-based instructional strategies that have been demonstrated to be effective with typically developing students and those facing particular challenges. Included among them are discrete trial, sequential, and student-initiated teaching methods that are especially well suited to teaching students with autism and related conditions. In this chapter we have described each of those three approaches along with a number of guidelines to help you succeed in preparing your daily lessons.

Discrete trial instruction is a formal approach to teaching specific skills on a trial-by-trial basis. The student needs to be attending instructions delivered in a simple, straightforward manner. The teacher needs to be patient in awaiting the correct response and, when it is given, must present rewarding consequences right away. When necessary, prompts can assist the student to provide the appropriate response. Additionally, the student needs to be supplied with numerous opportunities to repeat the correct response. Other considerations in discrete trial instruction include using short intervals to separate trials from one another, setting guidelines for the number of trials within a session that depend on the nature of the response, and deciding whether to mass or distribute practice opportunities. Nevertheless, introducing multiple lessons at once is to be avoided. One new lesson at a time is sufficient.

Sequential lessons lend themselves best to teaching complex skills that consist of many steps. We plan for sequential lessons by designing or choosing already developed task analyses. With sequential lessons, we need to decide in advance what event should cue the activity and plan to capitalize on those reinforcers inherent in the situation or to deliver them at particular points. That can depend on the exact nature of the activity and the student's history of exposure to it.

Student-initiated lessons capitalize on the natural motivators for the student. We can discover those by observing the student carefully to see what she approaches or chooses, or we can make new arrangements to entice the student's interest. With student-initiated lessons, we need to be familiar with the learner's history of responding in relation to the object or event so that we can build on and expand those skills. Additionally, we should teach ourselves to be very sensitive and responsive to unanticipated learning opportunities. While making hard-and-fast rules about the number of trials to repeat within a lesson is not advisable, often we may be able to provide for repeated practice by managing the student's access to preferred items and activities. An especially powerful way of accomplishing this is to involve peers in the student-initiated learning process.

In the next chapter we continue along the path of helping teachers develop and deliver behavior-analytic-based instruction. You will learn how to use prompts to get a behavior going and to use fading to see to it that the student ultimately can respond to the cues from within the natural environment.

Suggested Reading and Viewings

To	**READ**
Systematically choose programs for teaching	Taylor, B. S. & McDonough, K. A. Selecting teaching programs. In

young children with autism, apply the programs and assess progress along the way	Maurice, C., Green, G. & Luce, S. (Eds.) Behavioral intervention for young children with autism. Austin, TX: Pro-Ed, 63–194.
See what elements are important for parents to include to be able successfully to teach their children at home	Anderson, S. R., Taras, M. & Cannon, B. O'M (1996). Teaching new skills to young children with autism. InMaurice, C., Green, G. & Luce, S. (Eds.) Behavioral intervention for young children with autism. Austin,TX: Pro-ed 181–194.
Choose a curriculum and learn how to apply it in a center-based program or at home	Harris, S. L. & Weiss, M. J. (1998). What to teach and how to teach it. In Right from the start: Behavioral intervention for young children with autism. Bethesda, MD: Woodbine House.
Encounter an engaging series of examples and how-to's of teaching, dolphins dogs and people through differential reinforcement	Pryor, K. (1999). Don't shoot the dog: The new art of teaching and training. New York: Bantam Books, especially Chapter 6: Clicker training: A new technology, 165–183.
Design a pre-school program that incorporates discrete-trial, sequential and incidental training	Charlop-Christy, M. H. & Kelso, S. E. (1997). How to treat the child with autism (Chapters 9 & 11). Claremont, CA: Claremont McKenna College. Handleman, J. S. & Harris, S. L. (Eds.) Preschool education programs for children with autism, 2nd edition. Austin, TX: Pro-Ed, 157–190.
Choose when and how to use incidental teaching and teach others to use it	Fenske, E. C., Krantz, P. J. & McClannahan, L. E. (2001).In C. Maurice, G. Green & R. M. Foxx. (Eds.) Making a Difference: Behavioral Intervention for Autism. Austin, TX: Pro-Ed, 75–82. McGee, G. G., Morrier, M. J. & Daly, T. (2001). The Walden early childhood

programs. In Handleman, J. S. & Harris, S. L. (Eds.) Preschool education programs for children with autism, 2nd Edition. Austin, TX: Pro-Ed, 157–190.

TO	***DO***
Experience using behavioral methods to design and teach a lesson to your peers	Exercises in Sulzer-Azaroff, B. & Reese, E. P. (1982). Applying behavior analysis. (Chapter 8). New York: Holt, Rinehart & Winston.

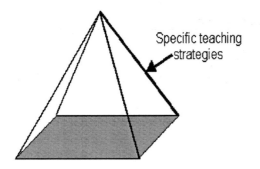
Specific teaching
strategies

9

Specific Teaching Strategies

"She is such a terrific teacher," Carlo's mom comments to her friend during a monthly parents' meeting. "Before he would just yell, scream, and kick, and we couldn't figure out what he wanted. It was a nightmare. Now he lets us know, with pictures, and sometimes even a word, what his issue is."

"If Kim could only do that, we'd feel like we'd won the lottery."

"Maybe she will. Give it a chance. She's only been here for a few weeks. They're teaching you how to follow through at home with her learning objectives, aren't they?"

"We're trying."

"I couldn't believe it the other day. We were in the mall, and he handed me his picture of a toilet and actually said something that sounded like 'toilet.'"

"So what happened?"

"Dan rushed him off to the bathroom. Seemed like that was what he needed."

None of Carlo's accomplishments had happened by chance. They were the result of his teacher carrying out careful "discrete trials" and generalization lessons. Through a carefully engineered series of steps, she had taught him to use pictures to request his favorite items and activities. She also had him respond to a picture of a toilet whenever there was a scheduled bathroom break. When he showed signs of needing to use the facility, a second teacher helped him use the picture to make a request (generalization trials).

Good teachers with all sorts of student populations are especially concerned with what people say and do in response to particular, not just any, cues: answering questions, analyzing events, generating solutions, using tools, developing particular motor skills, or responding to their own body cues. Good teachers do this efficiently and effectively.

The last chapter described various ways to design effective lessons in general. This one concentrates on ways to shift over prompts that currently work to get students to respond to the cues that should evoke those responses in the ordinary scheme of things.

Contrast this with the actions of a teacher who has a good deal to learn about effective teaching. "Andy, come here. Andy! Come here. Come here now! Come here. Come on, you can do it. Come here, Andy! Come here. Come on, over here."

One definition of insanity is doing the same thing over and over and expecting a different outcome!

—*Attributed to Albert Einstein*

Andy does not budge, or by the time he does, there is no way of knowing to which cue, if any, he had responded.

Unfortunately, that is a trap many of us have fallen into when we first began to teach. When something does not work, we repeat it, often louder and faster[1]

Is there a better way? Watch skillful instruction, and your answer will be "absolutely." Able teachers have learned how to arrange for the response they seek by doing the following:

- Presenting the natural cue and seeing whether that works, like asking Andy to come here *once*
- If that cue fails, supplementing with a prompt, such as a beckoning gesture, a different verbal form ("Come see what we're going to do next"), lavishly praising another student who comes when called, or, perhaps as a last resort, going to Andy and gently escorting him over
- Gradually eliminating those prompts over time while supporting the continuation of the particular response

As we emphasized in the previous chapter, one of a teacher's most important functions is to help students learn to respond skillfully not when prompted but when cued by the conditions natural to that situation. These cues may be direct and obvious, such as a stop sign, or more subtle, such as a raised eyebrow or the passage of time. When natural cues fail, teachers use prompts that also may vary in terms of how direct or subtle they are. Finding the right prompt to help the student act in a certain way is not the biggest challenge for

---

[1]The now-familiar extinction burst at work.

teachers, though. Rather, it is how to eliminate that prompt while the student continues to engage in the appropriate action. In this chapter, we will discuss different natural or contrived ways to promote the behaviors we are seeking, along with ways to dispense eventually with any artificial supports. In Chapter 10, we concentrate more heavily on instructional techniques for avoiding errors in the first place or for coping with then when they do crop up.

Prompting

Prompting is one of the most powerful instructional devices we know. As a strategy, it has been examined in great detail by behavior analysts working in the laboratory as well as in the field. It is tempting to use just any kind of prompting because it is easy and seems to gain the reaction we are looking for in the short run. Yet our concern is to produce learning that takes hold and maintains. Here the task is far more challenging because there is a lot to learn about effective prompting methods. We need to know what they are, which ones to choose, and where and how to use and remove them. Teachers who take the time to learn these important subtleties will be rewarded, though, by seeing their students' progress begin to accelerate.

Various Kinds of Prompts

There are many kinds of prompts (see Table 9.1) as well as a variety of strategies to move from one prompt to another or to change from prompts to natural cues systematically. It is important to understand that these prompts are not necessarily listed in terms of their importance, ease of use, or suggested place in a sequence. You do not need to start with the prompts at the top of

Table 9.1   Type of Instructional Prompts

1. Verbal (direct: "Come here"; indirect: "What do we need?")
2. Partial verbal ("Coo . . . " while prompting to say "cookie")
3. Physical (hand-over-hand assistance, putting your hand on a child's back with gentle pressure)
4. Partial physical (touching a child's hand or back)
5. Gestural (pointing to an area or item, tilting your head in a direction, touching an item)
6. Model (performing the act, saying a word, constructing the item, manipulating the material)
7. Augmented stimuli (brighter or larger visual, exaggerated tactile [e.g., sand over a letter], louder or more distinct auditory, lines on a paper, dotted lines, exaggerated aspects of a cue, overlapping visual cues)

this list and then move down to the bottom or begin at one prompt and move forward with any lesson. These are guidelines, however, for you to decide whether to use any prompt within a particular lesson and, if so, which one to apply. First, though, you need to identify what events ultimately are supposed to lead to a particular behavior.

Prompts versus Natural Cues

As discussed in the last chapter, **natural cues** involve those external or internal qualities that dependably activate a behavior, such as in the way a yellow triangular sign cues us to slow down or our bodily sensations suggest to us that it is all right to keep pedaling our bicycles. **Prompts** are those devices that teachers temporarily use to help learners begin to progress toward mastering particular skills, like "Remember, the "b" looks to the right, where the door is," or when Dad runs alongside and steadying the bike while junior is getting the hang of riding. The point of many lessons is to find and then remove those artificial supports so that the student eventually responds as everyone else is supposed to. The following sections describe strategies that teachers can use to identify the cues that ultimately should take control of a particular response and the kinds of prompts that can aid the process.

How to Identify Natural Cues.   A basic guideline of the Pyramid Approach to Education is that teachers should know what the final performance is supposed to look like before starting to teach it. Teachers must specify the cue that naturally will be associated with the skill before starting the lesson. For example, once a girl has learned to wash her hands, the cues that control her responses involve her hands, the soap, the water, the sink, and the towel. Notice that when she masters this skill, no verbal cues remain associated with the task. Therefore, before beginning to teach the lesson, carefully decide which types of prompts to use so that the youngster ultimately can respond to the natural cues in this activity. If verbal prompts are used while teaching the skill, then there must be a plan to remove them, because they are not naturally associated with this skill. Teachers do not want to create a situation in which the only way the girl washes her hands is when told to do each step. It is easier to avoid the use of verbal prompts in the first place than to remove them. If you do not put it in, you will not have to take it out.

On the other hand, consider a lesson on greeting people, where some verbal cues are integral to the situation. Greeting people politely can happen under one of several circumstances. For example, when Jane walks into a room and sees someone, it is polite for her to greet that person. However, if Jane is in a room and someone enters, then it also is appropriate for her to greet that person. Finally, if someone greets Jane with words or gestures, then she should respond with a greeting of her own. Only in this last instance was a verbal cue a natural precursor to greeting. However, to demonstrate complete mastery of this skill, Jane should greet people under all three conditions. Therefore, we should avoid using verbal prompts for the first two cases, but retain the natural verbal cues when we teach the last skill. (Table 9.2 provides some common activities and their associated natural cues. Some areas are left blank for you to decide how you might complete them.) Because a prompt is a way to give students extra help, the lesson is not complete until they can perform the task independently, that is, without the prompt. Therefore, whenever we use prompts, we want eventually to remove them. By recognizing where

Table 9.2 Cues Inherent in the Situation: Natural Cues

Activity	Natural Physical Cues	Natural Social Cues	Initiating Natural Cue
Washing hands	Hands, soap, sink, faucet, water, towel	"Wash hands" "Lunch is over" "Lunchtime" "Gee, your hands are dirty"	Dirty hands Finishing a meal Starting a meal
Tying shoes	Open laces Just put on shoe		
Making a PBJ sandwich	Bread, peanut butter jar, peanut butter, jelly jar, jelly, knife, plate		
Getting dressed	Shirt, pants, underwear, socks, shoes, buttons, zipper, snaps		
Stacking blocks	Blocks, possible properties of blocks (i.e., color, size, shape)		
Writing your name	Paper (possible lines on paper), pen/pencil, previous written letters		
Using a tape cassette player	Tape cassette, buttons, place for tape in tape player		
Greeting people	Someone else entering a room: you enter a room with someone else there; someone says "Hi" (or uses some other form of greeting)		

we are now—the current prompts—and knowing where we are going—the natural cue—we can begin constructing the roadway to allow prompts gradually to be diminished in favor of the natural cues.

Prompting Strategies

Researchers doing basic experimental studies of behavior deserve the credit for investigating methods for teaching their human and animal subjects to make very challenging distinctions. Can you tell which of the following objects is different?

Could you see that that the fifth one is more oval? How easy would it be to teach your students to differentiate that one from the others? Careful programming has enabled children with substantial developmental delays to accurately distinguish among shapes like those. In this and the next chapter you will find out about some of the prompting methods they created and how you can use them for your own instructional purposes.

Selecting Prompts.   When selecting a prompt, consider the following:

(1) Use prompts that work. Does the prompt actually help the student? Try it a few times. If it does not, try something else. To get a child to pick up an item, you may try pointing to it. If that fails, try tapping on the item. If that fails, try shining a light on the item. If that fails, picking up the item yourself may work. What you do is use a prompt only if it successfully leads to the response.

(2) Use prompts that are as close to the natural cues as possible. Having one's attention drawn to what the other children are doing is much closer to responding independently than is being physically guided. For any given situation, set up a hierarchy of prompts effective with that person, moving from those closest to the cue toward those further and further away. How to move through the hierarchy will be described later in this chapter.

(3) Model or demonstrate, when feasible, showing the pupil exactly what to do, when, and how. Be sure, though, that the child already

has learned to imitate modeled actions. If that is not the case, naturally it is very important to teach a child how to imitate because this is the essence of vicarious or observational learning. It is much easier to say, "Watch me (or them). Do it the way I (or they) do it," than to physically prompt someone through an entire activity.

(4) Three basic types of modeling prompts are often used in teaching:
   • Body actions, such as waving an arm, touching an ear, turning around, holding up one finger, and so on
   • Selection of objects, such as when the teacher picks up a ball, the student picks up a ball, and when the teacher picks up a spoon, the student picks up a spoon
   • Physical interactions with objects, such as pushing a button, scribbling with a crayon, turning a wheel, pulling a string, and so on

(5) When dealing with fine visual, oral, or tactile discriminations, consider **embedding** your prompts directly within the stimulus to draw the student's attention to the finer distinctions. If you want to teach a student the difference between the spoken words "stop" and "step," you might elongate the short "o" sound and/or make it louder; do something similar with the short "e" sound. To aid reading the word, you could draw a picture of an upheld hand around the "o" while placing a step beneath the "e" in "step." Or, instead, you could pair it with a hand gesture signaling "stop" and pretend to be climbing up the steps for "step."

(6) Use prompts that will be easiest to gradually remove, or **fade.** Suppose that every time a bell sounded to signal the end of an activity, you picked Andy up and carried him to the door. It would be very difficult to get him to line up independently. By contrast, it is easier to fade physical guidance, gestures, or other visual prompts. Our next section provides you with how to go about fading back from prompts to natural cues.

Fading Prompts.   Billy loves to listen to music on his tape cassette player. You want to teach him to put a cassette into the player and then push the "play" button independently. As you analyze the task, you recognize that when Billy has acquired this skill, the tape cassette, the tape player, and its buttons should be all he needs to respond to in order to activate it. No one should have to tell him what to do. You also know that Billy does not imitate others readily, so modeling is unlikely to prove effective. Therefore, you decide to assist him physically instead of prompting him verbally. The teaching question is, Although we can guarantee a successful action by physically guiding the entire sequence, how do we get Billy to do it independently? In this case, gradually reducing the amount of physical assistance provided will be the most effective strategy. The gradual reduction in the degree of support provided by a prompt is called fading. How a prompt is faded depends on the type of prompt.

Fading Spoken Prompts: Verbal prompts can be faded along a number of dimensions. For example, you can gradually reduce how loudly a prompt is said or slowly eliminate the number of words used within a sentence (e.g., "go to the door . . . go to the . . . go . . . "). Reduce even the proportion of a complete word, as in "Say 'chocolate' . . . say 'choco' . . . say 'choc'. . . . say 'ch.'"

Fading Physical Prompts: The degree of physical assistance provided can be reduced over a series of teaching trials. For example, begin with full, hand-over-hand guidance in pushing a button through a shirt hole. Across trials, gradually decrease the force exerted. Then use less physical assistance to guide the child's hand to the button itself. Fading physical prompts may also involve altering where physical contact is made with the student. For example, start **graduated guidance** with hand-over-hand prompting and then guide the child's wrist, then his arm, and then merely touch his shoulder. Of course, even the faintest physical prompt (e.g., a finger on a shoulder) provides help that must be eliminated. Therefore, physical prompts are successfully faded only when all contact has been removed.

Fading Gestural Prompts: Gestural prompts may involve pointing to some environmental object or event, including a part of the student's body. Another example is pantomime/gesture, such as moving your arms and hands in an upward fashion while saying, "Stand up." Increasing the distance between your fingertip and the object is one way to fade a gestural prompt like pointing. Over time, reduce the degree to which your hand, and eventually finger, is extended. Gestural prompts can be faded gradually by reducing exaggerated motions until they disappear altogether.

Fading Modeling Prompts: Modeling prompts can be faded by demonstrating fewer and fewer aspects of the full action—change from clapping many times to clapping once to beginning to clap but not connecting hands and so on.

Modeling the selection of an item is different than modeling an action with an item. Therefore, how modeling prompts are faded depends on the goal of the lesson. For example, Morris has learned to imitate when his teacher picks up an item from a set of common toys and objects. His teacher now uses modeling to teach Morris how to use each object. However, his teacher teaches Morris only one action with each item—scribble with a crayon, roll a ball, rub a tissue on his lips, and so on. Now, when his teacher picks up an item, Morris immediately picks the same item and performs the learned routine. Is Morris imitating his teacher's action? Most likely, he is only imitating her selection because he now knows what to do with each item. In order to be sure that he is imitating her action, she must teach him at least two actions with each object. Thereafter, he must watch what she selects and what she does with that item in order to successfully imitate.

Fading Augmented Stimuli: At times, pictorial prompts are temporarily added to a feature in the environment to guide a student's performance, as when dotted lines are supplied over which students can trace a letter. In time, the dots are faded by diminishing the number of dots, decreasing the intensity with which the dots are printed, or decreasing the size of the dots. Furthermore, the lesson could begin with a dashed line and then fade to a dotted line.

In other situations, an aspect of a natural cue is enhanced and then faded.[2] For example, in teaching a child to distinguish between the letters "p" and "q," accentuate something associated with the letter ("q" is for "queen"; she looks at the door) or the directions in which the letters face ("p" faces the pig outside the window), like that shown in Figure 9.1. You could fade by making the lines of the pictorial prompts thinner and thinner, moving back in steps until the only remaining hint was the nose.

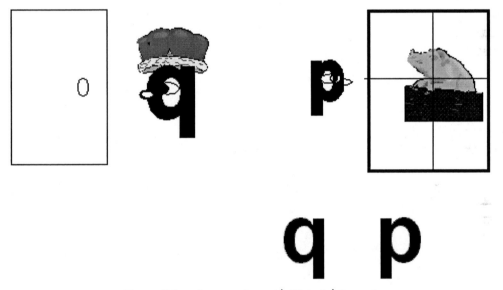

Figure 9.1   Augmenting with Pictorial Prompts

Within the Picture Exchange Communication System (PECS) training sequence, a student may have difficulty placing the "I want" symbol on the left-hand side of the sentence strip. Perhaps this is because the child is only three years old and cannot make such left-right discriminations at this point. One form of enhancement is to add a red line around the edge of the "I want" card

[2]E. P. Reese, Skills Training for the Special Child (1971). Cambridge Center for Behavioral Studies, 336 Baker Avenue, Concord, MA 01742. See also L. Schreibman, The Effects of Within-Stimulus and Extra-Stimulus Prompting on Discrimination Learning in Autistic Children, Journal of Applied Behavior Analysis 8 (1975): 91–112.

Figure 9.2   Fading Visual Placement Prompts

as well as a red lined box on the sentence strip. Over time, we fade the red line, as in Figure 9.2, and the child eventually places the symbol correctly using only natural cues.[3]

Another example (Figure 9.3) demonstrates how elements of a picture, such as enhanced circles (resembling an "O") added over the lenses, can be faded until only the printed word remains.

Some students may encounter real difficulty progressing from the real object to its pictorial image. Try superimposing a small picture or some other two dimensional representation on the three dimensional symbol while slowly making the latter less and less visible (Figure 9.4). Gradually enlarge the overlapping picture until it completely covers the object Use this combined symbol as before until student once again is performing at a satisfactory level.

Figure 9.3   Fading Visual Prompts for Reading the Word *Look*

Prompt Hierarchies

When you plan to use prompting strategies such as those just described, you have a couple of choices. You can provide hardly any help at all, adding assistance as needed. Alternatively, you can provide a good deal of support, gradually removing it bit by bit. Each serves separate purposes.

---

[3]L. Frost, and A. Bondy, The Picture Exchange Communication System Training Manual. Newark, DE: Pyramid Publications, 2000.

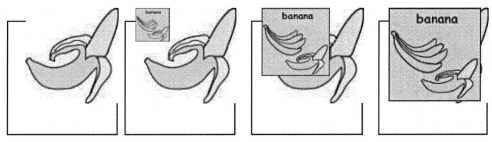

Figure 9.4   Stimulus Overlapping

Least-to-Most Prompt Hierarchies

In some cases, a student may be able to perform some of the actions necessary within a sequential activity. You assess performance by providing as little assistance as possible. Should you need to help, begin in the least intrusive way before gradually escalating support. This strategy forms the basis of the **least-to-most prompt hierarchy.** If you elect to use this strategy, decide the following in advance:

- Which types of prompts you will use.
- In what order you will present the prompts.
- How long you will wait before prompting. The length of the pause may reflect characteristics about the student (e.g., one student may benefit with five second pauses while for another student waiting for more than three seconds hardly ever succeeds).

Suppose you want to teach a toddler to stand up when you say "Stand up" so that you can help him get dressed. After giving the instruction, pause for five seconds (if that is the interval selected). Then use a hand signal (gestural prompt) and wait five more seconds. If that does not work, model the action and again wait to see what happens. Finally, physically assist the child to stand. The sequence of prompts is set, and so too is the length of the pause used between prompts. Of course, when the child stands, give him praise and possibly other rewards.

One challenge in using this strategy is deciding when the child simply needs a little more time to do something independently versus when the child is waiting for you to provide assistance. For example, when teaching a child to set the table with four sets of plates, forks, spoons, knifes, cups, and napkins, if there are five-second pauses between each of four types of prompts for each item, the table would hardly ever be set. This may lead into a type of stop-and-go pattern throughout a task: the child independently completes three steps, then pauses for the next step (waiting for a series of prompts), then completes five steps before pausing again, and so on. This herky-jerky pattern delays the acquisition of a fluid task sequence. Be sensitive to students who may need extra time to complete a difficult task while avoiding unnecessarily long waiting periods for those who do not.

Most-to-Least Prompt Hierarchies

Sometimes a pupil is almost entirely incapable of completing any aspects of a sequence. Different varieties of prompts are used, to no avail. Obviously, she needs assistance all along the way. In such cases, choose initially to provide as much help as necessary and over time gradually reduce the number and intrusiveness of the prompts. For example, in teaching a child to load a dishwasher, begin the lesson by using physical guidance as the child puts each item into the dishwasher. Over trials, switch from full physical guidance to merely touching an arm or hand. Later, only point to the items to be loaded. In this case, you would be reducing the successive intrusiveness of the prompts from full physical to a partial physical and finally to a gestural prompt. One advantage of this strategy is that it allows little room for mistakes because the appropriate action is ensured by providing the necessary prompt.

When physical prompting of this type is provided within a sequential task, it also is preferable to prompt from behind the student. For example, two teachers collaborate in Phase I of PECS. One entices the student by holding a desired item. When the child reaches for the item, the second teacher, stationed behind the child, guides the child's reaching hand to pick up a matching picture. Together they give the picture to the communicative partner, who immediately gives the child the desired item in exchange[4]. At first, the second teacher will need to use full physical prompts to have the child pick up the picture, reach it toward the teacher, and release it. Over trials and as quickly as possible, the second teacher begins to use less physical guidance, typically by going from full physical to partial physical prompts. In time, all physical prompts are removed and the child does the exchange independently.

Another example of effectively providing prompts from behind the student involves the use of visual schedule systems to help the student move through the activities of the day. Such prompting strategies are used for individual pictures as well as sequences of pictures. [5]

---

[4]If the teacher who is enticing the child also provides physical prompts, she may cause the child to become overly dependent on those prompts. Perhaps because prompts from behind the student are outside the child's field of vision, they are easier to eliminate.

[5]For a detailed description of this strategy, see L. F. McClannahan and P. J. Krantz *Activity Schedules for Children with Autism: Teaching Independent Behavior* (Bethesda, MD: Woodbine House, 1999).

In some sense, the most-to-least prompt strategy is similar to fading; that is, assistance is gradually reduced over time. However, in fading we reduce the level of a single type of prompt, while with the most-to-least strategy we gradually reduce different types of prompts. In the next chapter, in the section "Errorless Learning," we offer several additional examples of fading methods.

Delayed Prompting

A student may respond appropriately to certain types of prompts but not others. For example, some children almost always imitate a word modeled for them. Others reach for whatever picture someone merely points to or touches. Other children always retrieve the item corresponding to one displayed to them. In each case, the goal of a lesson is to transfer control from these currently effective prompts to natural cues (or other less intrusive types of prompts). **Delayed prompting** can be helpful in these cases. In this strategy, two distinct types of signals are used: the prompt that is already effective and the natural cue.

Two basic types of delayed prompt strategies are constant and progressive delay. As with all delayed prompt strategies, first we identify the currently effective prompt and the intended natural cue. For example, without any additional help, Henry is incapable of choosing his candy according to the color named by the teacher, say, "Red" or "Blue," when both are presented simultaneously. However, whenever his teacher points to the red one, he always picks up the red candy. When his teacher points to the blue candy, he picks up the blue one. In this case, a gestural prompt is effective, while spoken words are not.

Delayed prompting involves inserting a time interval between the two types of prompts. In **constant time delay,** a fixed time interval, such as four seconds, is always used. Henry's teacher says "Red" and then waits four seconds before pointing to the red candy. Each time candies are offered, his teacher waits the same four seconds between her spoken word and her gesture. Notice that Henry cannot fail at this lesson—either he responds to the spoken word "Red" or he responds to the point.[6] In either case, he gets candy. Over time, Henry begins to respond correctly even before his teacher has pointed. In all likelihood, he switches from the prompt to the spoken cue because he gets his reinforcer sooner.

---

[6]Research has shown this technique to be very effective with a wide range of learners. See P. E. Touchette and J. S. Howard, Errorless Learning: Reinforcement Contingencies and Stimulus Control Transfer in Delayed Prompting, Journal of Applied Behavior Analysis 17 (1984) 175–88, and in R. Sulzer-Azaroff and G. R. Mayer, Behavior Analysis for Lasting Change (New York: Holt, Rinehart & Winston, 1991), Chapter 18.

A variation on this strategy is to use **progressive time delay.** In this case, rather than using a set duration between the prompt and the cue, you begin with no delay; that is, you simultaneously present both signals and then, over a series of trials, gradually increase the delay between presenting the cue and presenting the prompt. For example, when Mariana is shown a picture of a spoon, she immediately gets a spoon. However, when her teacher says "Spoon," she does not respond correctly. Her teacher begins by saying "Spoon" while simultaneously showing her the picture of a spoon. Next, her teacher introduces a half-second delay between the spoken word and showing the picture. Then her teacher increases the interval to one second, two seconds, three seconds, and so on. As with constant time delay, Mariana responds either to the spoken word or to the picture. In neither situation is she likely to commit an error. This progressive time delay strategy is used Phase V of PECS training. In this case, control is transferred from pointing to an icon, "I want," to the spoken question, "What do you want?"

Delayed prompting works only when an effective prompt has been established previously. Some younger students lack many currently effective prompts, thereby limiting the applicability of this strategy for them. However, once any type of prompt proves effective, whether physical, gestural, verbal, or modeling, then this strategy becomes very appealing and promising.

Sequential Lessons

A number of strategic questions arise when we teach sequential lessons. Should we teach all steps of the sequence at the same time? Should the first steps or the last steps become the focus? Although there are no universal answers, often some choices need to be made along the way.

Whole or Partial Task

For many activities, the entire activity is to be completed each time it is taught. For example, hand washing requires carrying out the entire sequence, from turning on the water to drying hands, each time. The **whole task** needs to be taught. On the other hand, some activities permit separating segments in the sequence. For example, a student can practice putting clothes into the washing machine without having to run the machine every time it is loaded. This example uses a **partial task** approach. Concentrate on the more difficult aspects of the sequence when using this method. However, not all steps within the same task are amenable to partial task presentation. For example, while washing clothes, it is not practical to have the student repeatedly put liquid soap into the machine because if it were then turned on, the results would be disastrous.

Forward or Backward Chaining

As was noted earlier, sequential tasks can best be thought of as a behavior chain where each element is linked both to its previous step (as a reinforcer) and to the next step (as a discriminative stimulus). Furthermore, completing some tasks can be naturally rewarding for the student, while extra rewards need to be added for completion of others.

As chains have two ends, teachers have a choice as to which end they want to first teach. In **forward chaining,** the first steps are taught from the beginning of the lesson with full support provided for the remaining steps. For example, George's teacher wants him to wash his hands. With this strategy, George is first taught through prompting and fading to turn on the faucet and pick up the soap. Then his teacher provides full assistance on most of the remaining steps. So, next she helps him wet his hands. At this point he independently rubs them together and needs to be guided to move on to the next steps of returning the soap, rinsing his hands, and so on. In general, as George learns the initial steps, the teaching focus changes to the next set of steps.

Other sequences may be better taught by focusing on the last steps first, using **backward chaining.** This strategy may be necessary when the first steps are more difficult to teach. For example, to ride a bike, Nancy must get on the bike before pedaling to keep her balance. Teaching her to get on the bike first will be difficult because without pedaling, she cannot stay upright. Instead, her teacher helps her onto the bike and then holds her (helping her keep her balance) while she begins to pedal. As she gains control over her balance, her teacher lets go and carefully watches to see whether she stays upright. Only after she has mastered pedaling and balancing is she taught how to hop onto the bike and get going on her own.

Backward chaining also may be preferred when there are very powerful natural consequences. For example, putting on sneakers results in an opportunity to run. Thus, the last step—pulling the looped laces tight—is strongly reinforced by the immediate opportunity to use the sneakers. Therefore, Sam's teacher uses full assistance to help him complete all steps in tying laces except for the very last one. Once Sam learns to pull tight the looped laces, his teacher says, "Nice tying your sneakers! Go ahead outside!" During subsequent lessons, his teacher gradually expects him to learn to independently complete the steps just prior to the last one, carefully moving back in the sequence over time. The lesson always ends with Sam running outside.

Within the training sequence for PECS, after the children can exchange a single picture, we teach them to place two symbols—"I want" and a picture of the desired item—on a sentence strip before exchanging it with their partner. The final performance involves placing both pictures on the strip. A backward chaining approach is used because the final step—affixing

Is Combining Procedures Okay?

Sometimes strategies may be combined to maximize effectiveness. For instance, differential reinforcement may be used with delayed prompting. In such cases, when a student responds to the currently effective prompt, the reinforcer is provided calmly. However, when the student "beats the prompt," that is, responds to the natural cue, then enthusiastic praise is provided. Both cases continue to result in reward; it is only that independence earns more powerful ones than prompted responding.

the second symbol and giving the strip to the partner—leads to immediate reinforcement. Therefore, when we begin this lesson, the "I want" symbol is already on the sentence strip (sequence A in Figure 9.5). The child only needs initially to learn what to do with the single picture of the desired item. Rather than presenting it immediately, we teach him or her to place the picture on the sentence strip and then to give it to the partner. After they learn this, we teach them to affix the "I want" symbol (sequence B in Figure 9.5). At that point, the student can smoothly complete the remainder of the task by placing the symbol corresponding to the desired item on the sentence strip, as previously learned.

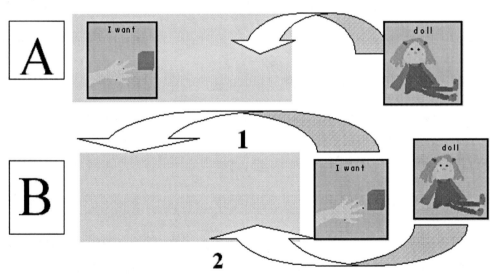

Figure 9.5   Backward Chaining Sequence to Teach Sentence Strip Use Within PECS

Summary

Most of our educational objectives consist of students learning to respond in one way to a particular cue and differently to other cues: following directions, answering questions, making the right choices, solving problems, and many more. When our students fail to react correctly, often we are tempted to try the same thing over and over again, often faster and louder. An alternative is to interpose a prompt, demonstrating, telling, gesturing, guiding, or whatever else works to get the student to respond correctly. Prompting can produce the behavior we are seeking, but ultimately, if our students are said to have really learned the right response, they must act independently of such guidance.

The way to approach the situation is to examine the objective to find out when, where, and under what conditions the behavior is supposed to happen. In other words, we need to be clear about the cues that should call forth the response under natural conditions. Then our task is to select those prompts that work and yet are as close to the natural ones as possible. Among the strategies often shown to be effective are demonstrating or modeling a particular bodily action or our own selection from an array or our manipulation of a particular object. Embedding prompts directly within the stimulus can work with those discriminations involving sight, sound, or touch. We must remain mindful of the fact that these ultimately will have to be eliminated, though, and consider this aspect when first selecting specific prompts.

We need to examine the nature of each prompt because we realize that our job is not done until all such prompts are eliminated. Then we can act accordingly. Spoken prompts may vary along a few dimensions, like loudness or completeness, so we can diminish the intensity of the sound. Physical prompts can be faded by diminishing the forcefulness or location of our guidance. Gestures and modeling prompts can be compressed and augmented stimuli made smaller and dimmer until they gradually disappear. Interposing a fixed or variable delay between the prompt and the natural cue is an especially effective way to proceed, as students typically begin to anticipate the cue in time.

Our task of removing prompts will be easier if we supply only those that are absolutely necessary in order to generate the response we are seeking. If we have the patience, we do that by starting with no help and adding it slowly and patiently, a bit at a time (least to most) until we get what we are looking for. That way we will have identified the minimal prompt intensity necessary. Alternatively, if we want to be absolutely certain to achieve the behavior we are seeking, we can prompt away in most-to-least fashion so that the student makes few errors. Then we remove those prompts slowly but surely.

Another valuable instructional tactic to use is chaining, or teaching lessons containing sequences of tasks. Depending on what the student already knows, the reinforcing features inherent in the task, and other aspects, we can begin by teaching either the initial portions or those at the end. While starting at the beginning seems the logical place, going backward can just about guarantee that the student will complete the job and come in regular contact with reinforcers every time. We all win.

Suggested Readings and Viewings

TO   READ

Define, describe and apply methods for chaining and shaping behavior

Sulzer-Azaroff, B. & Mayer, G. R. (1994). Achieving educational excellence: Behavior analysis for school personnel. San Marcos, CA: Western Image, 110–140.

Examine and learn about applying antecedents to motivate and teach students with autism

Luiselli, J. K. & Cameron, M. J. (1998). Antecedent control: Innovative approaches to behavioral support. (Especially sections IV & V). Baltimore, MD: Paul H. Brooks.

Use prompts to get responses to occur and transfer those prompts to natural antecedents

Cooper, J. O., Heron, T. E., & Heward, W. L. (1987). *Applied behavior analysis.* Englewood Cliffs, NJ: Prentice Hall. (chapter 13).
Cuvo, A. J. & Davis, P. K. (1998). Establishing and transferring stimulus control. In J. K. Luiselli & M. J. Cameron. (Eds.) Antecedent control: Innovative approaches to behavioral support, 347–369.
Baltimore, MD: Paul Brooks Publishing Company.
MacDuff, G. S., Krantz, P. J. & McClannahan, L. E. (2001). Prompts and prompt-fading strategies for people with autism. In C. Maurice, G. Green & R. M.Foxx. (Eds.) Making a difference: Behavioral intervention for autism. Austin, TX: Pro-Ed, 37–50.
Sulzer-Azaroff, B. & Mayer, G. R. (1991). Behavior analysis for lasting change. (Section III.) Atlanta: Wadsworth Group: Thompson.

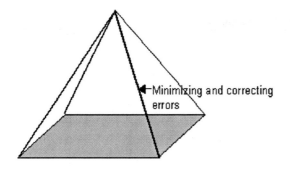

Minimizing and correcting errors

10

Minimizing and Correcting Errors

"Practice makes perfect." "Learn by trial and error." People familiar with these phrases might be shocked to learn that scientific evidence calls these age-old statements into question. Practice makes perfect only if we practice perfect or improving actions and if those are reinforced. If we repeatedly practice something the wrong way and get credit or some other form of reinforcement for doing it, we will learn to continue to do it imperfectly. If you are practicing hitting a tennis ball, you could be using poor form yet get it over the net. That could firmly establish the poor form and get in your way in the future. If you overbroil a hamburger but your guests declare it delicious, you may never learn to make a tender, juicy one.

The same thing goes for learning by trial and error. Sometimes errors are reinforced, and when they are, they are apt to reoccur. A better way to learn concepts or skills is by having our more successful efforts reinforced. An effective coach would be sure to reserve positive comment for a perfect (or at least improved) tennis swing or a reasonably juicy (or improving) quality of hamburger.

> Reinforcing perfect and improving practice makes perfect

Do we need to discard these sayings altogether? No. Just modify them a bit. Restate "Practice makes perfect" as "Reinforcing perfect and improving practice makes perfect."

Similarly, the phrase "Learn by trial and success" is more accurate than "Learn by trial and error." In both instances probably you have noticed that shaping can be an important part of the successful instructional process (for a review of shaping, see Chapter 4). Shaping is a wonderful teaching tool and we use it whenever appropriate. There are times, though, when a response cannot be shaped because there is no way to improve on it. Either it is right or it is wrong. A "6" is not a "9." A "W" is not an "M." Hugging family members or friends is fine, but one does not hug strangers in the mall. Sticking wires into electrical outlets, running into a street full of traffic, or eating pills from the medicine cabinet is unacceptable.

How do we teach rights and wrongs of those kinds? By presenting choices and (1) reinforcing the correct answers and (2) either withholding reinforcement from or correcting the wrong ones. This kind of **differential reinforcement** does teach learners to make proper distinctions or, technically speaking, **discriminations.** Reinforcing repetitions of the correct choice should allow students to learn the correct discrimination.

Teaching that way sometimes causes problems especially when our students have a very difficult time learning to tell slight but important differences between very similar stimuli. First of all, every time they practice the wrong response, there is a risk of reinforcement occurring by chance. The student or even the teacher might fail to note the inverted letter and accept an "M" where a "W" belongs. That can happen even to us. You may have used a poor strategy in a card or board game yet won often enough. Now you have learned a better method, but you are playing in a tournament and the pressure is on. You lose the game because you returned to your old, faulty ways.

The need to correct errors sometimes can create a second problem, particularly among special student populations. A certain side effect, sometimes called an **extinction burst,** may result when the student commits an error and, as appropriate, reinforcement has been withheld (technically, the error has been placed on extinction) or corrected (technically punished). Extinction bursts can take the form of real or symbolic anger, aggression, escape, and/or total inaction, thereby interfering with the learning process. Trying to teach a new skill to a screaming child or one who has tuned you out does not work very well and is punishing to you as a teacher as well. Is there another way? Yes. Remember that people learn best by trial and success. Errors are not essential.

Errorless Learning

Interestingly, if a response is perfect from the very beginning, the results will be even better. There would be no need to shape or correct errors. The advantages here are many:

(1) Reinforcement can be very dense because the response is right every single time. There is no need to correct or ignore any of its aspects.

(2) Extinction bursts are avoided.
(3) Also averted is establishing bad habits—accidentally getting stuck at a level of imperfection ("No matter what I do, my golf ball hooks to the left").

According to researchers and educators, students whose development is delayed thrive when they learn without making errors. Always to be right in a learning task is exciting and wonderful; a rare and heady experience. Reading, math concepts, and many other academic and social responses can be programmed for errorless learning. So can social and other kinds of skills.

How Do We Design Errorless Lessons?

As described earlier, we conclude that students have learned a skill or concept when they consistently demonstrate the following:

- A brand-new behavior, like zipping up a jacket
- A new form of a behavior, like combing one's part on the left instead of the right
- An older behavior under new conditions (now zipping slacks) or for longer time periods (assembling boxes for an hour instead of a minute), more intensely (brushing teeth until they really shine), at a faster rate (getting dressed in five minutes instead of an hour), or more accurately (filling in every space correctly on a job application)
- A set of behaviors rearranged in a new order (making a shopping list, purchasing the items, bringing them home, and putting them away)

Just as there are different types of learning, many of the kinds of teaching methods we read about in the last chapter (and elsewhere in this book) attempt to minimize or totally check errors from the start of the lesson. All these errorless strategies, of course, work best when we apply the rules for effective reinforcement discussed in Chapter 4.

Teaching for "Errorless Learning."   Teachers now have many techniques available to them for helping students avoid the pain of making errors by hardly ever producing them in the first place. Among these are some already familiar ones and a few new to you:

(1) Blocking errors: In some situations, parents and teachers prevent an action to avoid severe punishing consequences. We place covers over electrical outlets and never allow our children near streets with busy traffic unless they are holding our hands. In such cases, we would not know

whether the child has learned until he was no longer prevented from responding, that is, what he would do when electric outlets are not covered or if no one held his hand at a street corner. Maybe in these cases we do not care just how independently he acts, as long as the youngster can remain protected until he has matured sufficiently to make us feel more comfortable about gradually removing our safeguards.

(2) Shaping: When trying to teach a new form of an activity, shaping is a highly effective strategy. As noted earlier, the key to successful shaping is to make progressive changes in the response requirement large enough to encourage the student to advance but small enough that she can continue to do the task correctly. In shaping, no response is punished, while just about every response is reinforced.

(3) Physical guidance: Another way to help create new forms of behavior is gently to physically guide the student to perform the action perfectly and then gradually to withdraw or fade the degree of help we provide.

(4) Graduated guidance: Sometimes, rather than fading the degree of support within one type of prompt, it is helpful to shift from one type of prompt to another. Graduated guidance involves starting with sufficient physical support to ensure a successful action and then subtly introducing a different type of prompt or natural cue. Instances include reducing the amount and kind of physical guidance you use while teaching a student to set the table or moving from physically guiding a movement like sweeping with a broom to a demonstration and eventually to a spoken instruction to no prompts other than the natural cue of debris on the floor.

(5) Fading: Of course, we may be able to support a new form of action completely with prompts other than those involving physical contact: visual prompts, modeling, slow motion demonstrations, and so on. Once it is clear that these fully support the new behavior, we begin to diminish the number or strength of the prompts.

(6) Teaching discriminations errorlessly: As we saw in the last chapter, when teaching students to choose correctly between things that they "perceive" (see, hear, touch, taste, or smell), we can arrange our instructional stimuli so that making the wrong response becomes very improbable. With this strategy, teachers organize the array of materials in such a way that selecting one is very likely, while selecting the other is not. For example, you might place two objects on a tabletop: a ball immediately in front of the child and a spoon across the table and almost out of reach. Ask for the ball—the child is very likely to give you the nearest object. Each time the child responds correctly, you can provide some reinforcement. Very gradually, as in shaping, begin to move the two objects closer together while continuing to ask

for the ball. This arrangement is only the beginning of a discrimination lesson. In order to ensure that the spoken word "Ball" reliably results in the response of choosing the ball (in technical language, the choice is "under stimulus control"), the child will need to give you the ball when it is one of several equally available items and not give you the ball when you have asked for something different.

(7) Expanding: Some parts of an action need to be expanded. Helping a child throw a ball farther, walk quietly down a longer hall, go a greater distance across a room to ask the teacher for help, speak more loudly, place a stamp more neatly in the corner of the envelope, and fill the soda machine more quickly all depend on the student's possessing some current degree of skill. Each of these lessons can be accomplished without the use of prompts by having the teacher shape minute changes in the criterion for reinforcement. Thinning the schedule of reinforcement also involves no apparent prompts. Successfully implementing these strategies requires careful monitoring of information, such as the distance involved, the number of required repetitions, the duration of a response, or its frequency of reinforcement.

(8) "Slicing":[1] When a student hesitates or has difficulty with a portion of a sequential response, you can take that part and slice it into smaller parts. Then you allow the learner to practice each portion over and over until it looks automatic. Recombining it into the larger part becomes much easier later on. Suppose that a youngster was having difficulty tossing a ball into a basket. By examining the performance closely, you note that his wrists are placed on the ball at the wrong angle. You show him where they should be and practice just throwing short distances, forgetting about the basket for a while. After he continues to repeat this new position time after time after time (fluently), you now return to coach throwing toward the basket.

(9) Graduated guidance of sequential elements: You can use graduated guidance to ensure that the difficult parts of a sequential lesson are done correctly. As in the case of teaching a student to make her bed, each step may require a different degree or even type of prompt. However, the aim is to help the student smoothly complete the entire sequence. Over time, the teacher can withdraw physical and other help, shadowing (holding one's hand above the student's without making actual contact) for a while the actions of the student, thereby remaining close enough to prevent any long pauses or errors from taking place.

---

[1]The term for this form of teaching was suggested by Dr. Kent Johnson, director of the Morningside Academy in Seattle, Washington.

Planning instruction for errorless learning can be challenging and time consuming. Nevertheless, currently available computer graphics capabilities can ease the process substantially. In addition to the kinds of pictorial cues illustrated in the last chapter, we can subtly adjust other properties of the prompts, fading them out slowly in a series of steps until none remain other than the critical differences. Notice that the position of the two different letters is switched randomly in order to avoid the student's using position as an erroneous cue.

Fading Color Cues

You may decide that you want to change the color pictures your student uses to communicate to ones that are black and white (in part, to help reduce the cost of the pictures). In this case, you can gradually reduce the color saturation of the pictures in the manner shown in Figure 10.1.

Fading Size Cues

While teaching a student to discriminate pictures within PECS, you decide to take advantage of the child's tendency to reach for bigger pictures. In this case, when pairing an item that is highly desired (e.g., cheesies) versus minimally reinforcing (e.g., socks), you start by making the cheesie picture much larger than the sock picture. As soon as the child reliably uses the larger picture, you gradually change the relative size of the pictures in the manner shown in Figure 10.2.

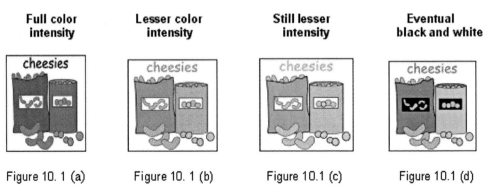

Full color intensity	**Lesser color intensity**	**Still lesser intensity**	**Eventual black and white**

Figure 10. 1 (a)   Figure 10. 1 (b)   Figure 10.1 (c)   Figure 10.1 (d)

Figure 10.1   Fading Color Saturation

Large *Cheesie* Picture
Small Picture of Socks

 vs.

Large *Cheesie* Picture
Somewhat Larger Picture of Socks

 vs.

Large *Cheesie* Picture
Somewhat Larger Picture of Socks

 vs.

Pictures of Equal Size

 vs.

Figure 10.2   Manipulating Size

Altering Intensity Cues

You may have found that one student can successfully choose between the picture of the cheesie only when it is paired with a **blank distracter,** that is, a card the same size as the picture of the cheesie but with nothing on it but its white background. As quickly as this pairing leads to successful selection of the cheesie, you gradually introduce a faint picture into the blank card—a picture of a sock. Over trials, the intensity or darkness of the sock image is gradually increased until it is just as dark as the picture of the cheesie (see Figure 10.3).

Figure 10.3   Increasing Intensity

But Suppose They Do Make Mistakes: Coping with Errors

A key goal for teachers is to minimize the errors their students make. However, despite our best intentions, sometimes mistakes do happen. You ask Bill his name, and he answers, "Soda." Michelle walks out of the bathroom into your classroom, and you hear the water still running. One way to react to these errors is to fix them. To Bill, you say his name, and he immediately repeats it. He now has said his name. You tell Michelle to go back into the bathroom and turn off the faucet. She does so, and the water stops running. In each case, the problem has been repaired: Bill said his name, and the water stopped running. However, what did the children learn? Most likely, Bill did not learn anything—he already knew how to imitate his name—and if Michelle acquired any new skill, it probably was that she should turn off the water when her teacher tells her to.

How, then, are teachers supposed to react to such errors? Just as we reviewed different types of lessons in order to design various errorless teaching strategies, so too will we need to link **error correction strategies** to the type of error made within a lesson. As opposed to quick fixes that the teacher chooses to repair the mistake, error correction strategies create small learning opportunities. At the same time, the teacher quickly and frequently assesses what the student actually learned.

The key to error correction is focusing on the goal of the original lesson. For Bill, the lesson was "Answer the question 'What is your name?'" For Michelle, the lesson was to complete a full hand-washing sequence in the bathroom. To select an error correction strategy, first identify the stimuli

("What is your name?"; running water) that are supposed to control the behavior ("My name is Bill;" turns off the water). Then develop and follow a plan to reestablish the appropriate stimulus control.

Discrete Trials: The Four-Step Error Correction Sequence

Step 1: Model/Demonstrate/Show the Correct Response. The error that Bill made took place within a type of discrete trial lesson. A simple stimulus, "What is your name?" should have been followed by a simple answer, "Bill," followed by a reinforcing consequence (e.g., "Yes!" or "Glad to meet you, Bill"). Instead, Bill said, "Soda." The teacher naturally would model, or demonstrate, the correct answer. When Bill imitates, should we move on, assuming that the problem was licked? No, because Bill's imitation of the word "Bill" is not the same as answering the question "What is your name?"

Step 2: Promote the Response Again (Prompt/Cue). Therefore, the teacher now asks his name again. Bill is very likely to respond correctly at this point. However, should we stop the lesson here? From Bill's perspective, he has just said his name twice in a row—once imitatively and once in response to the question. When he said his name the second time, could we say for sure whether he was listening to us or simply repeating the last thing that worked? Repeating a response that just got reinforced is a very good strategy for any learner; but if that is what Bill did, then his response was not under the stimulus control of the question but more likely was cued by his own previous response.

Step 3: Switch. How, then, do we check that he is truly listening to us? The teacher now introduces another simple instruction: switching to a different question. For example, the teacher holds up a known item, such as a cup, and asks, "What's this?" Given that this response is very familiar to Bill, he is likely to successfully respond. The teacher provides him with only a small reinforcer, such as praise, because his answer is not a new one.

Step 4: Repeat or Return to the Original Prompt/Cue (or set up for the lesson). Now the teacher repeats the original cue by asking, "What's your name?" If Bill says "Bill," the teacher can feel more confident that the reply was under the stimulus control of the question and not Bill's own prior response. The teacher also provides a big reinforcer at this point.

This strategy also is used within discrete lessons involving discrimination training. For example, within Phase III of the Picture Exchange Communication System (PECS), you may offer the student a choice between a cookie (i.e., a preferred item) versus a sock (i.e., a nonpreferred item). If the student gives

you the sock picture, you would offer the sock. When the student rejects taking the sock the four-steps would involve the following:

(1) Tap on the picture of the cookie (i.e., demonstrate).
(2) Hold out your hand near the cookie picture (to prompt giving you
    that picture).
    Praise the student, but do not give the cookie yet.
(3) Switch to another skill that the student knows.
(4) Repeat the initial step by reenticing with both the cookie and the sock.
    If the student gives you the cookie picture, immediately give the
    cookie and praise.

Hints about Switches.   The switch could involve having the child do
something different, such as pointing to a known body part. As with a spoken model, the lesson should not stop at that point. Selecting an item or picture that someone else just pointed to is not necessarily the same as choosing
correctly between an array of items or pictures. The switch in this case requires
distracting the student from staring at the item just selected and assuring ourselves that the target stimulus is truly controlling the response by introducing
different items or distracters.

It is helpful to switch to things that the student already knows. That way,
you also have an opportunity to provide the student a bit of reinforcement (i.e.,
praise for a correct answer) as an antidote for the consequences of the
mistake. Those reinforcers may help establish what is called **behavioral
momentum**—making future correct responses more likely.[2] A switch to
something the student knows well also gives you an opportunity to check
whether the student is paying attention at all or is just not making an effort.
Suppose you ask a child to touch his nose, and you are absolutely certain he
knows how to do this (because he has done this so many times before), but
he touches his ear instead. We should assume that something is wrong with
the overall lesson, not just with the target skill within the lesson. A teacher also
may consider switching to a completely different type of response—from a lesson target of giving a spoken reply to an imitative or instructional motor act.

Finally, if some of your students have not yet learned other reliable responses at this point in their education, pointing to something on the floor, or
even pausing for five or six seconds should provide the necessary distraction
prior to the teacher's repeating the primary cue.

Although our instructional example involved a spoken response, "Bill,"
suppose the lesson had involved teaching **receptive language,** where the

[2]Mace, F. C., et al. (1988). Behavioral momentum in the treatment of noncompliance. Journal
of Applied Behavior Analysis, 21, 123–141.

goal is to select a particular picture or item, rather than **expressive language,** where the objective is for the student to produce a spoken response. In that case, modeling could be conducted in the form of a demonstration or show of the correct picture, such as pointing to or tapping on the picture.

What Happens if the Student Continues to Make Errors?

At this point, you may be wondering what happens if the student makes another mistake at the repeat step? You might duplicate the entire four-step error correction sequence. However, suppose that the student makes yet another mistake? You could keep on looping through the sequence forever. To guard against this, repeat the four-step sequence only two or three times at most before stopping the lesson and moving on to something else. The more errors that build up, the greater the likelihood of a problematic behavioral episode. Here you can either stop the lesson at the point of the switch (e.g., "You're right! Let's get a drink of water") or greatly simplify (or even eliminate) the choices provided. In either case, the session ends on a successful note.

Correcting Errors in Sequential Tasks

Backstepping. Michelle was involved in a sequential activity when she made an error: leaving the faucet open. Her teacher noticed the problem when Michelle entered the classroom; but it is clear that the error was made in the bathroom. What should be the appropriate stimulus control for turning off the faucet? In part, that will depend on the task analysis—the plan for the order of the steps involved in washing hands. For example, the sequence may be as follows:

(1) Turn on faucet
(2) Pick up soap
(3) Rub soap on hands under water
(4) Put down soap
(5) Rinse hands
(6) Shut faucet
(7) Pick up towel
(8) Dry hands

In this sequence, "rinse hands" is the step that proceeds "shut off faucet" and thus should come to provide the proper stimulus control over turning off the water. However, Michelle is in the classroom with you. Her teacher must now go back in the sequence to the step before the error if Michelle is to learn the proper sequence. The teacher says, "Wow! Let's try that again!" while walking Michelle back into the bathroom. The teacher re-creates the proper conditions: soapy hands and water running. At that point, the teacher uses a gesture to prompt Michelle to turn off the water once she has rinsed her hands. Now, Michelle has a good chance of learning when to shut off the faucet.

This same backstepping strategy can be used to refine various flawed sequences, even when these are not part of a formal lesson. Suppose, along with the paper waste, that a child throws her spoon into the garbage. Many teachers would ask her to retrieve the spoon from the garbage can. Although she does need to learn to hold on to the spoon while dumping the garbage, she does not need to learn to retrieve spoons from inside garbage cans. Thus, she needs to take her tray and utensils back to her seat and learn to hold the spoon while dumping the garbage. Suppose that a boy bolts out the door and runs down the hallway. Rather than having the child walk back up the hallway and walk down slowly, the key is recognizing that the child needs to learn to associate going out the door with walking slowly. Thus, the boy's teacher would lead him back into the room, teaching him to leave the room through the door and walk down the hallway. A child using PECS places an attribute card in the wrong place on the sentence strip ("I want the ball blue"). Instead of pointing to where the picture should go, have the child re-create the entire sentence strip, ensuring the correct placement of the card at the correct point in the sequence.

Both the four-step sequence and backstepping require a fair degree of diligence from the teacher. Given the effort required at the time of the error, you may wonder whether it is worth the bother. A familiar adage may help remind you of your choices: Pay a little now or a lot later. Either create a learning opportunity through your error correction strategy, or you will see the error appear over and over again.

Anticipatory Prompting. While backstepping is an effective error correction strategy for sequential tasks, you may encounter situations in which it simply is not possible to stop the sequence and go back to an earlier step. Events during instructional activities based in the community may be beyond your immediate control. You take Jake on a public bus. He is supposed to take money out of his wallet and give it to the driver. On this occasion, Jake takes out his money but walks past the driver. An immediate backstepping procedure would require you to ask the driver to stop so that Jake could exit and reboard the bus while you then would prompt Jake to give the driver his money. Imagine the look the driver would give you.

In such a situation, your next opportunity to address the error will occur the next time you take Jake onto the bus, maybe the following week. You know where in the sequence Jake probably will make the error: that is, you can anticipate the error. Therefore, you can use an **anticipatory prompt** to prevent the error from reoccurring. As Jake is taking out his money, you may prompt (remind) him about the next step: give the money to the driver. How you prompt will depend on what you already know about Jake. A verbal hint will be effective with some students—either direct (e.g., "Give the money to the driver") or possibly indirect (e.g., "What will you do with the money?"). Gestures or pictures may work better with others.

As always, you need to eliminate those prompts over time. One way is to use the anticipatory prompt earlier and earlier in the sequence (before boarding the bus you might remind Jake, "Now, remember to give the money to the driver"). The intensity of the anticipatory prompt also may be faded over time (a spoken reminder, to pointing to Jake's wallet, then to the driver and so on).

Some sequential tasks contain reoccurring sequences of actions. For example, a vocational task may involve collating three pieces of paper, stapling them together, folding them in thirds, putting the set into an envelope, sealing the envelope, placing the envelope in a "finished" box, and then repeating the entire sequence. Suppose that a student consistently pauses at a particular step in the sequence. For example, Bart pauses after putting the filled envelope in the finished box. His teacher typically waits a few seconds and then tries subtly to prompt him to repeat the cycle. No matter how delicate the prompt—a finger flick or a slight nod of the head—Bart's continued performance remains prompt dependent. Because his teacher knows where in the sequence the error is likely to occur, she can use an anticipatory prompt. At first, while Bart is still sealing the envelope (but before he has put it into the finished box), his teacher touches the pile of papers that start the sequence. While the teacher prompts, Bart looks at the pile of papers but also puts the filled envelope in the right location. He then immediately starts the cycle over. Over time, his teacher moves the anticipatory prompt to a point earlier in the sequence and reduces the intensity of the prompt. In time, she completely removes it, and Bart cycles through the sequence until all the materials are used or the end of the work session is signaled.

Commonalties among Error Correction Strategies

Teachers always should seek to minimize errors in their design of lessons. When the goal is to establish stimulus control over a particular action, errors typically involve either responding to the wrong cue or not responding at all to the correct cue. When the focus is on establishing stimulus control, it is not a good idea to modify the lesson to allow prompts to remain. Choosing between pictures within a discrimination task is not the same as picking a picture tapped by the teacher. Answering a question is not the same as imitating the answer. Hanging up a coat after looking at a picture on a schedule is not the same as hanging up a coat following a verbal or gestural prompt. Teachers need to be prepared to use error correction strategies when the focus of the lesson is correct responding to given instructional or natural cues. Common among all error correction strategies is a sequence within which the intended stimulus (i.e., the instructional, natural, or chained cue) is arranged to connect with the target action. While it is best to apply correction opportunities as quickly as possible, circumstances may prevent repetition of the response sequence until the next opportunity arises naturally, as in the case of the bus rider.

| Prevent errors whenever possible and plan for appropriate error correction when necessary. |

Furthermore, by recognizing the nature of the lesson being taught, a teacher should be able to predict the type of error apt to emerge. Errors within discrete trial lessons tend to differ from those encountered in sequential lessons. Although teachers do their best to minimize errors, they should not be surprised when some crop up. In their lesson preparations, they should include a plan to apply appropriate error correction strategies, if needed.

Summary

Many learn successfully enough by practicing a skill repeatedly and through trial and error. The problem with these approaches is that repetition of errors can establish the wrong as well as the right aspects of the behavior. As we have seen, there are better ways, especially for students who encounter major difficulties in learning. These errorless learning methods have the advantages of avoiding the necessity of correcting errors, extinction bursts, and the development of bad habits. Behavior analysts have designed numerous errorless teaching methods that, when combined with powerful reinforcement strategies, can accomplish wonders. Included are blocking errors, shaping, physical and graduated guidance, fading, and teaching discriminations without allowing errors to intrude.

Nevertheless, errors are bound to happen. When they do, it pays in the long run to see to it that they do not become firmly established. Fortunately, another arsenal of strategies is available to us. The four-step error correction sequence—of modeling and then prompting the correct response, switching to another skill, and then repeating the prompt followed by a powerful reinforcer—works well with discrete trial instruction. In sequential lessons, backstepping to an element earlier in, or even to the beginning of, the sequence helps. When necessary, anticipatory prompting can be used temporarily to cue the correct response until the student includes it regularly. Eventually, fading these prompts is essential if the student is to perform the task appropriately and independently.

The important thing to remember when teaching the kinds of advanced skills described here is to remember not to become discouraged. If preventing errors altogether has not worked, you now have a number of ways to correct them. Like a good scout, do not let unanticipated errors throw you. Be prepared to cope with them by having a correction plan readily at hand.

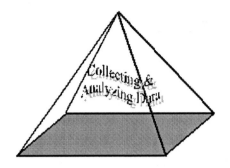

11

Collecting and Analyzing Data: The Why and How of Data Collection

A severe pain to your midsection jolts you awake at 4 A.M. You wait for it to subside, but it does not. Is it your heart? Gallbladder? Indigestion? In desperation, you call your physician, reaching the answering service. A few minutes later, you are still hurting and getting more worried by the moment. Finally, the doctor returns the call. Suppose, after you described your symptoms, that he simply advised that you to take a couple of aspirins and go back to bed. What would be your reaction?

Hold it. You were not asked any critical questions, like if you had a fever or what the thermometer read. Were you prompted to check your pulse and blood pressure or gather more information about other signs and symptoms? Would you not expect your physician to collect relevant information or data to help decide whether you should go back to bed or to the emergency room?

Respected specialists often are those who collect and review important data and use it appropriately: the garage mechanic who uses pressure gauges and other instruments to assess how effectively the various parts of your auto are working, the tailor who carefully takes your measurements to produce a perfect fit, or the carpet installer or wallpaper hanger who checks precisely how many square feet of material will be needed to complete the job with as little waste as possible. These experts appreciate the value of using data to help them decide how to proceed.

Why Collect Educational Data?

Educators need to pay the same attention to detail as those in any specialized field because students deserve the best. In their concern with student progress in gaining skills and decreasing problem behaviors, teachers can use sound, relevant data to guide the way they design and change their lesson strategies; to monitor student functioning; to analyze, design, and carry out educational plans; to track student progress; to overcome problems; to support their own and one another's efforts; and to demonstrate the relation between what they do and the outcome.

Designing and Changing Lesson Strategies

Effective teaching is hard work. While teachers put a great deal of effort into planning and implementing lessons, there is no guarantee that those efforts will be successful. If the student is not learning, the teacher is not teaching, and something about the lesson needs to change. Therefore, teachers need to collect information to find out whether their strategies are working and whether they should continue or change their lesson strategies.

It often is tempting to rely only on informal observations. Yet when the instructional steps are very small, as they tend to be when students have special needs, minor signs of student progress might well be overlooked. Some students progress so slowly that they may appear not to be moving along at all. Collecting data at such times can be extremely important. The information will affect decisions about whether to change lesson or behavior intervention plans. Suppose that a task analysis for laundering a shirt has 25 steps. In the absence of objective data, the teacher might easily overlook actual progress at the rate of about a step or two a week and be tempted to change her lesson strategy prematurely. By collecting data, she will uncover how effective her instruction actually has been.

Analyzing the Environment

Data should also serve as the central problem-solving piece when investigating how the elements of a complex system, like those in the home, school, community, or workplace setting, affect what students do. Then we can analyze the data to help guide decisions about whether and how the system should be changed. Consider, for example, prosocial behaviors. Data could be collected on factors known to influence that category of behaviors, including the type of activity, who is present, or the frequency of encouragement or praise from adults that supports positive interactions. We then can measure which people or which actions do the most to encourage or discourage the child to practice particular social skills.

Who Collects Data?

Observers need to be trained to be consistent in the way they score behavior so that the information they gather remains objective and reliable. Regardless of who wrote the program, though, the whole team, including paraprofessionals, takes responsibility for deciding how data are to be collected and analyzed. For example, both the teacher and the speech pathologist might collect information about the Picture Exchange Communication System (PECS) or speech performance at various times. However, each of these team members also might collect data on vocational objectives, such as how well a student requests missing materials for a job.

Resources, of course, dictate who might be in the best position to collect data on a behavior or its results. Progressive organizations will include technical support staff whose job includes collecting, summarizing, graphing, and analyzing data. In the absence of such personnel, you might be able to recruit others to do the job. They do need adequate training and supervision, though, until all are confident that their data are reliable and valid. In the absence of that kind of support, professional personnel, the teachers themselves, their peers (other teachers and aides), parents, capable students, and supervisors need to learn to fulfill this role successfully.

No matter who records, the method of data collection must remain accurate and consistent. In this chapter, we describe methods for maintaining this rigor by periodically scheduling simultaneous observations by a second person. Reliability needs to be monitored fairly often, especially in the beginning, so that differences in scoring can be used as a basis for refining definitions and training.

What Student Data to Collect

On a day-to-day basis, the two most important pieces of information for teachers are the functional skills their students are developing and how successful they are being at reducing problems. Other information will help them continue to do the best job possible.

Functional Skills and Problem Behaviors

Even when all your attention seems to be focused on problem behaviors, recall that the Pyramid Approach to Education emphasizes teaching functional skills and functionally equivalent alternative responses to inappropriate behavior. Therefore, although it might be tempting to limit data collection to problem behaviors, a teacher should concentrate most heavily on promoting students' skill development.

Nevertheless, we can make a similar case for recording changes in problem behaviors. Assisted by an aide, Charlie is integrated for several hours a week into a regular second-grade class. In the meantime, he has been learning a vocabulary that allows him to get food and take a break. On this very hot June day, he suddenly begins to throw whatever he can get his hands on across the room. Had data not been collected on the number of Charlie's outbursts and the type of requests he has learned, everyone might be tempted to agree that the inclusion program was a failure. His data sheets (Figure 11.1) give us our first clue as to where the problem might lie. We see that Charlie has yet to learn how to get a drink, yet at this time the weather has turned warmer.

When we plot the words learned and his CIB episodes, as in Figure 11.2, we see that the more words Charlie has learned, the lower the number of CIBs. What would you do if you were to see those kinds of data?

Vocabulary	Fully mastered	In progress	Not yet taught
Cracker	✓		
Banana	✓		
Bathroom		✓	
Break	✓		
Water			✓
Juice			✓

Figure 11.1   Charlie's Vocabulary Chart

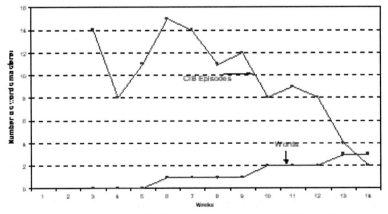

Figure 11.2   Vocabulary Mastered versus CIB Episodes

Actually, collecting data serves numerous useful purposes:

- Determining the *current status* of the student or others. For instance, a standardized language assessment is administered to discover (1) whether a student's placement in an educational program seems reasonable or (2) the average functioning level of the students in a given program.
- Tracking *progress,* as in a student advancing through the phases of a language-training program like PECS. Some teaching objectives will be broadly defined, while others will be broken down into very fine steps. Be certain that the type of data you collect reflects the size of the steps you are teaching.
- Supplying evidence of direct *accomplishments,* such as the number of contextually relevant requests a student makes or the number of words she reads per minute.
- Monitoring correlated *improvements* (e.g., downward trends in problematic behaviors, such as acts of aggression, self-abuse, or withdrawal).
- *Assessing* and *diagnosing* the origin of problems, as in assessing the function of aggressive or self-abusive episodes.
- Yielding information about curriculum, resources, and educational strategies to use as a basis for deciding what to use and how to use them.
- Serving as a *source of useful feedback* to students and teachers.
- Providing a basis for setting long-range and interim goals.

Specific Yardsticks

Just as we use a ruler to measure the length of an object, a scale to assess weight, and a thermometer to measure temperature, depending on our purposes, a number of different behavioral assessment instruments are available. Examples include the form, shape, or **topography** of a response or its results, frequency, rate, duration, and intensity.

Form of the Behavior

Often we count behavior by its form, shape, or topography: what it looks like when a student is doing something like clapping his hands, how he holds his pencil, or how closely the product of his effort conforms to a set of standards (e.g., how round the circles or straight the lines are when writing). Response topography is illustrated by the contents of checklists of the kind we see in Figure 11.2 and those based on task analyses. We also can collect topographical data on problem behaviors, such as the form or location of a head hit, the place on his hand that the youngster bites, how severe the bruises are, the objects a student with pica ingests, or the people he knocks off balance.

Form versus Function.   Two or more behaviors may have different topographies but the same function. An entire array of problematic behaviors, including hitting, spitting, pushing, rocking, screeching, and others, may all form part of a single response class because one is functionally the same as the next. Collecting data in such cases can be simplified if you collapse all those behaviors into one category, such as "aggression." On the other hand, a single behavioral topography may have two or more different functions. In such cases, it is important to separate behaviors with the same form but a different function, as when a student is spitting out food that is spoiled rather than spitting it at another child or when a teacher is patting a student on the shoulder in a manner that has the effect of reducing rather than increasing the behavior it follows.

Frequency

Sometimes we are concerned with how often a particular behavior happens. Giving the right answer to a multiplication problem once or twice is not the same as giving the right answer 30 times, nor is sorting the laundry properly the same as repeating it a dozen times. Similarly, there is a big difference between knocking one's baby brother down a time or two versus 20 or 30 times. Frequency is measured by counting.

It is easy to count when a behavior has a tangible outcome, such as the written answer to a multiplication problem or several piles of soiled laundry. When a behavior does not leave a lasting result, we need to measure it while it is happening (concurrently) or right afterward. You can tally the number of different words spoken or pictures used by keeping an inventory by date and adding to the list each time the student uses a new word appropriately. Provided that they have a distinctive beginning and end, you can record the number of a child's temper tantrums. You also can take frequency measures on your own performance, say, recording the number of times you conduct a particular type of lesson.

Just counting the frequency of presenting pictures or hitting actually gives us only the most basic information, though. What would be the meaning of a report that the child used 10 pictures correctly or hit himself 10 times? That is impossible to answer. We need to know more, such as over what period of time these events happened (their rate), how long they lasted (their duration), or how powerful or intense the behaviors were.

Rate

This measure adds the important time dimension to frequency. Rate can be defined as the frequency of the behavior per a given amount of time. Using 10 pictures or hitting oneself in the head once a week would be very different from once a minute. If you think about it, often we separate successful from unsuccessful students by noting their learning rates. Levels of mastery or fluency may be noted only by recording a behavior's rate. Being able very quickly to calculate the correct answers to multiplication problems is quite different from doing so slowly and hesitantly.

Remember, though, that if you use a rate measure, keep the time duration and other circumstances constant. Otherwise, you will not know whether a change in the measure was a function of the behavior, nor would you know the number of times it occurred or the conditions under which it occurred. A child may say "Hello" 10 times during the first 10 minutes of the day but not again until the end of the day. If we compared the rate of saying "Hello" without regard to the time and place, then the rate during the first 10 minutes would be dramatically different than the rate obtained across the first four hours of the day.

Many educators find rate to be the single most important type of information about a behavior. To be certain that your recordings of rate changes more closely represent what truly is going on, whenever you take behavioral frequency data, include details such as the place, dates, and times when you begin and end data collection.

Duration

A behavior's duration, or the length of time over which it persists, sometimes can be the main issue. Crying briefly after scraping a knee would not be regarded as something extraordinary, but continuing to weep for hours would be. The length of time an individual continues to perform a job task can be critically important. Working for one minute and stopping for 10 would be regarded as far more problematic than the other way around. Many lessons include as their goal expanding the duration of a behavior. Time on task, waiting, or remaining seated are examples. The objective is simply to stretch the length of time over which the behavior persists.

Similarly, shortening the duration of a behavior may be the goal when dealing with CIBs. Crying when hurt or imitating a television commercial for a few moments is reasonable. When our main purpose is to shorten the length of time a behavior persists, assessing duration becomes our sole data requirement.

Intensity

Sometimes your concern is with the forcefulness of a behavior. For instance, we may be satisfied with the rate and duration of a child's speech but unable to get the full message because the volume is too low. A different youngster may operate equipment correctly but push the buttons and switches with such force that he breaks them off. A student who jumps up and down, loudly shouting out answers, is disruptive to the rest of the group. In each case, assessing the intensity of the response will aid most in our efforts to change the behavior.

Qualities of Useful Data

Formal data collection is reserved for important educational purposes, not just for the fun of it, because the process can be costly. Educators need to balance the purpose and importance of the data with the methods yielding the most valuable information for the smallest investment. If the goal is simply to get a rough estimate of progress, precision may not be crucial (although realize that the results could be way off base). The following discussion assumes that the object is to get as closely as possible to the real truth.

Validity

To be of value, whatever data are collected must be valid; that is, the numbers must mirror exactly and accurately what they are supposed to be measuring. The more valid data are those with very carefully defined and tested objective definitions of the events being measured. That means avoiding one's subjective feelings or impressions. Instead either a completely objective mechanical instrument, like a tape recorder, or one or more unbiased observers are necessary. Standardized tests (e.g., individual intelligence tests) or teaching protocols (e.g., PECS and Direct Instruction) spell out very clearly what constitutes a "correct response," and users are trained to apply those definitions consistently. Under those circumstances, validity is less of an issue.

Sometimes it takes a major investment to design valid measures. Definitions may have to be defined, refined, and redefined repeatedly. Often, though, as we have seen, function may be more important than the form or topography of the behavior. So what needs to happen is to describe clearly the function of a whole set of related behaviors (i.e., a **functional response class**). Differentiating between a self-hit, bite, or head bang may not be the most important concern. All could be included under the functional heading of "avoidance or escape responses." More important is what any member of that response class appears to accomplish for the student. Similarly, the data taken could just as well relate to the effect the student's behavior has on objects (projects completed or windows broken) or on other people present (causing them to laugh, to cry or to surrender a toy).

Reliability

To be considered reliable, a data collection method needs to consistent over time from one observer to the next. In looking at ongoing student or teacher behavior, arrange for two people independently to collect the same behavior samples at the same time. What do you do if you find that each one scores an event quite differently from the other? Suppose that one says a student is spontaneously initiating a request to play with a given toy and the other says she is responding to a prompt. Deciding what to do next would be difficult. Should you fade the prompt or concentrate on promoting initiations toward a greater variety of toys? The problem is that the data do not truly represent what is happening; they are unreliable, useless. Problems like this can be fixed by the following:

(1) Revising and clarifying the definitions of correctness, including conditions, timing, rate, and other qualities or dimensions. Teaching teams are ideally suited for this purpose because everyone is familiar with the situation and knows where issues and confusions arise.

(2) Retraining the observers—having them observe, compare, receive feedback from trainers, and so on until all agree very closely among themselves not just once but on a number of occasions.

Here is an example:

Old definition: Student initiates a spontaneous choice.

New definition: When presented with two different toys placed equidistant from each other and with no instructions or gestures from the teacher, the student reaches in the direction of one of the toys within 10 seconds.

As a quality assurance strategy, check the data-scoring methods periodically by having two observers collect the same sequence of data (at least 10 or so repetitions) at the same time. Of course, the observers need to make sure to avoid communicating with one another during the process. They then can calculate an *index of agreement* by examining each item, one by one, to see whether the observers agreed or disagreed. They then count the number of times the scores (As) or disagreed (Ds). The proportion of the time the observers agreed is determined by dividing the number of times they agreed by the total number of times they scored, regardless of whether they agreed (A) or disagreed (D). To express the estimate of reliability as a percentage, multiply by 100—just move the decimal points two to the right. The formula, found over and over in the research literature (where they are very fussy about reliability and validity), is shown in Figure 11.3. An appropriate goal is to achieve a reliability index above .90 (or 90%). If it is substantially below .80,

$$\text{Percentage of agreement} = \frac{A}{A + D} \times 100$$

Figure 11.3   Determining Reliability

there are too many disagreements. In such cases, get the team (including supervisors) together to discuss the nature of the problem and work out further refinements.

Behavioral Recording Procedures

Many procedures are available when it comes to collecting behavioral data. Some are relatively simple; others more complicated. The choice depends on the behavior observed and the effort required to collect adequate information about it. Two fundamentals, though, are crucial to deciding what system to use:

(1) That any data collected are meaningful
(2) That any data collected are used

Getting Started

Do not try to do it all. Be selective because data are only useful if you use them. Forms piled on desks or jammed unread into cabinets just take up space. Record only what you are reasonably certain will be used. Often that means setting priorities. Probably this is a team decision, dictated by individual education plan (IEP) considerations. Mutually set priorities indicate what informational needs are most pressing. Do not begin with minute process measures, those nitpicking details about who did what, when, and how, unless the more gross ones do not tell you what you want to know. Do begin with those data that are easiest to obtain reliably, like the steps mastered in a training program or lists of new words spoken.

Should you encounter a roadblock and cannot figure out what is getting in the way, then you might begin to collect more challenging data, such as something about the instructional process or behaviors of the student that interfere with learning. Suppose that you are wondering whether you are providing the cues too soon in a delayed prompting procedure. You could have a peer count the seconds you actually wait between presenting a toy the student likes to play with and saying its name.

Other instances might be observing how closely teachers adhere to the protocol for displaying and using the student's daily schedule in the classroom or determining the steps that parents are conducting correctly in a PECS routine in the child's home. Are the timing of trials, placement of materials, nature and frequency of prompts, or other antecedents or consequences arranged optimally? A student's temper tantrums seem to have increased during discrete trial training. You could get some valuable information about how to improve the way you organize those sessions by measuring the nature of the tantrums and the conditions that appear to set them off or keep them going. An even better choice would be to examine more closely those antecedents and consequences that tend to support the smoothest, most efficient progress.

So, rather than plunging into taking data for data's sake, always ask yourself in what way the data will be meaningful and useful. If critical information is missing or inappropriate methods are selected, the data will lose value. Instead, we need to be as certain as possible that these elements are covered.

Crucial Identifying Information

Regardless of the system, the following information needs to be included when any data are collected:

- Date
- Time
- Location
- Name of the observer(s)
- Name of the person or group being observed
- Any atypical physical and social conditions in effect, such as other activities going on, unusual furniture arrangements, others present, and so on

Next we describe the two most common methods for recording behavior. One is based on its ongoing process; the other on its immediate results or products.

Observational Recording

When the behavior of concern leaves no enduring immediate product, like a worksheet, completed sandwich, or neatly organized toy shelf, we have no choice but to capture it while it is going on. That means that someone has to be present and watch either all the time or according to a schedule that permits the behavior to be accurately represented.

Continuous Observation. When faced with a particular challenge that requires us to know exactly how often, when and where a behavior occurs or some other measure of it, we need to count and record it every time it happens. We must be careful not to overlook or double-count instances. If a student hurts himself or someone else or damages property only rarely, we should be able to prepare an incident report and total such episodes reliably.

If, on the other hand, a boy rapidly and continuously hits himself or others, we may find it difficult to get an accurate count. Subtle but important changes might then easily be overlooked. As described here, a better alternative in such cases is to use a representative sampling system, checking the presence or absence of the behavior within a given period of time.

Certain kinds of classroom learning activities lend themselves especially well to continuous observation because they are discrete events with easily identified beginnings and ends. Included are the following:

- The total number of items performed correctly during discrete trial training.
- Progress through a task analysis, like one for bed making. You have a checklist containing each item broken down into its individual elements. Either the item is performed correctly or incorrectly or it is missing or in the wrong order.
- Items completed correctly per number of opportunities provided.
- Number of correct and incorrect responses by prompt level during carefully programmed instructional programs or in classrooms arranged to heighten incidental teaching opportunities.
- Number of correct or incorrect spontaneous (unprompted) responses during formal instruction or when the classroom is designed to heighten incidental teaching episodes.

When teachers control the pace of the lesson, counting and totaling is easy. At the end of the session, they can calculate a percentage correct, allowing them to see degrees of progress made over time.

Sometimes you might want to tally a behavior but cannot take the time from your ongoing activity to do that. Use an audio or video tape recorder or some other way of preserving the event until you have the time, perhaps after school.

Behavior Sampling. Is it necessary to record every response during every single teaching session? The answer depends on how essential or useful the information is. If you use it to make a decision about how to adjust aspects of your instruction, the more information you have, the better. However, if you want simply to use it as a basis for judging progress over time, probably a periodic probe will be sufficient. Remember that if the data are neither meaningful nor useful, the time spent taking them probably can be spent to greater advantage elsewhere.

When a behavior happens so often that it is impractical to record it every time, ask yourself whether it is really necessary to count every single response in a lesson or occasion the student gets up from the table. Instead, maybe you could take **representative samples,**[1] choosing as a reference a standard block of time, such as an hour, a half hour, five minutes, or a minute, and record whether the response of concern happens at all within each particular time block.[2] All you need to monitor for, then, is the first instance of the behavior, ignoring repetitions within that time interval. Alternatively, you can set a timer or use a sound, light flash or vibratory signal to cue you to monitor, score, and record at that moment.[3] Although these samples can over- or under-estimate reality, eventually they can give you valuable information. You will become increasingly confident that your tactics are succeeding when results show more and more blocks scored for the absence of a behavior that you hope to see diminish, like five 10-minute periods without any self-hitting; or for the presence of a behavior that you are encouraging, like playing inter-actively with a peer.

When resources are limited, even results of discrete trial instruction can be sampled, say, by scheduling someone to record every x sessions or time blocks. Most important is that the data represent what actually is happening as accurately as possible, a decision best made by a team including someone with expertise in this area.

Recording Results of Behavior

When the behavior we are attempting to teach leads directly to a product or other result, it may be possible to bypass observational recording of ongoing behavioral data. In fact, sometimes it matters little how a person does a job; just that the job is completed to standards of satisfaction. Once a student has learned the steps in a task analysis involving filling envelopes or cleaning rooms, our interest is in the number of envelopes filled or rooms cleaned, not

---

[1]Beware of sampling based solely on convenience because you may find yourself cued to observe by something the student is doing. Instead, decide ahead of time when the behavior is to be sampled and stick to the schedule.

[2]This system may be referred to as a **partial interval time sampling system** or an interval **spoilage system.** For a thorough description of various behavior sampling methods, see B. Sulzer-Azaroff and G. R. Mayer, *Behavior Analysis for Lasting Change* (Atlanta: Wadsworth, 1991), Chaps. 6, 14, 22.

[3]The name for this variation is **momentary time sample.** Pyramid Educational Consultants, Inc., markets auditory signaling tapes for educators who elect not to prepare their own.

in the motions that produced the results. In a classroom, behavioral products can include the numbers of workbook pages or problems the student completed, the pictures in a communication book used appropriately, or the total number of pieces of furniture broken or facial bruises seen. Computerized instructional programs may be designed to provide the number right or wrong, percentage correct, rate, and other important elements of the learning process. All we have to do is record that information.

The obvious advantage of using data based on products is that we need not engage in the time-consuming or possibly distracting process of observing the student while the behavior is ongoing. The presence of observers also can cue or otherwise influence various aspects of the behavior. Cleaning one's room or dressing for work while someone stands there with a checklist is very different from producing a clean room or being appropriately attired while no one is there to observe. If the ultimate objective is for the person to perform a task independently, it is best to assess under natural conditions those that match as closely as possible the typical environmental circumstances.

We can record information about the products of our own efforts just as well, such as counting how many student schedules we have posted or observational forms we have submitted. We could look at the way the physical environment is arranged for instruction: placement of chairs, table, pictures and so on. We can count the number of times the supervisor initialed and dated classroom charts. Written compliments could be tallied just as readily. Data like these can supply valuable information about our actions as teachers or supervisors as they relate to student progress.

Making Use of Data

Meaningful data can be used in a number of important ways, among others, to investigate the relation between the behavior and its consequences, immediate antecedents, and other contextual factors; to monitor and report student progress; and to evaluate the utility of instructional methods and their costs and benefits. Here we detail some of those.[4]

Assessing the Function of a Behavior

To determine the functional relation between a behavior and the environment, data must be collected on each element of our three-term contingency: specific

---

[4]Two other important uses, beyond the scope of this book, are experimental research and staff management. Numerous examples of these can be found in scientific and professional journals, such as the Journal of Applied Behavior Analysis and the Journal of Organizational Behavior Management.

behaviors and their antecedents and consequences. We want to know whether the student who presents a picture of a ball actually "knows what it means." We say, "It's time to go outside and play"—the antecedent. The child chooses a picture of a ball from an array of pictures and gives it to the teacher—the behavior. The teacher says, "Go get it," and the child gets a ball before going outside to play with it—the consequence (Figure 11.4). Because the child selected both the picture and the ball, we are more confident that he understands the meaning of the selected picture. Now, if we record a dozen or more instances in which that relationship is consistently maintained, we can feel more confident of the child's "understanding" of the relation between the card and the ball.

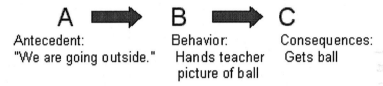

Figure 11.4   The Function of a Behavior

As mentioned earlier, if you have determined that a number of behaviors tend to happen together, like the group mentioned earlier under the heading of "aggression," you can handle them as a single set when assessing their function. When the same behavior has different functions, though, you will need to separate them from one another, depending on the antecedents or consequences. Presenting the picture of the ball just before recess would be very different from presenting the same picture at lunch. Head hits following a teacher's reprimand versus head hits while running a fever (perhaps elicited by the pain of an ear infection) are quite distinct and should be counted separately.

We need to measure all behaviors targeted for reduction in the behavior intervention plan from a functional perspective. Along with its rate or some other measurable attribute of the problem, we also systematically measure any variations in broad environmental conditions that might relate to the following:

- The presence or behaviors of teachers, supervisors, parents, and other students
- Suspected physical variables, such as the particular room and its arrangement, temperature, noise level, crowding, and so on
- Internal conditions of the student, including physical ailments and time since the last meal or break (Figure 11.5.)

In terms of specific antecedents, examples might include teachers' instructions or gestures or their presentation of written material, objects, or

Figure 11.5   Possible Sources of Data to Collect
from the Student's Wider Learning Context

pictures and similar items or events. Possible consequences might be scolding, ignoring, giving tangible objects, praising, hugging, complaining, and so on.

Assessing Student Progress

Report cards represent a long tradition of recording information on student progress and communicating it to parents and others. Just how valid and reliable report card data might be in any given case is open to question. Besides, standard report card measures represent major chunks of progress. Fine details are missing. Broad-brush measures of the relatively slower progress of students with special needs may mean very little. More sensible, as described in the chapter on functional objectives, is breaking skills down into their parts and determining in advance just what standards constitute mastery of the skill. Now there is a more reasonable and accurate basis for measuring and reporting progress. These data then can be inserted in the students' records and communicated to the students themselves, parents, supervisors, future teachers, and relevant groups.

Data on student progress also can inform educators about the appropriateness of the categories, difficulty level, and size of learning steps. When progress is very slow, probably objectives are too challenging or not relevant to the student's functioning or reinforcement has been too sparse. The program needs to change. If, on the other hand, the student is acquiring minor objectives by the bucket full, there is a good chance that objectives can be made more challenging.

The feedback inherent in reporting progress data also may serve a powerful reinforcing function for its recipients, especially when objectives and instructional methods are carefully adapted to the individual student. Many take advantage of this fact by issuing progress reports more often than the typical quarterly report card: monthly, weekly, or even daily. When objectives are listed in advance, inventorying progress becomes a simple matter of just checking them off.

Another related situation is when you want to monitor students' progress through a curriculum chosen to support their broader IEP objectives. Here, especially in the early stages, you want to determine what, if any headway the curriculum appears to be promoting. Figure 11.6 displays the number of pictures mastered by a student being instructed in the PECS. Here the purpose was to assess whether the decision to use PECS was justified and, if so, to determine just how well it was working. Notice that as time progressed and the student began to master new pictures, data were collected less often. Probing once in a while, thereafter, could reassure us that the progress we think we see taking place actually is.

Analyzing Instructional Methods

Concern with tracking accomplishments and progress of individual students is one thing. Another is to analyze instructional effectiveness by using data to help us plan the details of our teaching routines, to diagnose problems, and

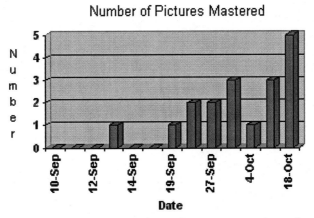

Figure 11.6   Assessing a Student's Progress through
PECS

to prescribe promising solutions. We know, for instance, that while the student is attempting to learn something new and difficult, like following her daily schedule, it is crucial for the teacher to provide lots of reinforcement. After the objective is mastered (when the youngster checks and follows the schedule regularly), reinforcement is supposed to be delivered less and less frequently because intermittent reinforcement is best for maintaining a well-established skill. In that case, we may want to monitor the teacher's frequency of reinforcement to ensure that the intended thinning of the schedule actually is taking place. We could count the number of praise statements delivered at the point of mastery, then probe at irregular intervals to determine whether the reinforcement rate were diminishing while the student's progress remained consistent. Figure 11.7 shows this relationship.

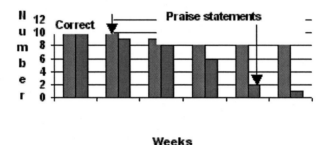

Figure 11.7   Ratio of Praise Statements to Number
Correct

Making a Case for Special Placement or Supplemental Resources

Clear objective data are essential in order to justify recommending placing students in a special setting or requesting supplemental resources. Review the kinds of evidence demanded by law or standard practice and supply it. One item of interest could be the students' rates of progress through their academic curriculum; another might be information about their social or emotional skills and deficiencies. It is one thing to say that the student has difficulty reading and another to count the number of new words he has learned to decode within a given week. Even more powerful would be those data showing rates of progress (or of maladaptive behaviors) per day or week over a number of weeks or months. If these are very different from those of the members of a criterion group, your chances of reaching a reasonable resolution are increased. Figure 11.8 shows an example.

Dealing with Limited Resources

If you are limited by scarce resources and have to sacrifice collecting data on some aspects of your program, maintain collecting and summarizing the most

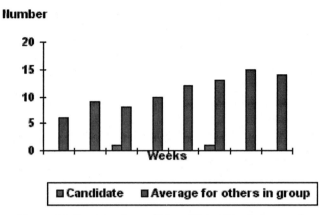

Figure 11.8   Number of New Sight Words Learned

important elements of a student's IEP. These could include individual objectives or combinations of closely linked objectives (see Figure 11.9).

Who Else's Behavior Is Assessed?

Typically, it is the student whose performance is being assessed, and that has been the main focus of this chapter. Nevertheless, if we are to take a broad view of the learning environment, we might also take data on the performance of instructional or supervisory staff, data collectors, parents, peers, and others. To illustrate, quantitative information could be used to track the following:

- Progress of an educator's mastering the skills involved in using the Pyramid Approach or a district's number of PECS personnel certified per semester
- Teacher accomplishments, such as the type of certifications a teacher has obtained
- Improvements in staff satisfaction, staff absenteeism, turnover, and so on
- Adhering to planned teaching routines

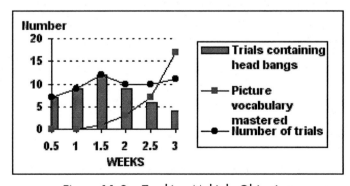

Figure 11.9   Tracking Multiple Objectives

Assessing Costs and Benefits Associated with Taking Data

Getting reliable, valid data consumes valuable resources. When deciding whether or how to collect any particular data set, always begin by asking, "How much will these data contribute to the students' educational objectives now and in the future? Will they accelerate rates of students' goals achievement? Do those benefits outweigh the costs my system will need to invest? Is there a simpler way to obtain almost the same results?" Consider, too, whether the student currently is in the process of acquiring the skill or just maintaining it at a steady rate. In the latter case, less frequent, more random samples are justified. Collecting data on seriously dangerous behaviors is crucial but on mildly annoying behaviors probably is not.

Here is an actual example of the misuse of data collection. A number of years ago, two observers were employed to see what they could do to stop the self-injury of a boy by recording every single time he hit his head. It took them a long time to differentiate between a bang, a tap, and a scratch. Thousands of data points were recorded, but they never were made use of. One would be hard put to justify the cost of obtaining those data even if they were used, especially because information that probably would have been just as valid could have been gathered by using a sampling method. Also, they could have combined all those behaviors into a single response class labeled "self-abusive acts." The main point is to use data to ask whether what and how you spend it is worth what you get in return.

> The best educational decisions are based on sound, relevant data.

Getting the Most from Your Data

We use data to make decisions. That is why it occupies such a central a position in the Pyramid Approach, filling the whole space. However, data are of value only if we use them wisely to provide us with important information by which to guide our actions. That is why graphing and sharing data can be so profitable. We need to guard against making data collection or its application punishing, though, because then its purposes no longer will be served.

Graphing Data

Looking at rows of numbers is one thing, but when we see the patterns the numbers form, we can derive more value from them. In an instance, a clear graph can show progress or its absence (and much more), as you have seen elsewhere in this chapter. For example, using data as a basis for setting interim goals is a good strategy. You decide what level you ultimately want to achieve—a long-term goal, such as a student's mastering a basic picture vocabulary. Then you record progress over time, as shown in Figure 11.10. Those data about what the student has accomplished then are used to set new goals for the next time period, such as a series of weeks. On the figure we show those interim goals as dashed horizontal lines.

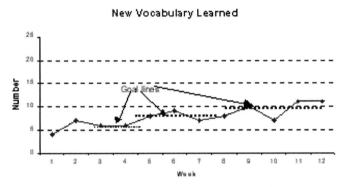

Figure 11.10   Using Data to Set Interim Goals: New Vocabulary Learned

Additionally, graphs posted in a prominent spot can prompt participants to give themselves or one another other feedback and reinforcement for progress. Reaching challenging goals is a cause for celebration, so at that point some powerful reinforcers can be made available to those involved, to students, and even sometimes to staff (notes of recognition, commendation for teachers or parents, rewards for students, and so on).

Data showing steady progress in the desired direction can be highly reinforcing to those responsible, energizing them toward promoting even greater gains. By contrast, data showing lack of progress or deterioration in performance tends to be punishing and may reasonably impel the teacher to change direction. We must be sure to give a new effort a reasonable try, though, before abandoning it. Some educational practices, such as ignoring troubling behaviors, testing new instructional styles, and so on, take a while to grab hold. Guard against giving up too soon by setting a reasonable trial period up front.

Data as a Reinforcing Tool

Now that you can see the value of using data to reinforce maintaining and accelerating positive change, as a final point, let us caution you against designing a data collection system that turns out to be punishing. That can happen when progress fails to occurs, when collecting, plotting, or interpreting data takes too long or requires excessively major changes in routines or extra personnel; or when others use the data as a basis for assigning blame. These pitfalls can be avoided by keeping the system easy, by avoiding attempting too much at once, by randomly sampling, and by using the data constructively in ways described earlier.

Shape data collection by setting priorities and beginning with the data that will give you information that is easy to obtain and that has the greatest potential for rewarding the data collection activity. That could mean delaying auditing other important facts, but it is best to have a dependable system than one that breaks down because of overload. Also, it is okay to discontinue collecting some kinds of data after a while, say, when an individual has firmly mastered a given skill; or, as we said earlier, you might begin to space out observations separated more and more widely in time. Do not forget the importance of feedback and recognition for your data collectors (even if you are the one doing it yourself). Stop from time to time and let the person know (or remind yourself of) the value of these efforts and even think about rewarding that activity from time to time in more tangible ways, say, with a luncheon invitation, a soft drink, a note, or some equivalent.

The Data Collection Plan

We have talked about the importance of validity, reliability, and practicality. Assuming that you are satisfied that these factors have been dealt with adequately, a few further issues remain. You need to plan who will gather what data, how, where, when, and how often, along with how much of it will be needed. Remind yourself of the purpose of collecting it in the first place: to make a sound educational decision. The exact nature of the particular decision being made, though, should influence how you design your specific data collection plan.

Summary

To do their best, teachers need to make informed decisions about how to enable their students to gain important skills and overcome problems. Clear, objective, reliable, and valid data provide the best basis on which to design and change lesson strategies. Data also can provide clues about what might be promoting and supporting problematic behaviors and how to change that state of affairs.

Various people, trained and supervised to remain objective and consistent, cooperate in collecting data on the current status of individual students to track their progress, supply evidence of their accomplishments and improvements, assess and diagnose the origin of problems, and provide a solid basis for making decisions and as sources of feedback and bases for setting short- and long-range goals. Different behavioral yardsticks may include the form, frequency, rate, duration, or intensity of the behavior, depending on the nature of the issue. Regardless of the measure selected, the information it provides will be valuable only to the extent that it fairly and consistently represents what it is supposed to.

Data are not collected simply for their own sake. They need to be meaningful and be used. Among the ways of ensuring this is to advance slowly, beginning with the simpler and moving gradually on to the more complicated forms. After crucial identifying information is noted, either the direct immediate results or the products of behavior can be assessed or ongoing acts recorded. Counting is possible when those acts are clearly distinct, having clear beginnings and ends. As long as the method produces truly representative information, sampling is better suited for those behaviors tending to persist over time.

Functional assessments include tracking the behavior(s) of concern and systematically measuring related variations in the student's (internal and external) environment. Findings then are used to redesign the individual student's program of instruction. Recording the nature of students' progress under various new conditions, such as changing when they provide how many of what kinds of reinforcers, reveals the best mix for the student. The outcome of cost-benefit assessments guides choices about the kinds of data that pay off sufficiently to justify continuing them.

Most educators want to know how their students are progressing over time. Graphing their data will help them get the most out of the data they have collected.

Because data collection has so many advantages, it is important for teams to systematically plan to gather and review the data. Developing and adhering to a meaningful, doable, systematic plan is the best way to make data collection work for you and your students.

Suggested Readings and Viewings

TO	*READ*
Become familiar with various ways to assess behavior and be accountable	Sulzer-Azaroff, B. & Mayer, G. R. (1994). Achieving educational excellence: Behavior analysis for school personnel. San Marcos, CA: Western Image, 19–59.

Learn how to measure, record, graph and analyze the results of behavioral interventions (t, bar)

Charlop-Christy, M. H. & Kelso, S. E. (1997). How to treat the child with autism. (Chapter 17). Claremont, CA: Claremont McKenna College.
Cooper, J. O., Heron, T. E. & Heward, W. L. (1987). (Part 7 & 8). Applied behavior analysis. (Chapters 4–9). Englewood Cliffs, NJ: Prentice Hall.
Sulzer-Azaroff, B. & Mayer, G.R. (1991). Behavior analysis for lasting change. (Chapters 6, 14 & 22). Atlanta: Wadsworth Group: Thompson.

TO

Practice assessing, recording, graphing data

Maurice, C., Green, G. & Luce, S. (Eds.) Behavioral intervention for young children with autism. (Chapters 5, 7). Austin, TX: Pro-Ed
Partington, J. W. & Sundberg, M. L. (1998). The assessment of basic language and learning skills (The ABLLS). (Appendix 1) Behavior Analysts, Inc., 3329 Vincent Road, Pleasant Hill, CA 94523.
Quill, K. A. (2000). *Do-Watch-Listen-Say.* Baltimore, MD: Brooks, 297–322, 396–398.
Sundberg, M. L. & Partington, J. W. (1998). Teaching language to children with autism or other developmental disabilities. Pleasant Hill, CA: Behavior Analysts, 163–170.

DO

Practice reading and analyzing the research literature; planning to use your own experimental analyses

Exercises in Sulzer-Azaroff, B. & Reese, E. P. (1982).Applying behavior analysis. (Chapter 6). New York: Holt, Rinehart & Winston.

12

A Typical School Day

Diane Black, M.Ed.

This book has explained many concepts that you may be familiar with and may use in your classroom. Most likely, others are brand new to you, and you are wondering, "How do I incorporate all that I have learned into practice?" Before becoming a Pyramid consultant, I was a lead teacher of a class composed of children with autism. During that time, I integrated the Pyramid Approach to Education into my daily classroom routine. I would like to share some of my experiences with you. Join me during a typical school day and discover how the Pyramid Approach can be incorporated within your program. To enable you to see for yourself how a scenario might play out, I will narrate the activity. The boxes isolate and describe the sequence of activities often incorporated within a pyramid classroom schedule. Boldface is used to signify technical terms from the pyramid model and the Picture Exchange Communication System (PECS).

Our model class consists of six students, three through five years of age, and three staff: one teacher, myself, and two paraprofessionals/teacher assistants. Figure 12.1 illustrates the kind of critical information posted about each child in the classroom. The students' likes (reinforcers) and dislikes, communication and reinforcement systems, and behavior management targets are listed.[1] All staff, including teacher-assistants, are trained to work with the students just as I do. They teach lessons and also collect data.

---

[1]For confidentiality, the names of the students and staff are fictitious.

Steven

Likes:	Dislikes:	Communication:	Reinforcement
Goldfish	Vegetables	Phase IV	System:
Popcorn	Water	Help	Variable interval (VI)
Pretzels	Pickles	Wait	Three minutes
Chips	Applesauce	Yes/no	Five tokens
Tornado bottle	Tomatoes	Attributes	
Trains			
Music books			

Doug

Likes:	Dislikes	Communication:	Reinforcement
Marshmallows	Fruit	Phase IV	System:
Raisins	Mustard	Wait	VI -3 minutes
Cheese balls	Water	Help	Five tokens
Chips	Skittles	Yes/no	
Toys that vibrate		Break	
Music		Attributes	
Ketchup			

Behavior Target:	Functional Equivalent Alternative Behavior:
Aggression	Break

Abby

Likes:	Dislikes:	Communication:	Reinforcement
Carrots	Chocolate	Phase IV	System:
Celery	Water	Wait	VI-3 minute
Candy	Squishy toys	Help	Five tokens
Cookies	Pickles	Yes/no	
Sand table	Break		
Juice		Attributes	
		Phase VI	

Behavior Target:	Functional Equivalent Alternative Behavior:
Self-injurious Behavior	Break

Mark

Likes:	Dislikes:	Communication:	Reinforcement
Pepperoni	Fruit	Phase II	System:
Skittles	Vegetables	Help	VI-3 minutes
Chips		Yes/no	Edible
Music Books		Phase IIIa	

Behavior Target:	Functional Equivalent Alternative Behavior:
Out of area	"Chase"

Figure 12.1   Classroom Postings

Robert

Likes:	Dislikes:	Communication:	Reinforcement
Grape juice	Licorice	Phase IV	System:
Cookies	Lemons	Attributes	VI-5 minutes
Skittles		Phase VI	Five tokens
Books		Wait	
Photographs			
Walks			

Gary

Like:	Dislikes:	Communication:	Reinforcement
Pretzels	Candy	Phase IIIa	System:
Animal crackers	Milk		VI-3 minutes
Juice			Edible
Cookies			
Magazines			

Behavior Target:	*Functional Equivalent Alternative Behavior:*
Self-injurious behavior	Break

Figure 12.1   (continued)

Arrival at School

The day begins by assisting the students off the bus and bringing them inside. This may seem like an easy venture for many, but some children have a very difficult time with transitions. Teaching begins as soon as the students step onto school grounds because some have a difficult time getting off the bus, and many others need to be prompted to walk to the classroom.

Each staff member is responsible for two different students each day. They bring reinforcers, the reinforcer menu, and the students' token cards out to the buses. Staff begin by asking their students what they want to work for.

As a way of promoting generalization, we vary staff-student assignments daily. Once all know their assignments for the day, we begin the morning routine. Every staff person also has a special job each morning. One puts together the students' pictorial schedule boards, another fills the reinforcer trays, and one sets up the first activity. The last thing I do before greeting the students at the bus is to turn on the **audio reinforcer reminder tape (ARRT).** Now we are ready to collect the children from the buses.

Today, I am working with Mark and Gary. Ms. J, one paraprofessional, is guiding Steven and Doug; Mr. B, the other paraprofessional, assists Robert and Abby. Since Mark has difficulty making the transition from the bus to the classroom, I begin with **"let's make a deal"** as soon as I reach the bus. I bring out a few of Mark's powerful reinforcers; ask him to choose one, and then begin the lesson. Mark chooses chips. I want to make sure that he is successful, so I begin by rewarding him with a small piece of a chip once he steps off the bus. Then, using a countdown timer, I keep rewarding him every six seconds (using a countdown timer) for walking next to me. Should he drop to the ground, as he often does, I remind him by displaying the chip—the item he is working for. Once he starts to walk again, I reset the timer for six seconds. If he runs out of the area, I then **backstep** by guiding him to the last spot where he was walking appropriately. I then display the chip and reset the timer for six seconds.

Since Gary, Steven, and Doug needed many prompts to walk to the classroom, we begin "let's make a deal" with them as well. Gary, who needs to earn a total of four tokens, receives his first as soon as he steps off the bus, the second halfway to the school, the third once he enters the school, and the fourth once he enters the classroom.

Steven and Doug, who need to earn five tokens, earn their first one by entering the school building; the second for entering the classroom; the third for hanging their book bags on the hooks, and the fourth for placing their home/school books on my desk in the basket. Abby and Robert walk to the class independently.

(Note: The ARRT is running throughout the entire day.)

Morning Routine

Once the students are inside the classroom, they must complete the first routine of the day. This includes taking off and hanging up their coats (if needed), hanging up their book bags, and getting their home/school books out and placing them in the basket on the teacher's desk. The last step is to go to the schedule board and see what the first activity of the day will be.

This routine should be taught without verbal prompts because verbal prompts may be extremely hard to fade. Therefore, in the beginning, when we need to, we use gestural and/or full physical prompts to finish this routine.

Mark continues with "let's make a deal" once he has entered the classroom. He is operating on a 1:1 reinforcement schedule for this activity, receiving a reward after each step of the routine. For example, I hold up a piece of a chip while Mark gets his home/school book out. Once the book is out of his book bag, I give him the chip. After he puts the home/school book in the basket on my desk, I give him another piece of a chip.

Since Gary was able to "cash in" his tokens for a reward when he entered the classroom, I then restart a deal with him. (Each time a student cashes out, the staff member has the student pick a reinforcer from a menu of pictures prior to beginning the next lesson.) Gary needs partial physical prompting to hang up his coat and book bag and full physical prompting to open his book bag. At this point he is able to get his home/school bag out independently, and I just gesture for him to approach my desk. Gary takes his home/school book out of his book bag, but this time he throws it on the floor. I gesture to him to pick up the home/school book, place it back into his book bag, and have him try again (**backstepping**). As he is pulling the book out of his book bag, I physically guide him to hold onto the book and begin to walk with him toward my desk. He completes the rest of the routine independently.

Steven and Doug both are continuing to earn their tokens during this routine. Doug is trying to open his book bag. Suddenly, he scratches Ms. J She immediately has Doug complete a "pickup"[2] task as a consequence of his aggression. (This plan has been discussed with all team members and is in place consistently during the day. Doug gets very frustrated during difficult tasks. The **functionally equivalent alternative behavior [FEAB]** we are teaching is *requesting help*.) While Doug is finishing the pickup procedure, Ms. J places his communication book[3] on the table by the coat hooks. Since it is apparent he is already agitated, she also places the "I want" icon on the sentence strip to enable Doug to have a better chance of succeeding on his next step. As soon as Doug completes the pickup procedure, he is directed back to complete the same task. Anticipating his frustration, Mr. B helps by physically prompting Doug to place the visual symbol for "help" on his sentence strip and then hand the sentence strip to Ms. J Doug reads it as he points to the pictures "I want help." Ms. J complies before Doug has the chance to become further frustrated. (Had Doug scratched the staff member again before he delivered the help card, the staff member would have repeated the pick-up procedure.) Because of his **contextually inappropriate behavior (CIB),** Doug does not earn his last token this time, but he still has the opportunity to earn it next time the ARRT sounds.

Steven and Robert independently complete the routine and earn their last tokens. Meanwhile, Abby is becoming upset while trying to get her home/school book out of her book bag. She starts to slap her face. Mr. B holds her hands down briefly for 10 seconds (Brief hand immobilization—this also is a behavior intervention that has been discussed and reviewed with all staff. The FEAB is "requesting help.") After the 10-second hand immobilization is complete, Abby is directed back to finish the task of removing her homework book from her bag. Because Ms. J wants Abby to be successful with requesting help and avoid any further frustration, she positions Abby's communication book on the table conveniently next to the coat hooks. She also places the "I want" icon on her sentence strip. Now Ms. J prompts Abby to place the visual symbol for "help" on the sentence strip and then hand the sentence strip to Mr. B She reads it as Abby points to the pictures. The girl does this without any additional problems. Mr. B helps her get her book out of her bag, and Abby completes the rest of the routine independently.

---

[2]This procedure requires the student to pick up 10 Popsicle sticks (one at a time) and place them into a container.

[3]All students in this classroom are using the PECS. If you are unfamiliar with PECS, refer to L. Frost and A. Bondy, *The Picture Exchange Communication System Training Manual* (Newark, DE: Pyramid Publications, 2000). I will refer to specific phases of PECS throughout the text as outlined in Chapter 5.

> ### Check Schedule—Bathroom/Waiting
>
> After putting home/school books on my desk, each student goes to his schedule board to see what the first thing on his day will be. It is bathroom. During this activity, each student sits in a "waiting" chair with a **wait card** and **wait toys.** The ARRT is running, and when the tone sounds, students receive reinforcement for "nice waiting." Mark and Gary are still learning which pictures represent each activity, so they do not have a schedule board yet. Instead, they are following picture directions.

Abby, Robert, Steven, and Doug all walk over to their pictorial **schedule board** and change the pictures to "bathroom." Abby, Steven, and Doug all sit in a waiting chair. Robert decides to explore the other side of the classroom. Mr. B guides him back to his schedule, has him again place the bathroom picture in the square marked "current activity," and physically leads him to a wait chair (backstepping).

Mark and Gary both are given a picture representing "bathroom" and told, "Go here." They are both led to the bathroom, where a larger version of the bathroom picture is attached to the door with Velcro. I physically prompt each student to place his own bathroom picture on the bigger one. I then announce that it is time for bathroom. Mark uses the bathroom first while Gary holds a wait card along with the others.

During this time, the ARRT is running, and each student earns a token for sitting appropriately. Those who are not in their seats when the timer goes off are shown a token to indicate what they did not earn during this time period and are reminded that they can try again. Once students earn all their tokens, they can cash them

> ### Check Schedule
>
> After all students use the bathroom, they go to their schedule boards to see what is next. It is breakfast.

in for their rewards. When the tape beeps, Mark receives his reward: his favorite collection of plastic animals to play with for a while. Everyone else receives a token. Steven, Abby, Robert, and Doug go to their schedule boards, change them, and move independently to breakfast. Mark and Gary are again given a picture of "breakfast" and told, "Go here." There will be an enlarged picture of breakfast on the table in the kitchen area. At this time, I am able to give the picture to both Mark and Gary and can fade my prompting about halfway to the table.

Abby, Robert, Steven, and Doug have reached the stage in PECS when they are learning to structure sentences (Phase IV). They are all working on following picture directions. Doug gets out of his seat and puts the sentence strip "I want cereal" into my hands. He points to the pictures as he reads them aloud. I say, "Okay." I then give him a picture of "bowl," then say, "Get this," and then lead him over to where the bowls are located and have him match the picture in his hand to the picture in front of the pile of bowls. I then prompt him to pick up a bowl while saying, "Bowl." Doug then walks back to his seat. I give him the box of cereal, which he sets to work opening and pouring into the bowl.

Breakfast

Breakfast is next. Student's work on requesting food items, asking for needed help, following picture directions, and appropriate eating skills. Food items are at the end of the table. On the counter by the kitchen sink, are a pile of plates, cups, and bowls, also baskets containing forks, knives, and spoons. In front of each set of items on the counter is a picture of the item. The staff have corresponding pictures at the table. They will use these for teaching picture direction following.

Abby has caught on very quickly to the breakfast routine and following the picture directions. She requests juice from Mr. B ("I want juice") using her sentence strip. Mr. B gives her the juice and then walks away. Abby proceeds to get up and independently get a cup from the counter. Because she has mastered this skill rapidly, we were able quickly to fade out the picture direction and any prompting. She brings the cup back and tries to open the juice bottle. Noting the difficulty she is encountering, Ms. J prompts her to hand the juice container over to Mr. B Mr. B says, "I want help," and opens the container for Abby and gives her a small amount in her cup. He then replaces the lid. A few seconds later, Abby requests juice again. Mr. B hands her the juice bottle. Abby picks it up and gives it right back to Mr. B, who says, "I want help," and opens it. The sequence is repeated. Before the next trial, Mr. B tells the other paraprofessional that he wants Abby now to learn to give him the "help" card after she hands him the juice bottle. So, on the next instance that Abby requests juice from Mr. B, he gives her the bottle of juice, and Abby hands the bottle back to him. Immediately, Ms. J physically prompts Abby to put the help card on her sentence strip, so it reads "I want help" and has her give it to Mr. B Mr. B reads the sentence strip as Abby points to the pictures and he then opens the bottle for her.

Steven gets out of his chair and requests cereal ("I want cereal") using his sentence strip. I give him the picture of bowl and say, "Get this." He walks over to the counter and gets the wrong item. I backstep him to the table and give him the picture for bowl again, repeating the direction "Get this." I then follow him to the counter and guide him to the correct picture and pile of items. Steven proceeds to take the bowl back to the table. He opens the box, pours the cereal into the bowl, and then looks about for a spoon. I give him a picture of the spoon, and he successfully retrieves it. At this point Ms. J begins to work with Steven on his appropriate eating skills.

Robert also has mastered this routine and is at the point where I am "sabotaging" the activity (as a way of encouraging him to initiate a request). After requesting cereal and getting his bowl, he proceeds to look for a spoon at the counter. I have put the spoons away and am working on Robert's asking for an item that is not there. As he is looking for a spoon, Mr. B places his communication book on the counter with a spoon picture on the front of the book. He gestures to the spoon picture, and Robert puts together the sentence ("I want spoon") and hands it to him. Robert points to the pictures as Mr. B reads it. Mr. B then gets a spoon for him.

Mark and Gary are both working on **traveling**[5], and are also beginning Phase III (nonpreferred vs. preferred choices) of PECS. Today I am going to work with Mark on traveling and with Gary on discrimination. I slowly begin to increase my distance each time Mark requests juice. By the end of breakfast, he is walking around the table to find me, holding the picture of juice in his hand. He successfully finds my hand and places the picture into it. Gary is working on discrimination.

Check Schedule
After breakfast the students move to their schedule boards to see what is next on their day.

At the conclusion of breakfast, a timer rings, signaling the conclusion of breakfast. Now it is time to check schedules. Mark, Gary, and Steven are to brush their teeth; Doug, Robert, and Abby are to change for gym. (Tomorrow Mark, Gary, and Steven will change at this time, and Doug, Robert, and Abby will brush teeth.) Following a gesture to his schedule board, Steven then moves independently to the shelf to get his basket of items. He then proceeds to the waiting chairs by the bathroom.

Gary and Mark both are given a picture of "brush teeth" and told, "Get this." They are then both prompted to their baskets and then to the waiting chairs. (Each of the six students has a distinctively colored picture and background. These correspond to duplicates of their distinctive pictures and colored backgrounds mounted on the basket of items.)

Brushing Teeth/Waiting
Students are at different levels of learning to brush their teeth. They earn tokens for "waiting" and are given a choice of wait items to play with at this time. A clipboard with data sheets is hanging in the bathroom. (Data should be collected at least once a week on each objective.)

Mark earns a token for wetting his toothbrush and placing it in his mouth. He has not brushed his teeth for many years and is very resistant to having a brush in his mouth. Our plan is **desensitization.**

While Mark is brushing his teeth, Gary is waiting. When the ARRT sounds, Gary earns a token. Now he is next in line to brush his teeth. I am working on teaching him this skill by using **backward chaining.** I physically guide him gently through all the steps of the task analysis until the last step and begin by teaching at this final step first (throwing the paper towel into the trash can). A gesture serves successfully to prompt him to discard the paper towel appropriately.

Steven has earned two tokens for waiting. I am using a **prompt hierarchy** to teach him the skill of brushing teeth. At this time the only hint he needs is a gesture to begin completing the sequence. He has done well learning this objective.

---

[5]Increasing the distance between the student and the teacher.

> **Dressing**
>
> While I have been teaching the other three to brush their teeth, Doug, Robert, and Abby are working on dressing skills. They are to change into sweatpants, a T-shirt, and different socks. Today, Ms. J and Mr. B split the group between them.

Meanwhile, Doug, Robert and Steven have independently changed their schedules to *dressing* and are proceeding to collect their clothes basket from the shelf. All three students have their reinforcer cards and communication books with them. Ms. J asks Doug and Robert to choose what they will work for. Doug picks raisins, and Robert chooses photographs. Mr. B asks Henry what he is working for, and he picks celery. The ARRT is running, and students are earning tokens or edibles for dressing or undressing when the timer sounds.

Doug brings his basket to the changing area. He starts to kick the baskets of clothes. Ms. J moves the basket away from him, gestures to his reinforcer card, and also holds up a raisin for Doug to see. Doug begins to take his shoes off. (As Doug begins to get undressed, Ms. J asks Mr. B to prompt a *break* after the boy has taken off both shoes.) Once his shoes are off, Mr. B physically guides Doug to pick up the break card and hand it to Ms. J She, in turn, says, "I want a break. Go ahead." Doug leaves the changing area and sits in his break chair. He sets the timer for two minutes and proceeds to look at a magazine. When the timer goes off, Ms. J reminds Doug what he is working for, and Doug returns to the changing area. He continues to get undressed. After he has taken his socks and pants off, Mr. B again prompts him to hand the break card to Ms. J The same sequence is repeated. After his second break, Doug completes the remainder of the activity without a problem. He does need gestures and partial physical prompting to put clothes on. (We remember to not prompt orally.) Doug earns tokens only when he is working on his dressing skills. He does not earn any tokens during break time.

During the time that Doug is requesting breaks, Robert is successfully undressing and putting on his "gym" clothes. Each time the ARRT sounds, he is earns his tokens.

Mr. B is working on dressing with Abby, a student who becomes upset very easily during this task. Abby begins to take off her shoes and socks. Then, as she tries to undo the fasteners on her pants, she shows some small signs of exasperation. (Mr. B quickly asks Ms. J to prompt Abby to request help. To ensure success, Ms. J places the "I want" stationary on the sentence strip.) Ms. J physically prompts Abby to pick up the visual symbol for "help," place it on the sentence strip, and give the sentence strip to Mr. B Mr. B, in turn, says, "I want help," as Abby points to the pictures, and Mr. B helps Abby with the fasteners. Abby again begins to have the same difficulty when putting her shoes on. The same sequence is repeated here. In both instances Abby's growing frustration has been detected soon enough to avert a tantrum. The staff have been able to anticipate her need for help. Abby earns tokens for undressing and dressing when the timer sounds.

She has earned all her tokens and is able to cash them in for celery.

A timer rings, signaling the end of that activity. Abby, Robert, and Doug independently move to their

Check Schedule

schedule and change it to the next event. Steven needs a gesture, and Mark and Gary are given pictures of gym and told, "Go here." They both hold the picture of "gym" as they walk from the classroom to the gym. Since Mark has difficulty walking in the hallways, he is rewarded every six seconds for staying with the group. (If he runs out of the area, he is brought back to the spot where he was last walking.) There is a larger version for the picture of gym velcroed to the gym door. Mark and Gary are able independently to match the picture in their hands to the picture on the door.

Students begin gym class by choosing what they want to work for. All students except Mark and Gary use pictures to choose the order. Since Mark and Gary are not discriminating pictures yet, they use three-dimensional objects. Both have a choice card containing four squares. Within the squares, he places a small object: a small ball in the first box for "throwing balls," a scooter in the second box for gross motor work on the scooters; a soccer ball in the third square for "kicking balls," and a "Barbie bike/small bike" in the fourth square for "riding bikes." This helps the two boys see what they have to do and in what order. Yes, there is an ARRT running in gym class too. Everyone earns tokens and/or snacks when the tone sounds.

> **Gym**
>
> Communication books, reinforcers, and reinforcer menus are brought to the gym. During gym, students are assigned four activities. Each student can choose the order in which these are completed.

In a tone different from that associated with the ARRT, a timer beeps to signal the completion of gym.

Doug, Robert, and Abby change their schedules independently and move to the chairs where their clothing baskets have been placed. Mark and Gary are given a picture of "puzzles" and told, "Go here." Mark is rewarded every six seconds for walk-

> **Check Schedule**
>
> Students gather their communication books and walk back to the classroom.

ing with the group in the hallway. They walk back to the classroom and need only a gesture to go to the table where the puzzles are. Steven changes his schedule independently and walks to the puzzle table.

All students change back into their school clothes without any disturbances, each earning tokens or tangible rewards when the timer sounds. Doug, Robert, and Abby change back into their "school" clothes. Steven, Mark and Gary work on puzzles until dressing is finished. If they are off task (just sitting; not dressing or working with a puzzle) when the timer rings, they are shown a token or edible and told

> **Dressing/Puzzles**
>
> Students change back into their school clothes. They earn tokens for getting dressed and undressed when the timer sounds.

to try again. During this time Doug spontaneously requests help ("I want help!"). After placing the sentence strip into Ms. J's hand, Doug orally reads the sentence as he points to the pictures. She complies immediately.

A timer sounds to signal the end of dressing and puzzles. Mark and Gary are given a picture of "circle" and told, "Go here." Both need a gesture to the circle area, and

> **Check Schedule**

both are able to match their picture with the larger version on the wall. Robert, Steven, and Abby change independently and sit in a chair for the circle activity. The ARRT runs throughout circle time. Robert's schedule is a variable interval (VI) 5-minute. He can receive a token when the timer rings. Gary's schedule is a VI 3-minute and he receives edibles at the sound of the timer. Each schedule is paired with a distinctive tone. The others are operating on a VI 3-minute schedule.

Circle Activities

Dressing "Alvin" for the Day
The students are asked to choose the correct color item, for example, when presented with two shirts, one red and one green. I have also interchanged this with *matching* the red shirt to the red shirt Alvin already is wearing.

Requesting a Song to Sing
An activity board contains the pictures of the songs. The board has an "I want" picture and sentence strip on one side but can easily be turned over to allow fewer pictures to be presented to those students still working on simpler discrimination.

Jobs for the Day/Name Recognition
There are six jobs: light helper (turns lights off when we leave the classroom), line leader, caboose, messenger (takes messages to other staff), teacher's helper, and recess helper (helps take balls and toys out to recess). Student names are posted on the board. Each child places the job description next to his or her name. Velcro is attached to each name card to permit varying the cards' positions. This helps avoid student's attending to the irrelevant aspect; the card's location.

Imitation
Students learn to imitate actions during the songs sung in circle.

I begin by letting the students request songs. Steven asks for "The Wheels on the Bus." He then uses the pictures on the activity board to request which action he would like to do first. He chooses "blinking lights." As soon as we all start to sing this song, Abby puts her hands over her ears. At this point Mr. B prompts Abby to pick up the "break" card and hand it to me. I then say, " I want a break." Abby leaves circle and sits in a break chair on the other side of the room. Abby does not like loud noise. Covering her ears with her hands is the first hint that a tantrum might follow. From experience we know her behavior would escalate next to slapping her ears and face. Abby's timer is preset for 2 minutes. All she has to do when she goes to the break area is push the button. The timer will then begin to count down to zero. When the timer goes off, Abby usually comes back to the present activity. Today the timer goes off, and she does not move out of break. Mr. B walks over to the break area with the reinforcer card in hand to remind her what she is working for. Abby stands up and walks back to group.

Next Robert requests "If You're Happy and You Know It." He puts the sentence "I want to sing 'If You're Happy and You Know It'" and hands it to me. I read it as he points to the pictures. While the staff sings the song, sometimes joined by Doug, the students are working on imitating our actions. Robert, Steven, Gary, and Abby are able to do at least a portion of each action. To earn a token, they must be imitating when the ARRT sounds.

Mark has difficulty sitting for long periods of time at circle. He is able to wander around the classroom, although he has no access to reinforcers at this time. To earn them, he would need to spend at least five minutes in the circle. I will prompt him to come to circle and participate in the last five minutes. (In the beginning of the year, Mark would come to the last 5 to 10 seconds of circle and be asked to do just one thing. He has now worked up to staying for five minutes.)

Students next work on **name identification.** I give the job of "line leader" to Steven. He should place it next to his name, but he misplaces it, next to Robert's name instead. At this point I use the **4-Step switch error correction procedure: model-prompt-switch-repeat.**

Doug reaches over and scratches my arm. Ms. J removes him from circle and has him perform the "pickup" procedure. After he completes this and returns to group, I give him his job, and he places it next to his name. When Doug returns to his seat, Ms. J physically guides him to hand me the break card. I respond by saying, "I want a break. Go ahead." Doug walks over to the break area, sets the timer, and looks at a magazine, *not* a powerful reinforcer for him. When the timer goes off, he returns to circle independently.

The final circle activity today is dressing Alvin, a felt doll. Students need to follow color identification directions, such as "Take the red shirt and place it on Alvin." Everyone succeeds. At this time, Mark is brought over to circle. He sits and participates

| **Check schedule** |

for the remaining five minutes. I set the timer to ring to signal the end of circle.

Abby, Steven, Robert, and Doug all go to their schedules and change them independently. They each then move to the designated center indicated on their schedule card.

Centers

Each day students rotate through three **centers,** devoted to communication, functional academics, or structured play. A staff member has been assigned to each.

Within the **communication center,** students work on activities designed to increase communication skills.

At the **functional academics center,** students focus on individual goals within functional activities.

Structured play involves teaching the students color identification, counting, how to appropriately play with toys, and how to imitate.

The centers last approximately 15 to 20 minutes.

For the centers activity, students are paired as follows: Mark and Gary, Abby and Steven, and Robert and Doug. Ms. J is running the structured play center, Mr. B is in charge of the communication center, and I am heading the functional academic station. Students are shown a picture of their center and told, "Go Here." Each needs minimal prompting to go to the designated location.

Center Rotation 1

Communication Center

Once the students get to their appropriate centers, the activities start. Mark and Gary begin at the **communication center.** Today they will continue to work on **discrimination skills.** During this time, an array of reinforcing items is displayed from which they may choose. If they make mistakes, then Mr. B will conduct the 4-step error correction procedure. There are many interesting items for each child to request. Both behave very well because of the reinforcing nature of the activity.

Functional Academic Center

In the **functional academics center,** each pair of students is going to work on one of the following: set table for lunch (following directions involving numbers and colors and setting table), making apple juice, and making grape juice (follow picture directions, object identification, and following one-step directions). Now Abby and Steven are present. I begin by showing them both a reinforcer menu to find out what they want to work for. Abby chooses candy. She places the picture of candy on her reinforcer card. Steven chooses "trains" and also places the corresponding picture on his reinforcer card.

Both are still learning the picture directions for making apple juice. The necessary items are a spoon, a pitcher, and an apple juice concentrate can. I give a picture of "pitcher" to Abby and say, "Get this." I then **shadow** her (follow right behind without touching her) over to where the pitcher is kept. She opens the cabinet and takes the pitcher out. (There is a picture of "pitcher" velcroed to the outside of the cabinet door.) I verbally label "pitcher" as she picks up the item. She then brings it back to the table. The ARRT sounds, and both students are on task, so both receive a token.

Next I give Steven a picture of "spoon." The spoons are in the same place as they were for breakfast. There is also a picture of "spoon" in front of the basket of spoons. Steven has learned its location but walks over to the counter and gets a fork. I backstep him to the table where I gave the direction. I again say, "Get this," and shadow him back to the counter. As he reaches for a basket, I direct him to match the "spoon" picture to the one already there. He proceeds to pick up a spoon. I label it aloud, and he returns to the table with the spoon. The ARRT sounds, and both students earn a token for on-task behavior.

I give the last picture direction to Steven. I hand him the picture of an "apple juice can" and say, "Get this." I then lead him to the refrigerator where the can is stored. I gesture for him to open the refrigerator and point to the can. I label the item as he picks it up. He brings it back to the table.

Next both students make the juice. I ask Abby to open the can. *Help* is a lesson that I am teaching her. As this part of the activity approaches, I quickly signal Mr. B to prompt Abby to hand me the "help" card. Mr. B leaves his center briefly to assist. Abby does hand the juice container to me, and then Mr. B prompts her to put the "I want" and the "help" cards on her sentence strip. Abby hands the sentence strip to me and points to the pictures as I read it. I then help her open the can.

After the can is open, Abby pours the concentrate into the pitcher. I give her the verbal direction "Throw away." Abby walks to the trash can and throws away the empty juice can. The ARRT sounds, and both students receive a token.

Steven's last job is to add water to the pitcher. I have drawn a red line inside the pitcher to signify where to stop. Steven takes the pitcher over to the sink and fills it with water. I give him the verbal direction, "Give the pitcher to Abby." I then give **partial prompts** to help him give the pitcher to Abby. Abby completes the activity by stirring the mixture. The ARRT sounds, and both students earn tokens for on-task behavior as well as having time to drink some juice.

Once this activity is finished, both students work on the recreation/leisure task, *puzzles*. The ARRT sounds, and both students earn a token for on-task behavior. At this point, Steven and Abby have earned all five required tokens and "cash in" for their reward.

Throughout this center activity, I have been taking data on the objectives. The clipboard is on the table, and each student has a separate lesson plan for which data are collected. I indicate the prompt level needed for following a picture direction and a "+" or "−" for following a verbal direction.

Structured Play Center

Meanwhile, Robert and Doug have begun with Ms. J in the **structured play center.** Today they are playing with the garage, airport, and wooden blocks. Ms. J begins by showing both students a **reinforcer menu.** Each student chooses what he wants to work for. Robert chooses photos; Doug chooses music.

Ms. J begins by working on color identification and counting with the wooden blocks. She holds out a red and yellow block and says to Robert, "Take the red block." Robert chooses correctly. She then holds a red and blue block in front of Doug and says, "Take the blue block." Doug's choice is incorrect, so Ms. J goes through the four-step error correction procedure with him. She continues this activity until both students have built half their tower.

Ms. J then begins to ask the students to take a certain number of blocks. She puts a handful of blocks in a pile on the floor and says to Robert, "Take two blocks." Robert takes three blocks, so Ms. J takes him through the error correction procedure.

Ms. J has a clipboard with her that holds the plans corresponding to the lesson she is teaching. As they work, she collects data on each objective. The lesson plan states the rate at which the student is supposed to be rewarded for this skill. Robert and Doug are both getting rewarded for each correct response. Each time they are correct, they are to earn a token (**continuous reinforcement schedule**). Both students are earning tokens toward their chosen reinforcer during this activity. Therefore, even though the ARRT has been running throughout, Ms. J's rate of reinforcing correct responses is so high that she does not give the boys tokens for remaining on task. Doug and Robert both earn all five tokens and are able to "cash in" for their rewards.

Center Rotation 2

Students now rotate to their next center. Steven and Abby go to the communication center, Mark and Gary to the structured play center, and Robert and Doug to the functional academic center. The objectives for these students while in the communication center are requesting, using attributes, and commenting. Since we know that the first activity is sufficiently reinforcing for both students, they are not using their reinforcer cards at this time.

Mr. B brings out the container that hold a little and big version of Mr. Potato Head. Steven begins by handing the sentence strip to Mr. B Mr. B begins to read the phrase "I want big" as Steven points to the icons. Mr. B then pauses after "big" to see whether Steven will finish the sentence (**constant delayed prompt**). Steven verbally reads "Potato Head." He then requests, "I want big arm," in the same way. Abby begins by requesting, "I want little potato head." She then continues with "I want little ear." On her third turn she requests, "I want two little arms and little eyes." Mr. B is delighted that Abby has independently put together this sophisticated sentence.

Steven continues by requesting, "I want two big arms and two big ears." Mr. B again lets Steven verbally fill in the words "arms" and "ears." Both students continue to request until each Mr. Potato Head is complete. The next communication activity requires Mr. B to see what each student wants to work for. He shows the reinforcer menu to Steven, who chooses trains. Abby selects celery. Now Mr. B is able to continue with his lesson.

Mr. B is introducing a **commenting** lesson to both students. His goal is to promote spontaneous commenting, so he really needs to have the students noting new and different things. Before the students arrived at school today, he has strategically placed items around the building. He takes the students out of the classroom to comment on those items.

Mr. B has placed needed vocabulary in each child's communication book. Both bring their books with them as they go for a walk around the school building. The first item they come to is an airplane hanging from the ceiling. Mr. B points to the airplane and says, "What do you see?" This is not the first lesson the students have had with commenting, so they both know how to respond to this question. Steven puts together the sentence strip "I see airplane." He hands it to Mr. B, and Mr. B reads, "I see," as Steven verbally reads "airplane." Mr. B, in turn, gives Steven a token. Abby also has put together the same sentence and hands it to Mr. B, who reads it as Abby points to the pictures. Abby also receives a token.

The students continue to wander through the hallways with their teacher. Each turn presents something different to comment about: spider, alligator, horse, and dragon. Each student earns a token for correctly commenting. After each student has earned five tokens, everyone returns to the classroom to cash out for their rewards.

Within my functional academic center, Robert and Doug work on making grape juice. They both choose a reinforcer before the activity for *following directions* begins.

I begin by giving Robert a picture of "spoon," saying, "Get this." Robert walks over to the counter and picks up a spoon and brings it back to the table. Next I give Doug a picture of "pitcher" and say," Get this." I then physically lead him to the cabinet where the pitcher is kept, help him open the cabinet, and retrieve the pitcher. The VI 3-minute ARRT sounds, and Doug receives a token.

Before I give the next direction to Doug, I notice that he is becoming slightly agitated. He has been working a while now during center time and has not been prompted to take a break. He is still learning how to request a break, so he does need to be prompted at this time. I signal to Ms. J to help Doug pick up the break card and hand it to me. After he hands it to me, I say, "I want a break. Go ahead." Doug walks over to the break chair and sets his timer for two minutes. When the timer sounds, he comes back to the activity. I remind him what he is working for and give him the picture of "grape juice" along with the direction "Get this." I again physically guide Doug to the refrigerator but then stop and allow him to open the refrigerator and get the can of concentrate juice. He then brings it back to the table. The VI 3-minute ARRT sounds and Doug earns his second token. When the VI 5-minute ARRT sounds Robert receives his first token.

I hand the can of concentrated grape juice to Robert and ask him to open it. He tries but is not able. (He has mastered requesting help.) Robert hands the can back to me and puts the sentence "I want help juice" together and hands it to me. I read it as he points to the pictures. I then open the can for him.

After Robert pours the concentrate into the pitcher, I instruct him, "Throw away." Robert begins to walk to the trash can but then something in another center catches his eye. He walks off in that direction. I silently guide him back to the table, give him the direction again, and then shadow him as he walks toward the trashcan (backstepping).

The VI 5-minute ARRT sounds, but Robert does not receive a token because of his recent exit from the area. I show him the token and remind him that he can try to earn it again. The VI 3-minute ARRT sounds and Doug receives his third token. I give Robert the verbal direction "Give the pitcher to Doug." Robert passes the pitcher to Doug. The last step is for Doug to fill the pitcher with water. I give him a picture of "water" and lead him to the faucet. There is a line in the pitcher that signals where to stop. I shadow Doug to the faucet, where he independently turns the water on and fills the pitcher. The VI 5-minute ARRT sounds, and Robert receives his second token. Doug brings the pitcher back to the table and both Robert and Doug take turns stirring. The VI 3-minute ARRT sounds and Doug receives his fourth token. Just like the previous group, both students get a small glass of juice after they complete the activity.

In the structured play center, Ms. J is working with Mark and Gary. She begins by asking each student what he wants to work for. Mark chooses chips; Gary chooses pretzels. Again Ms. J is going to ignore the ARRT and reinforce for correct responses. Both these students are moving toward using a reinforcer card. They are at the beginning stages of learning "Let's Make a Deal." Soon I will start them both on reinforcer cards. Right now they are receiving direct reinforcement, in the form of an edible, for correct responses.

Ms. J begins by working on imitation skills. She has the garage and airport on the floor, along with toy cars and airplanes. She chose these two activities because she knows that Mark loves toy cars and Gary loves airplanes. She wants to make this functional for both students.

Ms. J starts to push a car down the garage ramp. She asks Mark to do the same. He does and thus is rewarded with a chip. She then lets Mark play for a short time by himself as she works with Gary. Ms. J "flies" the airplane around in the air above the airport. She prompts Gary to do the same. He does and is rewarded accordingly. Ms. J directs her attention back to Mark where she begins to put gas from the gas pump in her toy car. She gestures to Mark to do the same. He does and is rewarded.

Gary appears to be getting a little frustrated because Ms. J keeps interrupting his "own" play. He starts to bite his hand the next time Ms. J tries to interrupt him. Ms. J follows the procedure in place for this behavior. Accordingly, as previously decided by the team, she holds his hands down for 10 seconds. The functionally equivalent alternative behavior (FEAB) that is being taught is "requesting a break."

After the procedure is over, Ms. J directs Gary to imitate her action. (During the procedure, she asks me to prompt a break as soon as Gary has imitated one action.) As soon as Gary complies, I physically prompt him to hand the break card over to Ms. J She, in turn, says, "I want a break. Go ahead." Gary walks over to the break area, sets his timer for minutes, and sits and looks at a magazine (not a powerful reinforcer). When the timer sounds, Gary sits in his chair and does not move. Ms. J walks over to him, reinforcer in hand, to remind him of what he is working for. Gary sees the reinforcer and independently walks back to the structured play center.

Gary is calmer and imitates the actions that Ms. J demonstrates. He earns his reward with each correct imitation. Mark also is imitating Ms. J's actions very well and is rewarded for each act he correctly imitates.

Center Rotation 3

Each group now rotates to the last center. Steven and Abby are now at the structured play, Mark and Gary are at the functional academics, and Robert and Doug are at the functional communication center. Mr. B's station (communication) begins with a reinforcing activity, so there is no need for reinforcer cards at this time. He opens a box full of different kinds of candy. There are different shapes, sizes, colors, and types. Mr. B also has an activity board that contains the entire needed vocabulary.

Robert starts by requesting, "I want one red fish candy." He hands the sentence strip to Mr. B and points to the pictures as Mr. B reads them. Doug begins by requesting, "I want two circle purple candy." He also hands over the sentence strip to Mr. B and says the words "purple candy" after Mr. B reads, "I want two circle." Both students continue to use very long sentences to make their requests.

Before the start of the next activity, Mr. B asks both students what they want to work for. He is going to ignore the ARRT during this time and reinforce correct responses instead. He shows the boys a reinforcer menu, and Robert chooses photos, while Doug chooses chips. Within this activity, both students will comment on what people are doing in pictures. To make the activity "novel," Mr. B brought in a magazine from home and is going to have them comment on pictures within it. Both Robert and Doug are learning pronouns, verbs, and objects. An activity board containing the entire essential vocabulary is available.

The first picture is of a man riding a bike. Mr. B asks Robert, "Tell me about the picture." Robert constructs the sentence, "He riding bike." (Each "word" is a picture.) Mr. B continues to ask questions to each student and each student, does well with this activity. Eventually Mr. B begins to fade out his question. At the end of the activity, each student cashes out for his reward.

Within my functional academics center, Mark and Gary are going to work on setting the table. I ask each student what he wants to work for. Mark chooses chips; Gary chooses pretzels. I begin by giving Mark the verbal direction "Get six place mats." Mark picks up six mats and then begins to place them in front of each chair at the table.

The ARRT sounds and each student receives a small edible treat.

I verbally direct Mark to "get three red cups." Mark picks up two red cups. I use the 4-step to correct this error. Mark chooses the right number of cups on the last step of the procedure and continues to place the cups above the plates at the table. I follow this with another verbal direction, "Mark, get three blue cups." Mark gets three blue cups and places them at the top of the remaining plates.

The ARRT sounds, and both students receive an edible.

The next direction given is to Gary. I tell him, "Get four forks." He gets the correct amount, and then I point to the place they go next to the plates. I ask Mark, "Get two forks," but he gets three instead. Again, I use the 4-Step error correction procedure. Once Mark gets it right, I gesture toward the spot where they need to be placed.

The ARRT sounds, and both students receive an edible.

I give the next direction to Mark, "Get five knives." Mark obtains the correct amount and also places them where they belong next to the plates. I tell Gary, "Get one knife." He does, and I need only point to where it goes next to the plate.

The last direction involves the spoons. I tell Mark, "Get two spoons." He does, and I use a gesture to show him where they are to be placed next to the knife. I then tell Gary, "Get four spoons." His counting skills also are correct, and all he needs is a gesture to prompt him to place them next to the knives.

The ARRT sounds, and both students receive an edible for nice work.

During this entire activity, I have been collecting data on each student's counting skills.

Ms. J is running her final structured play center for the day. She begins by asking what Steven and Abby would like to work for. Steven chooses trains; Abby chooses celery. Again Ms. J is going to ignore the ARRT and reinforce for correct responses.

Today Ms. J will work on color identification and counting. She begins by holding a red block and a blue block out to Steven and saying, "Take the red block." Steven is correct in his response and earns a token. She then turns to Abby, holds out a blue block and a green block, and says, "Take the green block." Abby, now earning a token for every two correct responses, also responds correctly. So Ms. J continues by holding out a red and yellow block, saying, "Take the yellow block." Abby does and thus receives a token. She also starts to build a tower with her blocks.

Ms. J turns her attention to Steven and says to him, "Take the yellow block." Steven does, and this time Ms. J asks Steven, "Take the blue block." Steven responds correctly, thus earning a token. Steven has also started to build his tower.

Both students continue with color identification and counting skills. Each is now earning a token for every two correct responses. If they had made an error, then Ms. J would have used the 4-Step error correction procedure.

A timer sounds to signal the end of center activities.

| Check Schedule |
All students except Mark and Gary move to their schedules independently and then to the waiting chairs outside the bathroom door. Mark and Gary are given a picture of "wash hands" and told, "Go here." They are led to the bathroom, where there is a larger version of the picture for "wash hands" just outside the bathroom door. Only after an adult gestures do they place the picture in the correct spot.

Mark is first to wash his hands. I am teaching him this skill using backward chaining. I fully prompt him through all the steps of the task analysis and begin by teaching him the last step first. At this point in the year he is able to complete the last three steps independently.

> **Wash Hands**
>
> Every day before lunch, the students wash their hands. Data are collected at least one time per week on this objective. Each student holds a "wait" card and is reinforced for nice waiting during this time. Since the wait could be up to 10 minutes, each student plays with a "wait" toy. The ARRT is running during this time.

The VI 3-minute ARRT sounds and all five students earn a token. (Robert is on a VI 5-minute ARRT.) Gary is next in line. I am also using backward chaining to teach him this skill. He has mastered the last four steps. Gary returns to his seat and the VI 3 and 5-minute ARRTs sound. Everyone receives a token at this time.

It is Abby's turn. She has a tough time with this objective. As she does not like to get her hands wet, we are shaping her behavior on this objective. So Abby is rewarded as soon as the water touches her hands. In the beginning she just had to put one finger under the running water. By now she places both hands under the water for a split second.

The VI 3-minute ARRT sounds and everyone except Robert receives a token.

Robert is now washing his hands in the bathroom. He does extremely well with this objective. After he is finished, the VI 5-minute ARRT sounds and he earns a token, as he sits back in the waiting chair.

While Robert is in the bathroom, Doug begins to get out of his seat and run around the room. Just as he leaves his chair, the VI 3-minute ARRT sounds. He is reminded what he is working for. He returns to his seat, but does not receive a token and is reminded that he can try again. Doug is next in line to wash his hands. He also does very well with this objective. As he returns to his seat, the VI 3-minute ARRT sounds, and he earns a token.

Steven and Abby "cash in" for their rewards at this time. Robert still has one more token to earn. Mark and Gary are earning edibles each time the ARRT sounds.

Since Steven is working for popcorn, he eats it and continues to wash his hands. Steven is learning this skill by backward chaining. He has mastered the last two steps of the task analysis.

The VI 5 and 3-minute ARRTs sound, and Robert earns a third token. Doug earns his last token. He "cashes in" for his reward at this time. The timer sounds, indicating that hand washing is over.

Lunch

Natural instances of requesting help occur during lunch. Some students bring box juice drinks and are unable to open them or put the straw in them. Some students have bag milk and need help with puncturing the straw into the bag milk. Finally, there are the Tupperware containers that students have trouble opening.

Check Schedule

Everyone walks to his schedule and changes it to *lunch*. Now we work on students' appropriate eating skills. Also, Mr. B takes his break at this time. Steven, Robert, Doug, and Abby all walk over and retrieve their lunch boxes and bring them to the table. Mark and Gary are given pictures of "lunch" and told, "Go here." Gary walks independently to the table and matches the small picture of lunch to the larger one on the table. He then proceeds to get his lunch box. Mark wanders across the room. I backstep Mark to the waiting chairs and give the direction again. I shadow him to the table for lunch. He matches his lunch picture with the larger version on the table. I then direct him to get his lunch box.

Each student opens his or her lunch box and begins to eat. Right away, Doug has trouble opening his juice box. He starts to scratch Ms. J According to his behavior intervention plan, Ms. J immediately has him perform a "pickup." As soon as Doug returns to his seat and again grasps the juice box, I prompt him to give the box to Ms. J and put together the sentence "I want help." I prompt him to hand the sentence strip to Ms. J. He reads the sentence aloud as he points to the pictures. She proceeds to help him.

Again, Robert has become very good at independently getting needed items for his lunch. For example, yesterday when he brought soup, he knew he needed a spoon. He knows where the spoons are kept, so he left his chair and got one on his own. Today he has brought hotdogs. I heat these and cut them into pieces for him. He proceeds to go to the basket for a fork but soon realizes that there are none there. I gesture to the "fork" picture on his communication book. He puts together the sentence "I want fork." I read it as he pointed to the picture. I, in turn, give him a fork.

Steven had rice for lunch. I am now able to work on object identification with him. I hold out a fork and a spoon and said, "Take fork." He chooses the correct item, and I mark a plus on my data sheet.

| Check Schedule |

Once everyone is finished with lunch, I set a timer to sound. Waiting chairs are lined up by the door. Everyone except Mark and Gary goes to the schedule board and sees that recess is next. They sit in the waiting chairs. Mark and Gary, who are sitting in wait chairs, are given a picture of "recess" and told, "Go here." Everyone leaves the classroom and heads for the playground. As Mark and Gary approach the doors to the outside, they can see a larger version of the "recess" picture on that door. Both students independently match it and go outside. Mark needs to be rewarded every six seconds in the hallway for staying with the group.

Now back from break, Mr. B oversees recess with Ms. J while I take my break. Mr. B and Ms. J encourage students to engage themselves with the play equipment. All of the students stay on the playground as they are supposed to; nor are there any other problems. Since both assistants cannot work with all the students, they rotate the youngsters with whom they closely interact each day. To-

> **Recess**
>
> Students are encouraged to engage themselves with the play equipment. Teachers involve students in learning experiences on a rotating basis.

day Mr. B works with Mark, who really likes to swing. He is also still working on learning to discriminate. Mark and Gary are taking turns swinging. Each time it is Mark's turn he must request which item he would like. He can swing or have a pickle. (Pickles are Mark's nonpreferred item.) If Mark chooses pickle, then Mr. B is able to do the 4 Step Switch with him. If he is correct, then he gets to swing even faster because he made a correct choice.

A timer sounds and signals the conclusion of recess. Mr. B gives a picture of "bathroom" to Mark and Gary and says, "Go here." They carry the picture in hand back to the classroom with the rest of the students. In the hallway Mark needs to be rewarded every six seconds for walking with the group. Steven, Robert, Abby, and Doug change their schedule boards and walk to the waiting chairs for bathroom. During this time Ms. J takes her break. All students earn tokens for nice "waiting." Everyone uses the bathroom.

Steven, Robert, Abby, and Doug independently change their schedules and walk to the art table. Mark and Gary are given a picture of "art" and told, "Go

| Check Schedule |

here." Both students need minimal prompting. Today the students are going to make a butterfly. Each student has a section to paint and then glue on. Each section is also a different size. There are small, medium, and large pieces of paper from which to choose.

For the students, I have prepared two activity boards containing vocabulary necessary for the lesson. The pictures for the items are displayed, as are the size, number, and color. I begin by finding out that Mark and Gary are working for chips and for juice, respectively. I pass the reinforcer menu to Mr. B and begin the activity with my two students. I know that Mark and Gary both enjoy painting, but they are both still working on learning to discriminate. I hold out a container of paint and pickles to Mark. (Pickles are his nonpreferred item.) Mark gives me the picture of the pickles. I give him the pickles. He pushes the bag of pickles away, and I perform the 4-Step error correction procedure. When I repeat, Mark hands me the picture for paint, and I give him the paint container. I then take this opportunity to work on object identification. I hold out a paintbrush and a comb and say, "Take the paintbrush." Mark is successful. The last statement I make to him is, "Take two pieces of paper." Mark is again correct. He begins to paint.

I now turn my attention to Gary, who has been sitting nicely with his wait card. I take the wait card from him and say, "Nice waiting." I then begin with holding out the same material as I did for Mark. Gary gives me the picture for paintbrush. I then give him a paintbrush but now he has to have paper to paint on. I tell him, "Take one piece of paper." Gary does that correctly.

At this time the other students have been asked what they want to work for and have begun the activity with the staff. Abby already has been prompted to request help with opening the paint container, and we are delighted when Doug has independently requested a break by using his "I want a break" sentence strip and asking for it aloud.

Robert has requested red and yellow paint, a paintbrush, and two small pieces of paper. The length of his sentences for requesting are very impressive.

Steven begins by requesting a color. Ms. J does a correspondence check with him, and his response is incorrect. (For the correspondence check, Steven requests a specific color, "blue." Ms. J holds out a picture of that color plus another colored yellow that had been affixed to the front of Steven's communication book. Ms. J says to Steven, "Take it." Steven takes the wrong item.) Ms. J removes the color picture from the sentence strip and places it back on the activity board. She then attempts to teach Steven the picture of the color he had reached for. His response is correct on the repeated trial within the 4-step error correction procedure, and he successfully matches the color he apparently had wanted.

The ARRT is running throughout this activity, and if on task, each student earns reinforcers when the ARRT sounds.

Check Schedule

The timer sounds to signal the end of art time. Mark and Gary are given a picture of "music" and told, "Go here." They both need partial physical guidance to get from art to the music area. The other students go to their schedule boards, change them to music, and walk independently to the music area.

Ms. D, the music teacher, begins by finding out what each student wants to work for. The ARRT is running during this activity, and students will earn tokens or edibles for participation. Next Ms. D hands the activity board to Robert for him to choose the instrument he would like to play first. Robert puts together the sentence strip "I want tambourine." He hands it to Ms. D, and she reads it as he points to the pictures. Ms. D hands Robert the tambourine.

> **Music**
>
> Our music teacher goes from room to room with her cart of material. She plays songs and has the students imitate her. She also has an activity board where all necessary vocabulary is placed so that students can request a song or an instrument.

Each student has a turn requesting the instrument he or she wants. After everyone has made a choice, Ms. D begins to play a selection of recorded music. While it plays, she directs students to follow particular actions. At one point the students have to raise the instrument above their heads, and then they have to either shake, bang, or tap the instrument.

> **Dismissal**
>
> The students put their coats on, find their communication books (**name identification**), place them in their book bags, and put their coats on. Once these three steps are complete, they sit in waiting chairs until everyone is ready to walk out to the buses.
>
> Each staff member works with the pair of students to whom he or she was assigned for the day. Again, we remember to use *no* spoken prompts, only gestures and physical prompts, to teach this routine and collect data on **name recognition.**

Throughout, the ARRT is running, and the students are earning tokens or treats for participation and appropriate behavior. Then the timer sounds to signal the end of the activity.

Mark and Gary are given a picture of "bus." They are partially prompted to move to the area where the book bags are kept, but both students complete the matching of the picture on their own.

The others independently change their schedules and begin to get their coats and book bags. Robert, Steven, Mark, and Gary do an excellent job of completing the routine, while Doug and Abby have some difficulty. As Abby carries her communication book to her book bag, she drops it on the floor and kicks it

Check Schedule

across the room. Without saying anything, Mr. B picks up the communication book, places it back on the table, and physically helps Abby pick it up. He then walks Abby to her school bag (backstep). Abby then places it in her book bag independently.

Doug has a problem closing his book bag, beginning to show small signs of frustration. So Ms. J quickly asks me to prompt "help." I physically guide Doug to pick up the "help" card and place it on his sentence strip. He then hands the sentence strip to Ms. J, and he reads it aloud. She then helps Doug zipper his book bag.

Once all the students are ready, they walk out to the buses. We members of the teaching staff are tired from our day of intense effort and concentration, but when we look over our data and see how far our students have progressed, we know that it has been really worth it.

Suggested Readings and Viewings

TO	**READ**
Become familiar with nine different preschool programs for children with autism: their structure and content; diagnostic and assessment approaches; staffing and administration; curriculum; integration; perspectives on aversives; family involvement; and outcomes	Handleman, J. S. & Harris, S. L. (2001). *Preschool education programs for children with autism,* 2nd ed. Austin, TX: Pro-Ed.
Enable you to develop a schedules of activities for students with autism, while in the process promoting their independence and choice	McClannahan, L. E. & Krantz, P. J. (1999). Activity schedules for children with autism. Betheseda, MD: Woodbine House.

Prepare you for pitfalls facing behavior analysts as they attempt to build effective programs of intervention and suggestions for achieving programmatic success

Foxx, R. M. (2001). Lessons learned: Thirty years of applied behavior analysis in treating problem behaviors. In C. Maurice, G. Green & R. M. Foxx. (Eds.) Making a difference: Behavioral intervention for autism Austin, TX: Pro-Ed, 183–194.
Lovaas, I. O. (1996). The UCLA young autism model of service delivery. In C. Maurice, G. Green & S. Luce. (Eds.) Behavioral intervention for young children with autism Austin, TX: Pro-Ed, 241–248.

Familiarize yourself with numerous methods for including people with difficult behavior within the community.

In Koegel, L. K., Koegel, R. L. & Dunlap, G. (1996). (Eds.) Positive behavioral support: Including people with difficult behavior in the community. Baltimore, MD: Paul Brooks Publishing Co.

Choose an effective treatment for your child; select what to teach and how to teach it; identify personnel to assist; obtain practical support; work with speech-language specialists and the schools

Maurice, C., Green, G. & Luce, S. (1996). Behavioral intervention for young children with autism. Austin,TX: Pro-Ed.